Praise for *Uncultivated*

"Andy Brennan is a stubborn, thoughtful original, and his apple memoir is powered by inspiring verve and irreverence. Loving apples or cider is not a prerequisite for loving this book. All that is needed is the willingness to follow a vibrant narrative voice driven by the pursuit of dreams."
— **ALICE FEIRING**, author of *Naked Wine* and *For the Love of Wine*

"Andy Brennan's new book *Uncultivated* is smart, wise, raw, generous, unapologetic, and poetic. As delicious to drink in and as profound as the unique and artful ciders he makes."
— **DEIRDRE HEEKIN**, vintner, La Garagista Winery; author of *An Unlikely Vineyard*

"Andy Brennan's *Uncultivated* could become the twenty-first century's *One Straw Revolution*. Forty years ago, Masanobu Fukuoka's 1970s classic helped define the thinking of thousands of us searching for a new way to look at farming and the world. Every cider maker in America will want to read *Uncultivated*, and everyone else should, too. Not only does Brennan explore the questions facing those of us who love to grow and squeeze apples, he also digs deeply into language, art, economics, and life itself. *Uncultivated* is provocative and fun. Whether you're a cider maker or not, read this book. It's a One Apple Tree Revolution."
— **JOHN BUNKER**, apple historian; author of *Not Far from the Tree*

"Part autobiography and part ecological meditation, *Uncultivated* presents the case for the rewilding of our agricultural imagination. Andy Brennan reflects on the relationship between authenticity, location, and commerce and finds his deepest truths in the dry farm cider of America's Northeast. Above all, this is a celebration of the power of the wild apple tree to express a sense of place; as it acclimatizes and adapts, so it tells us the story of the land."
— **FRANCIS PERCIVAL**, coauthor of *Reinventing the Wheel*

"This book captivated me—it's wry and artful, informative and soulful. In *Uncultivated* Andy Brennan throws down the gauntlet (or rather gathering tarp) for cider made from foraged wild apples, continuing hill town traditions of spirit and survival. He offers readers a new/old (revolutionary/conservative) way to think about community, business, and the living world. The book is bright with art, spirit, and daring."
— **JUDITH MALONEY**, cofounder, West County Cider

"Andy Brennan's journey with the fruit of our desire is wildly inclined in ways that are going to surprise and delight. Dare I describe my cider-making friend as *raucous*? That this word-loving hooligan is the one orchardist among us who presumes to *ungrow* the apple? Open a bottle of your finest, and make a date with *Uncultivated* this very evening. The time has come to ponder the dignity of the apple tree."

—MICHAEL PHILLIPS, author of
The Apple Grower and *The Holistic Orchard*

"Every community has its visionaries. At times, they inspire and enlighten. At others, they vex and confound. But they always push you to think more deeply, reevaluate your judgments, and become more intentional, while making you feel a little uncomfortable in the process. I believe Andy Brennan is a key visionary for contemporary American cider. In *Uncultivated* you learn that while Andy was helping to shape and elevate the national conversation about cider and apples, he was also evolving in profound and personal ways. Idealistic and provocative, rebellious and vulnerable, Andy is both cider's conscience and a thorn in its side, and we are the better for his work."

—ELLEN CAVALLI, editor and publisher, *Malus*

"With regards to growing apples and making cider, *un*cultivation is a concept that excites me, particularly coming from an American author. Andy Brennan's *Uncultivated* argues a case for 'natural cider', and his approach to it is something I hope to see grow as craft cidermakers aim to express individual quality and identity. Philosophical, haughty, and enjoyable, Andy's approach embraces what American cidermakers strive to understand: American terroir."

—BILL BRADSHAW, coauthor of *World's Best Cider*

"American cider has traditionally been deeply regional, dependent on ungrafted seedling trees like those lining the rocky farm fields and sandstone ridges of the Hudson Valley in New York. Andy Brennan and Polly Giragosian name their 'locational' ciders after some of these foraging sites: *Neversink Highlands*, *Shawangunk Ridge*, *Mamakating Hollow*. Theirs are tannic, rich, full-bodied, complex drinks. As Brennan writes, 'Cider making is a responsibility'—to the trees, the land, good food, and the community. *Uncultivated* is a wonderful, timely reminder of all that this drink can be at its best."

—DAVID BUCHANAN, owner, Portersfield Cider;
author of *Taste, Memory*

Uncultivated

Uncultivated

WILD APPLES, REAL CIDER, AND THE COMPLICATED ART OF MAKING A LIVING

ANDY BRENNAN

FOREWORD BY ROWAN JACOBSEN

CHELSEA GREEN PUBLISHING
White River Junction, Vermont
London, UK

Project Manager: Sarah Kovach
Project Editor: Benjamin Watson
Copy Editor: Laura Jorstad
Proofreader: Deb Heimann
Indexer: Shana Milkie
Designer: Melissa Jacobson

Printed in Canada.
First printing May 2019.
10 9 8 7 6 5 4 3 2 1   19 20 21 22 23

Our Commitment to Green Publishing
Chelsea Green sees publishing as a tool for cultural change and ecological stewardship. We strive to align our book manufacturing practices with our editorial mission and to reduce the impact of our business enterprise in the environment. We print our books and catalogs on chlorine-free recycled paper, using vegetable-based inks whenever possible. This book may cost slightly more because it was printed on paper that contains recycled fiber, and we hope you'll agree that it's worth it. *Uncultivated* was printed on paper supplied by Marquis that is made of recycled materials and other controlled sources.

Library of Congress Cataloging-in-Publication Data
Names: Brennan, Andy (Andy Crown), author.
Title: Uncultivated : wild apples, real cider, and the complicated art of making a living /
    Andy Brennan ; foreword by Rowan Jacobsen.
Description: White River Junction, Vermont : Chelsea Green Publishing, [2019]
    | Includes bibliographical references and index.
Identifiers: LCCN 2019004503| ISBN 9781603588447 (hardcover : alk. paper) |
    ISBN 9781603588454 (ebook)
Subjects: LCSH: Apples. | Cider industry. | Wild foods. | Farms, Small.
Classification: LCC SB363 .B693 2019 | DDC 634/.11--dc23
LC record available at https://lccn.loc.gov/2019004503

Chelsea Green Publishing
85 North Main Street, Suite 120
White River Junction, VT 05001
(802) 295-6300
www.chelseagreen.com

MIX
Paper from
responsible sources
FSC® C103567

Dedicated to the wild apple trees.

CONTENTS

FOREWORD

I first tasted Andy Brennan's cider in New York City a few years ago while working on a book about heirloom apples. It was remarkable. And what made it so was not just the flavor (which was excellent) but the audacity: Here was a minimalist bottle with a label so simple it could have stepped out of the 1800s, holding 500 milliliters of lively but unrefined cider, and it wasn't cheap. Like Alice Waters famously serving a perfect, plain peach for dessert at Chez Panisse, the message was clear: There is something in this bottle that comes straight from the countryside, and it's worth paying attention to, even in Gotham. *Especially* in Gotham.

Since that time I've enjoyed Aaron Burr Cider many times, and it always helps set me straight. I've made my own simple farmhouse cider in Vermont for many years, and have sampled the wares of many other amateur cider makers. Andy Brennan's is a part of this family, but it's always better. Andy knows how to use his painterly skills to frame his subject, to point to its inherent wildness in a way that underscores its meaningfulness. He knows how to make cider more than the sum of its parts.

Now it turns out he knows how to do this in the medium of words, too. Like Aaron Burr Cider, *Uncultivated* is an important and necessary work, and much of that importance is because it makes no attempt to be important. Andy likes to work intimately, on a small scale, and *Uncultivated* is no exception. These glimpses of a life with apple trees don't try to exert themselves upon the world. Instead they require you to lean close, but when you do, they offer little windows into an alternate world interlaced with our own: a culture where cash is not king.

"I personally can trace much of my inspiration, many of my ideas, and many of my insights to simply being with wild apple trees," Andy writes in *Uncultivated*. "I place their highest value in the pricelessness of companionship. In this sense wild apple trees live in *other* economies, ones that prioritize beauty, uniqueness, nutrition, taste—just to name a few things that are often in direct conflict with a growing financial economy."

These are dangerous ideas, and *Uncultivated* is a dangerous book—not to you as an individual, but to a system that depends on capital being the sole arbiter of value. Agriculture was long ago subsumed into capitalism, but every now and then a little piece of it breaks free—and apple trees are paragons of escape. Unlike our other domesticated plants and animals, we haven't yet broken them. They are forever slipping away to the woods and pastures of an older, unmonetized world to establish their own economy—one based on sugar and sunlight and relationship.

Andy Brennan dances on the edge of that world. Yes, you can pay real money for his cider, but every time you do, you are trafficking in a wild system that threatens to upset the established rules of what's good and bad, what's worth our precious time and love. As a chronicle of that domain, *Uncultivated* will help you to enjoy every bottle of real cider you encounter in the future. But it might just do more than that. Like the spirits of the old orchardists on Andy's farm, it will haunt you. The past is more alive than you have been led to believe.

When I think back on the piercing poignancy of that first bottle of Aaron Burr Cider, I finally understand something Andy explains in this book: The taste of a cider matters, but the taste of the experience of making a cider matters more. Every bottle holds the lingering ghost of that relationship, and though it isn't something that will ever turn up in the tasting notes, it just might be what we're looking for.

—ROWAN JACOBSEN
Calais, Vermont
January 2019

Prologue

hen I was almost three years old, I said my first word: "Apple." This was in the autumn of 1973, nearly 100 miles from Washington, DC, in the rugged landscape of western Maryland where the Appalachian ridges ripple like a series of long waves, unfolding one after the next toward the headwaters of the Potomac. Dotting the hillsides were homestead farms, and below in the valley floors there remained old brick villages that appeared just as they had when General Lee stormed up, bringing the fight to Union soil. Outside the town hall in one of these hamlets, a giant pome sculpture served as the focal point of the lawn just the way an obelisk or water fountain would. It was this sight, the giant apple, that piqued the interest of the boy in the backseat. Most children are saying full sentences long before their third birthday, but I was waiting for the vision of an apple to start talking.

This book is a continuation of whatever excitement woke in me that day. And if I succeed in relaying the importance of apple trees, you might say this book is *also* a continuation of the excitement awakened in Eve and Adam after their famous run-in with apples. I make these efforts not as a professional writer, but simply as a longtime observer of naturalized apple trees. I don't assume readers to be focused on the fields of nutrition, art, farming, or farm businesses, but I take for granted that (1) these are profoundly connected subjects, and (2) as a unified subject it is of great concern to us all. The apple tree, it just so happens, is the perfect connector.

If what I saw today was a true cultural appreciation for apple trees and their importance to the general public, I would have no reason to write these letters. But what I see instead is a growing rift between laypeople and apple trees, while pomological expertise given to professional growers and academics serves to further and further divide us. A few years ago

I thought a rekindled cider market could bridge this isolation; now it, too, is governed by an oligarchy of specialists. My goal is to rethink this distancing and possibly weaken the barriers that keep us from assimilating, or at least sympathizing, with the natural world for the sake of caring for the future. And this happens to be the apple tree's great gift to us! It has long been our ambassador for this purpose. Though I will relay some practical information regarding apples, cider, and farm businesses, I ask that the reader absorb this information empathetically with the lives and experiences of apple trees. Think of them anthropomorphically.

This might sound like a weird request, but I've become convinced, by piecing together hundreds of apple metaphors (dating back many centuries), that the trees have been attempting to communicate with us. Their message, as representatives of nature, sometimes speaks poorly of Modern humankind's decisions, but it can still provide us knowledge about ourselves and make us more satisfied with this world. There's no obvious translation of this message; Google won't help, and worst of all would be to study the apple species with a removed, academic gaze. Rather, if we want to hear what our onetime friend the apple tree is telling us, we need to truly reconnect with her and spend time observing how she relates to the real world. Most of this *cannot* be done on apple farms or in research stations. It *must* be done by incorporating apple trees into every location. Luckily, reconnecting is easier than it might first seem, for this is the way it always was. We simply need to look at forgotten wisdom.

I'm not sure how I became so sensitive to apple trees. Perhaps it's related to the above three-year-old's story: Verbal language came to me with difficulty. Instead of through words, I developed visually and struggled through grade school with only my art teachers to encourage me. From the age of nine, I took private painting lessons and I ended up majoring in art at college. Art was my sanctuary from the time of my earliest memory all the way into my early adult years. But truth be told, I don't recall noticing apple trees during those two decades. Only after I moved to New York City in the early 1990s did the apple tree become significant to me. Over the following 10-year span, 1993 through 2002, the art world, and the city itself, offered me much, but I found them to require constant engagement. As an introvert, I could not sustain this year-round. Luckily for me, during that decade I was able to return to Maryland each summer to a fishing shack on the shore of the Chesapeake Bay, one that a friend and I rented from a farmer. This location re-introduced me to apples after the 20-year absence.

"The cottage," as Steve and I called it, had no insulation, no TV, no phone, and obviously no internet; it offered only an outhouse, an outdoor shower, and the great outdoors for exploring. Driven by thrift, we studied mushroom identification, foraged for berries, and gleaned corn from the neighboring fields. And in the evenings we'd gather with the neighbors to shore-cast from the beach, hoping to hook anything from flounder to skate. By the light of a driftwood fire we'd recount winter tales, drink homemade wine, and eye our fishing lines as they faded into darkness over the calm waters. We were content with or without action, though if one of those lines suddenly twanged we'd have a little excitement and a dual purpose for the fire.

But the summers always faded, and the neighborhood went quiet when school started up. Everyone moved back to their permanent homes, leaving me with the two nicest months, September and October, all to myself—and nothing can please an introverted artist more. Whereas in the hot months the community focused east on the expansive waters of the Chesapeake, in the fall my gaze turned westward to where the setting sun fell into the most beautiful thing on earth: an abandoned apple orchard.

Words can only hint at the importance of that orchard to me. Yes, I would gather the apples, and yes, those trees became the subjects of my landscape paintings, but I never entered the orchard expecting anything out of it. Just the opposite: When I tunneled past the towering blackberry walls rimming the apple grove, I went in only to explore and "become one" with the trees. This eventually happened, but only after I reached the profound realization this was the same goal of *all* the creatures and vegetation beginning to inhabit the 10-acre abandoned site.

Dappled light seeped in from the overgrown canopy, and breezes would rustle the rust-spotted leaves. I set up my easel and began each new canvas hoping to capture the whole of the experience, not merely to depict what I saw. How does one paint assimilation? Little by little apples would fall with a thud in the high grass. Losing track of time in the golden glow of autumn, I also lost a sense of myself.

Sometimes there was pure silence, broken only by the periodic sloshing of my brush in the turpentine cup. And sometimes I got the eerie feeling that I was being watched. I'd quickly turn my head to find I was right: A pack of wild dogs known to live in the swamps beyond the tobacco field frequently came to spy on me while I was painting! God, what a perfect little world this was. I wondered if the dogs understood this place to be a special refuge for the feral.

To modern folks apples are considered a healthy snack, and not much more. But beyond the tempting fruit, the tree has long held a special place in our collective unconscious. It continues to emerge and reemerge, as it has for thousands of years. The tree is mysteriously part of who we are, even now, well into the Modern era. (Note for future reference: I use the capital *M* to differentiate the regular use of the word *modern* from the cultural movement that started in the mid-1800s, as in *Modern art*. The capital-*M* Modernism movement by no coincidence parallels the shift in Western civilization from agrarian society toward industrialized.)

The easiest way to appreciate our cultural connection to apple trees is to draw similarities between two species: *Malus domestica* (the modern apple) and *Canis lupus familiaris*. The latter, the common dog, is our *companion animal*, while the former, the common apple tree, is our *companion plant*. One is "man's best friend," and the other is "the giving tree." Although we immediately relate to the animal kingdom, we can also relate to the plant kingdom in profound ways. We are all living beings with shared goals. The relating is slower, and more obtuse, but we have developed a great language for relating with apple trees, greater than with any other plant. No doubt we still have uncommon compassion for them.

If you're still reading by chapter 8, you'll find that I'm obsessed with this connection. How rare is it that we can empathize with a plant! But what's important to this prologue is that after thousands of years, this relationship did not die 200 years ago with the start of the Modern era. Though hardly anyone lives with apple trees anymore, the bond still strongly exists. And what great satisfaction it brings me to see examples of this reunion, like when property owners begin clearing land and discover an apple tree. Determined as they are to chop down everything in sight, suddenly the chain saw goes silent when they happen upon an apple tree! Even very old, sick trees are spared and nursed for dozens of years.

I'm a sucker for this. But a frightful proposition rises in me: As the general population expands and we are increasingly removed from farming, how will that empathy erode? And if it vanishes for the apple tree, what does that say of our empathetic connection with other living beings? Fearful as that is for me, I can also imagine the opposite happening: Couldn't we also expand upon our empathy for apple trees (as we seem to for dogs) and allow that compassion to reach other living beings, endangered creatures, and *all* of nature?

The new millennium brought economic development opportunities and suburban growth to that part of Maryland where "the cottage" was. Those timeless days exploring nature in the warm months abruptly ended in 2002. I won't go into detail about the fate of the abandoned orchard, it's too grotesque, but I will say that after losing that place I found a new direction for my life. Determined to regain that connection with nature (via apple trees), I started looking for land of my own. After saving 80 percent of each paycheck for the next four years, I found what I was looking for 90 minutes northwest of New York City. Ironically, this Hudson Valley / Catskill location is very similar to the Appalachian landscape where I spoke my first word.

Later in the book I will talk more about how my experiences with apples have changed now that I'm a property owner and a commercial apple farmer, but everything I do as a grower will forever be held in context with two things: (1) I came from an art background, and (2) I formed a relationship with wild apple trees first. This bond predated anything I read or heard about *Malus domestica*, which turns out to be extremely important because my pomological teachers were dead wrong about some things. I had examples of an alternative story. More so, I could not have endured so many agricultural setbacks without faith in the trees. As an outsider to farming, coming at it late in life (in my mid-30s), and as someone with very challenging soils, I had a severe disadvantage (compared with family farmers or experienced academics), but by relating to the uncultivated trees outside the system I found courage and inspiration. I would follow their lead and acclimate to an alternative scenario.

Now I'm also a professional cider maker and a small business owner. As both, I am either successful or unsuccessful depending on what the expectations are. To those who grew up watching the TV program *Shark Tank*, I'm sure my business is laughable. But expectations can be natural or unnatural, just like apples. In an effort to strike a balance with my land and avoid living precariously above or below subsistence, I have become a proponent of natural apple farming, natural cider making, and maintaining a natural business *only*. To succeed in these practices this way, I have learned that it's essential to take a consistent approach throughout (rather than, for example, following nature's example in one practice and humankind's expectations in another). I reject forced growth such as we see in agriculture's fertilizers, winemaking's "stretching" (of volume), or the use of outside capital infusions. Essentially, I'm opposed to anything turbocharged to override the pace of natural acclimation. What unites and distinguishes natural practices is a look away from predetermination. I want to look toward nature, where things happen, they don't happen, or they happen in unexpected ways. Natural practices seek acceptance with these facts. If I want my business and products (cider) to be natural, I, too, must accept this in all parts.

Land is limited, success is fleeting, seasons change, and multiplicity is a healthy adaptation for survival. These are all natural principles that conflict with Modern humanity's modus operandi: constant growth, limitless absorption, specialization, the need for certainty. My goal in writing this book is not to rebuke the businesses or farms that float Modern people (in fact, at this point they seem required); I simply want to remind myself and others that another way exists. I've been lured down that path and I've discovered personal success by emulating the apple trees along the road. They are becoming wild.

PART I

Between Cultivation and the Wild

ONE

Apples

*T*he slope is severe, almost 30 degrees, and I'm breaking a sweat scampering up and down this wooded mountainside. Making it all the more difficult is the unruly state of the understory: Thorny wild rose thickets, fallen tree limbs, and 4-inch-thick grapevines threaten me at neck level like draping boa constrictors. But the most challenging thing about this slope is that my feet are never firmly planted. Decomposing leaf mulch slides under my boots. And to top it all off, Bill, the farmer who owns this property, has recently taken up cattle farming again (after decades), and he's been pushing his herd through these woods all summer long to escape the heat. Now cow patties are everywhere.

But for me it's worth it. There, in the gullies formed by protruding tree roots, are piles of apples that would otherwise keep rolling downhill if it weren't for the low root walls. It's easy to collect the pre-gathered fruit as I fill my buckets in preparation for the hard haul back uphill to where my beloved 1991 Toyota pickup is stashed beyond these woods. The bed of the truck holds 50 of these 5-gallon buckets, 20 pounds each, so it's going to be a lot of schlepping this morning. Such is life in the Borscht Belt: hardscrabble. But this is not only how I make my living; I live for this.

Let me make it clear that this was a *non*descript patch of forest when I first discovered it 10 years ago. I studied forestry as a New York State volunteer woods assessor, but even with a fair amount of knowledge I still wouldn't have given these woods a second look had I not come here exactly at the right time of year. That was the spring of 2008. After a long winter the duck-house at our homestead farm was unimaginably gross and I needed fresh straw to reline the floor. My auto mechanic wrote down the number of an unadvertised hay farmer up near the top of the mountain, and when I first arrived at Bill's farm that Easter weekend the trees surrounding the fields were still gray and dormant. But something about them caught my eye. Up in the high canopy were little white blossoms dancing around in the breeze like fireflies in the intertwined branches. I had seen flowers like this on understory trees before—on dogwoods, ironwood, or pin cherry—but never had I seen them up so high.

Curious, I made my way toward them, nearly hypnotized by their swaying. This was a few years before Bill had cows, so there were no barbed-wire or electric fences to contend with. As I approached I peered into the dark of the woods to study the trunks of the trees, finding what anyone would expect to see in the northern reaches of Appalachia: oaks, pines, maples, hickory—all shooting up 50 or 60 feet like telephone poles. But upon closer inspection I also noticed something silvery and smooth about a number of the boles. This wasn't the bark of birch or cherry trees, though those trees bore the closest resemblance to them. Instead the glimmering skin belonged to something I recognized, just never in this context. I was looking at my first stand of assimilated truly wild apple trees.

Apple trees are not mentioned in forestry class any more than forestry is the subject of apple farming, yet here they were, two worlds overlapping at one of the more memorable *Of course!* moments in my life: Apples are a tree; trees grow in the forest. Why should this be surprising? I felt like an idiot for not having thought of this before: Here I was, a young apple farmer, and the only way I could comprehend an apple tree was in a meadow setting?

Back at the barn Bill threw bales of hay down to me and instructed me how to interlock them on the bed of my pickup so they wouldn't tumble out on my way home. I had to ask: "Hey, Bill, I noticed all those apple trees out in the woods just now. Was there an orchard here long ago?" But his response surprised me. "I don't know how the apple trees got there, but I don't know how *any* of those woods got there— including the oaks and maples. That used to be all pasture when I was a kid. It was cleared when my grandfather was a kid and cleared when my great-grandfather was a kid. And when my great-great-grandfather started this farm in the mid-1800s, he had nothing but grazing fields all the way to the ridgetop."

Sure enough, there are ancient photographs to prove it: This mountain was a bald bulge of grass rising above New York's Hudson Valley, like a huge wave emerging from the west. It was dotted with cows, but not trees.

"It was too steep for the tractor on that slope and we stopped cutting the grass. I guess the trees just grew back at a certain point," Bill continued.

But this didn't answer my question: Why were there apple trees in the mix? There was more history to learn.

As we reconsider the progress of *Malus domestica* (the common apple tree), we discover how Bill's pippin forest (*pippin* is one of those great old-fashioned words referring to a surprise apple tree born from seed) reveals a different narrative for apples in America. This history counterbalances assumptions that the tree has been on a controlled, linear path toward greater and greater efficiency. One of the last things Thoreau wrote in 1862 was that he felt sorry for people 100 years hence, for they would not have wild apples to pick anymore. And yet even with 50-plus years tacked on to his predicted doom date, wild apples still survive. They prove the sum is greater than the parts, succeeding without all the agricultural props given to their farmed cousins. This defies scientists, who claim their success is dependent on human intervention, and it even enrages many commercial orchardists who have attempted to round up the wildlings (also a word for a seedling tree, along with *pippin* and *volunteer*) for fear of a contaminating influence. But like Christmas to the Grinch, they keep finding a way of coming.

The history of *Malus domestica* in America is, in fact, more complex than the explanations offered by modernity. But there was a time in American history when the soul of the tree, its inquisitive and independent nature, was better understood and cherished as next to godly. To be able to see this takes a different mind-set. Johnny Appleseed is famous for shedding light on this subject, but we downplay the importance of his service and focus instead on his trivial oddities. He was, in fact, eccentric, but his service as an ambassador for the apple tree simply captures the reverence common in America during the 150 years prior to his time. His spiritual devotion to the apple tree was not odd, and it is still justified today.

Chance occurrences in nature have been layered in time and intertwined with countless unconsidered variables to result in the pippins along roadsides, in pasture edges, and amid woods like at Bill's. These trees exist by relating to the whole of the forest system, including the geology, the wildlife, and the climate. They have even adjusted to our human progress. The variables are so infinite, so wondrous, that even at specific locations like Bill's it's impossible to explain how they came to be. It would be hubris even to try. Still, to love the trees is to want to know more about them. So let me offer aspects of apple history that I think are important to America's still-wild trees. And it all starts with the aptly named *Mayflower*.

America's Fruit

Many people don't know this, but the common apple tree is not native to the northeastern United States, where it was first declared "America's fruit." This surprises anyone who has driven these country roads, because there are so many uncultivated trees visible without even leaving the car. In fact the fruit is so perfectly suited for our cold climate that I once heard a friend compare the wild apples of Maine to the abundance of tropical fruit popping out of the vegetation along roadways where she grew up in Kenya.

This scene of natural abundance wasn't always the case, not in the Northeast, not before the mid-1600s. If any apple tree grew here prior (though it's not assumed they did), it would have been the small and mealy *Malus coronaria*, a crab apple that by the 1800s was reported growing only west of the Northeast colonies, over the Appalachians. *M. domestica*, the larger apple we're all familiar with, is an immigrant just like us. It is part of the whole of Western culture that arrived by boat in the 1620s, and it has evolved here in tandem with Western culture ever since.

However, the Pilgrims did not bring live trees across the Atlantic; they brought only apple seeds with them. They planted them en masse, just as Johnny Appleseed would later do to create seedling trees. Trees from seed—pippins—are very different from modern apple trees in that their genetic variety is unique (not cloned, as with grafted trees). Every apple has five seed cells in its core. Not only will each of those seeds develop into a unique apple tree (uniquely different from its parent), but each seed will also develop a tree distinct from the ones produced from the other seeds in the core. Loaded with thousands and thousands of apple seeds, a single tree can launch tens of thousands of potentially new varieties and test the environment where those seeds end up. With the right combination of genetics and environmental suitability, one of those seedlings is bound to survive and find itself perfectly suited for a particular location.

But did the Pilgrims feel the same way about themselves in their new location? This is not an unrelated question. I try to imagine what went on in the heads of those religious separatists as they crammed onto wooden ships and set sail for a two-month voyage across the ocean for the New World: It must have been like boarding a spacecraft with a one-way ticket to Mars. And things didn't get any easier once they "safely landed," either. In fact, those first few years the settlers had to adjust to brutal cold and snow unlike anything they were used to in temperate Europe. In addition, the terrain and the soil were much rockier and more difficult to cultivate than what they had hoped for. Things were hard. There was no way around it.

A religious people, they might have read this as God's rebuke. They could have extrapolated that the difficulties were the Lord's way of telling them that the elements of Western culture were not suitable for this new land. Such thoughts would surely creep in and affect morale, and as we all know, sometimes morale is the only thing to carry us through trying times. Beaten up by the weather, fighting rock and snow, as well as frightened of "savage" attacks, the settlers needed a sign for inspiration. That sign eventually came in the form of an apple.

Simultaneous to the struggles of the Pilgrims, apple trees were also trying to define themselves in the New World. While it was unnoticeable at first, the settlers soon realized that something interesting was occurring with these trees. Not only did they seem okay with the harsher temperatures and rocky soils, but after a decade or two growing to fruit-bearing age, proof eventually came that the trees were more suitable here than in old England. The apple tree, having worked its roots around heavier, rocky soil, produced a fruit with superior taste-intensity, becoming the first element of Western culture to surpass Europe's nurturing. Finally, empirical and divine proof that Western civilization could succeed in North America! The goal was clear: Follow the apple.

The success of the tree in the Northeast is not surprising to us now that we know more about the extended history of *Malus domestica*. Pomologists (those who study the science of apples) currently believe they originated in Central Asia in the foothills of the Tien Shan Mountains where the climate, latitude, and terrain more closely resemble the extremes of New England than they do old England. But having the fruit do better here became America's original boasting point. It became known as America's fruit, sort of like a colonial *In your face!*

Over time American apples only became more highly esteemed, and even as war was brewing with the mother country, apples were being exported back to England. Their praise was sung by famous men and women on both sides of the Atlantic. And by the end of the nineteenth century, American apple varieties were being grown worldwide. Even today American cultivars (short for "cultivated varieties"), including some of those early heirloom varieties, disproportionately dominate global markets. The apple is unquestionably America's fruit—that is, if America starts with Western culture.

Nature Versus Nurture

Despite our tendency to choose perfect apples, there is an advantage to stumbling across imperfections in the grocery store. The flaws reveal what is otherwise covered up: a history that speaks of the farm, the farmer, the weather, and the ecosystem behind that piece of fruit. I'd like to call to attention a double standard: Some apples, especially wild apples, are not perfect. But neither are people.

The character of every individual tree, and subsequently the character of its fruit, is shaped by two variables: (1) the environmental influences (including the biological community, rock type, climate, and more), and (2) the genetic traits of that particular tree (defining factors such as apple variety, growth tendency, and fungal susceptibility). Nowadays customers rarely hear about the environmental influences, but these can drastically affect the apple tree's development, thus in turn drastically affecting how the apple tastes. Anyone who has suffered through Psych 101 knows this as the nature-versus-nurture debate. The question, applied to humans, seeks to determine the dominant sources of *our* character. If I grew up in a violent city, would my character be the same as if I had grown up on an Amish farm? Probably not. Advantage: nurture. But regardless of which location I hail from, had I been born an extroverted, cerebral female (as opposed to an introverted, emotionally sensitive male), my history and my experiences would surely shape me differently, right? Advantage: nature. There's really no winning this decades-old debate. Both nature and nurture are monumental in shaping human character.

I had heard similar things from apple farmers, too: You don't want to grow a Granny Smith up north; you don't want to grow a Mac in the foggy valley; you don't want Spitzenburg in a hot and humid climate. And so on, and so forth. All these things suggest that environmental factors are just as influential as genetic factors in the character of the fruit, despite the fact that only the fruit's variety is mentioned in grocery markets. You almost *never* hear about the growing conditions when you read flavor profiles of an apple (or cider), and yet if you visit the actual tree these factors are unmistakable: You can see the fruit's connection to the tree, the tree's connection to the soil, and the soil's place in the larger environment and climate. You can feel all those interconnected things as they influence your own experience there, so how could they *not* be factors in an apple's taste, too?

As someone who travels to different sites to forage apples, I am particularly advantaged to study the environmental influences that location has on apples, but the cultural obsession with genetic varieties dominated my early explorations, too. It wasn't until I first foraged at Bill's farm that I realized nurture's full influence on apples. His farm sits on the ridge above my orchard, no more than a five-minute drive away, but with a 1,000-foot change in elevation there exists a night-and-day distinction: When I stumble out of my truck I find the rocks, the sun, the wind, the temperatures, the moisture, the forest, and soil ecosystems all strikingly different. I feel it, the trees must feel it.

Over the years I've been collecting Bill's wild apples, as well as the wild apples from down in my valley, and when milling them separately, I saw the first obvious distinction: After handling the valley apples my hands were dirty, almost as if I was wearing black latex gloves, but while touching apples from up the mountain my hands remained clean. The reason for this is sooty blotch. In the valley, fogs set in overnight and don't clear until midmorning, allowing airborne fungi to colonize the surface of my home apples and give them a dull, dark gray coating. Bill's apples have none of this. In the bright, windswept hilltop not one of his apples suffers from this condition. Wind and sun (UV rays), as all growers know, help deter the fungal set.

Coincidentally, this was about the time I was introduced to the natural wine enthusiast and writer Alice Feiring, who subsequently lured me down the rabbit hole of her expertise with her emphatic arguments. And her red hair. I'd see her from time to time in New York, but the more I read from her work the more I questioned the role of growing practices not just in apple cultivation but in cider making as well. She turned me on to the concept of terroir, and I became more and more focused on studying this element of cider rather than the art of blending varieties. I soon applied my experiments to my two main foraging sites and divided our Homestead Apple cider between Shawangunk Ridge and Mamakating Hollow ciders. I wanted the two microclimates to have their own bottlings rather than take the best apples from each location and use them as components in some master blend. But to prove the environment was affecting the taste of the two I needed to conduct a more scientific study, which meant I had to start grafting to eliminate the genetic variables that clearly were factors, too (given that every wild apple is its own variety).

The solution was to clone. In the winter of 2012, I gathered live shoots of wood from some of Bill's apple trees and grafted the scions onto trees down in my orchard. Would the same variety remain sooty-blotch-free in the fog belt? Then in 2015 I was finally given the opportunity to compare genetically matched fruit when the trees bore apples on both my farm and his. The results were mixed: Some of the uphill varieties were sooty-blotch-free on both farms but other varieties from Bill's farm had the fungal footprint only when grown in the valley. This proves that *both* nature and nurture can contribute to sooty blotch (and presumably other environmental susceptibilities), but it also opens up other cans of worms. On the varieties that were sooty-blotch-free on both uphill and downhill trees, there were new measurable differences, too: The uphill apples were smaller and had a greater density of flavor (also higher measurable sugars); the same varieties on my farm were heavier and slightly blander tasting. Although my apples looked larger (and yielded a higher volume of juice per apple), the flavor was missing many of its interesting qualities. The dry bitterness, bright acidity, chalkiness, and intense aromas of the apples from Bill's original trees faded when grown on my trees, despite being genetically the same apple.

What was happening in the shift between the wild tree and my farm? Had I really conducted a scientific experiment capable of isolating the factors that lead toward taste? The more I thought about it, the more I concluded I had just scratched the surface in terms of eliminating potential variables. My trees were younger than the original: What influence does the age of the tree have on the apple? What about the different root systems, the different flora and fauna, or even the slight variations in the relationship between the trees and the sun? How am I, or how is anyone, supposed to describe the taste of an apple if the factors behind the growing conditions are so diverse? With so many unknowns it's no wonder apple marketing focuses just on variety!

Now every time I describe an apple, whether it be the variety or the terroir (which is the focus of our "locational" ciders), I'm certain that I am grossly oversimplifying the factors leading to taste. The individual apple tree, with its relationship to soils, ecosystem, and seasons, is just too diverse to predict. So now what?

Even if I'm a little disappointed in the loss of character I witnessed between my cultivated orchard setting versus Bill's wild hilltop, I'm not about to start all over again with new grafts. Instead, I want to focus more on the soil and the surrounding ecosystem. I suspect in 40 years' time as the trees get older, the apples will taste different than they do now, perhaps more in keeping with Bill's original trees. But I am now convinced I've been looking at taste the wrong way. If fruit varieties or terroir are about stating how something will taste (Hudson Valley apples taste this way, Loire grapes taste that), then I'm part of the problem, explaining not exploring. No one can say what the character of a person will be at birth, and no one should try! The same goes for an apple. But the problem with us humans is that we feel compelled to try anyhow; then consciously or unconsciously we make great efforts to make predictions come true, a self-fulfilling prophecy.

I said earlier that wild apples are not perfect, but neither are people. I hope exposing this double standard helps to lift the unfair expectations put on apple trees, their farmers, and their cider.

The Blank Canvas

Even as an apple lover it feels awkward boasting about how well the tree does in America. Because apples are a symbol of our (Western) success, they could also serve as a reminder of our defeat of the native culture. Though the apple is not an invasive species, it's hard not to see it as a symbol of our conquests. But this needn't be the case, and, in fact, it shouldn't be—the apple could have easily taken another path. Don't blame the tree if the operator of the bulldozer drops a core in his wake. Only with tight, controlled parameters do many of our statements escape scrutiny. Calling the non-native apple America's fruit was (and is) much like today's European Americans' opposition to immigration: It's an absurdity based on a limited view of history.

The limited view, in this case, being that America started with the *Mayflower*. For many that's when this continent started to become "successful," if success means taming, progressing, and being globally powerful and wealthy. But in actuality these values are indicative of a narrow worldview, and championing them says a lot about our core being. Above all else, I'm inclined to think this understanding of "success" is tied to a compulsory need for order. Furthermore, I can't help but notice that this concept of order seems at war with nature, too. And interestingly enough, as someone with an art background, I might be the most guilty of this compulsion.

My upbringing was as a painter. Before buying the farm I spent 25 years painting and drawing, which of course explains why I chose a blank canvas as the metaphor for examining the compulsion to eliminate variables and create a fresh start. In painting that's what a blank canvas represents, but you could look to other fields to see the same pattern (everything from agriculture to architecture to medicine). But it's worth noting that Western cultures did not always exhibit this compulsion. In fact, before the Renaissance Western paintings were integrated within the architecture of cathedrals or other interiors (or caves, if you want to go back that far); sculptures, too, were created and juxtaposed with buildings or parks. There was a direct subject-matter connection between the art and the place, striving to integrate with the environment, both in content and in form. But then roughly 500 years ago painting started to become studio-based and movable on stretched canvases. Artists built their creations from a blank slate, a tabula rasa of sorts, and over the centuries the content of paintings became isolated from the influence of their eventual surroundings. By the Modern era we had turned 180 degrees from the cave art origin: Today most artists envision their work placed in white-walled galleries or museums where the architecture is designed to minimize the effect of external influences when viewing art.

This is our order, and I'm not sure it isn't hardwired into our being by this point, like the herd instinct of a collie. Nonetheless, it's something we can work on. And rather than fret over the decisions we've made in the past, I'd like to reflect on the agricultural history of apple trees with this order compulsion in mind.

Looking back it sounds so idyllic: a landscape of small diversified farms, or what we now nostalgically call homestead farms. This was the early European American's vision and hope for independence, an agrarian system that launched itself from the evolution of European agriculture. The farms weren't just complex and bucolic—in many ways they were also interwoven within the surrounding culture where whole communities and towns were designed to support one another on the homesteads. No isolated family could accomplish certain things, for instance, so they often exchanged labor when building barns or during harvests. They also borrowed or shared equipment to lessen individual financial exposure, and because farms grew or made just about everything a person needed—food, lumber, alcohol, wool, and so forth—they were able to barter for goods and services in town. They met with a favorable balance of trade when in need of other things like medicine and manufactured goods (tools, ammunition, and the like). How idyllic this sounds to a modern farmer!

But beyond the idealized vision painted by George Henry Durrie or Thomas Cole, where the American homestead farm seems blissfully interwoven with nature, there is a dark side. The implementation of our agrarian society required a shocking number of horrors. It was disruptive, it was unjust, and it was violent, and I'm not just talking about our abuse of the Native American peoples. The violence also prevailed over everything that got in our way, from the rock, to the water, to preexisting vegetative and animal cultures. Our vision of an American independence was pinned to a preconception at war with many of North America's ecosystems. We set out to replace what existed with favorable conditions, a process exactly opposite acclimation—a blank canvas.

It started slowly along the coasts, but in 150 years' time Western culture had begun penetrating inland. In New York, for example, before the War of Independence colonists had just started to settle the Catskills (not far from where I live today), but this development sped up with industrialization in the 1800s, and by the American Civil War all of New York had been "tamed." Settlers cleared the forests for pasturelands along the way, so it's anyone's guess how much of the freshly exposed soil now sits at the bottom of the Atlantic Ocean.

Clichés come to mind: "Cutting off your nose to spite your face," "Not seeing the forest for the trees," and more. The Modern era, born out of industrial innovations, ushered in faster and faster change until it snowballed into the no-turning-back marriage we now have with progress. Rapid and endless development became an American assumption, if nothing else, because it was required just to hold on to the accomplishments from the previous generation.

Agricultural history, particularly as it pertains to our compulsions to clear the land, amend the soil, fence off the lots, and kill off weeds, bugs, and bacteria, exhibits a clear blank-canvas compulsion. But in all fields, from apple growing, to manufacturing, to science, philosophy, religion, and art, we have a hardwired start-from-scratch mentality. It's the perfect metaphor for our early approach to agriculture, but it's only become that much stronger as agriculture has progressed. It's who we are. And if farming is too much of an abstraction for you, ponder what your compulsion as a backyard gardener is. Do you amend the soil? Do you weed? No one is above the blank-canvas compulsion; there are only degrees to which we all participate.

By the way, I'm not hating on Western culture when I point this out, I'm only doing so because we ought to be aware that this approach is simply a choice. Do we go with it, or do we fight it? All I know is that it's not smart to ignore possible alternatives when things aren't working, and it seems to me we are fast painting ourselves into a corner with agriculture (or apple farming, at least). To avoid getting stuck in that corner, it's necessary to evaluate the starting point and plan out the progress—that's all I'm saying.

And speaking of starting and end points, I began this discussion by saying the apple tree could have taken another turn; the remarkable thing is that it did—it *did* defy our own progression. Yes, there are blank-canvas-farmed trees, but in some places there are cave-painting trees, too! Drive down Route 15 in Maine, the Green Mountains in Vermont, or the Catskills in New York and tell me the trees are modernized! Trees like these are the ones early settlers admired and wanted to emulate. They represented success in assimilating to the New World, but now the question is: Which trees are we more likely to emulate, the wild trees or the farmed ones? Are we neatly organized specialists working behind 8-foot-tall fences, or are we inspired to make a prison break and assimilate with our natural surroundings?

The Five-Second Rule

Bill looks exactly like you'd expect a farmer to look. He's about 6 feet tall, in his late 60s, thick-boned, with hands the size of oven mitts. I'm afraid my knuckles will shatter mid-handshake. The boots on his feet are broken in, scratched and rubbed by stone and dirt, achieving a patina that rivals the handles of an old scythe. He has a blue baseball cap that has been bleached by the sun. And his flannel shirt is frayed at the edges with buttons stretched to contain his barrel chest.

He's friendly, and usually cheerful, and although he is clearly German in heritage, he has smiling Irish eyes that penetrate while he speaks. He does so in short sentences. What you will hear is reminiscent of ages past:

fair but firm opinions guided by a conservative compass. His warmness combined with wisdom makes me, born from urban progressive stock, want to slow down and consider things more carefully. And I enjoy this challenge, I seek it out to remind myself of the good in people, but I also must confess it makes me a little nervous. Perhaps I sense an incongruity within my own character? I can bet you anything, though: If I were to confess this to Bill, he would belly-laugh like Santa Claus and say that's just my "city way" of making too much out of nothing. That's Bill.

Recently he's taken on beef farming in addition to his hay operation. To rotate the small herd between pastures, he's now rimmed his fields with electric wires that I must cross before driving up to the apple trees. He tells me to come any time I'd like, and he shows me how to operate the fence gate, which is a series of live wires stretched on springs over the road. He grabs the insulated handles with confidence (it takes him just a few seconds to unhook all four coils), but when I return the following week I find the whole ordeal highly unnerving. It's like Operation, the board game, with greater consequences. I know that if the jolt can contain a 2,000-pound steer with a thick hide, it ain't going to feel pleasant.

I make my way up the steep tractor road to the midway point of the east-facing slope and an open field where I find Bert and Ernie. One is a squat apple tree and the other a tall pear tree. They are growing so closely together, about 16 inches on-center, that it's nearly impossible to make out which limbs belongs to which tree in the tangled mess of branches. But this year, being an on-year for both trees, the fruit itself will make this clear. And Bert, the pear tree, needs to be harvested now, in September. (The *Sesame Street* names I've assigned them tell of their body types, but in general this is true regarding the different growing habits of pear and apple trees: Pears tend to grow sky-high while apples extend out more, and don't usually get as high.)

Bert pears are small, about 2 inches top-to-bottom and about 1½ inches wide at the fat part of their teardrop shape. They have a yellow ocher base, sometimes with a rosy blush from the sun, and they are specked with dark polka dots. Scab. This doesn't affect the integrity of the fruit, though, which is still very hard. The thick, glossy skin is so protective of the sweet, Brazil-nut-tasting flesh that it takes a bashing to compromise the outer layer. And the degree to which Bert pears are tannic, especially just below the skin, is mouth numbing. Why, or how, the cows eat them, I cannot say. The fruit is so bitterly astringent that no human can stomach a second bite, but nonetheless the cows *are* eating them, and I panic.

I want these pears for my perry like a prospector gets gold fever (*perry* is the traditional name for cider or wine made from pears). No cultivated pear—not even the ones specifically cultivated for perry—can come close to matching these properties, which culminate in an exceptionally long-lived, surprising roller coaster of a drink. But the cows are gulping them down at a rate faster than I can pick them up. And to make matters worse, they are making a mess of the foraging site with fresh poop. Let's hope the FDA doesn't see what coats the fruit when it gets milled.

I jump out of the truck and give them my best "Yah!" to get them moving along, but they either can't hear me or don't give a damn. They exploit my lack of herdsman confidence with indifferent tail swats. I'm guessing they know how scared I am to be surrounded by animals of this size, but I'm hanging my safety on the look in their huge doe eyes. "Come on, Fatso!" I yell with my arms flailing. I fake an aggressive charge, but only the little ones move. The big cows have a funny way of feigning cooperation by bending their front knee for a second, but they don't even lift their heads as they continue to Shop-Vac my pears. That's it; I've got to get Bill.

I never finished 10th-grade horticulture, I was expelled from high school in mid-November, but I recall something from that class: Plants produce fruit around their seeds to attract the restless creatures from the animal kingdom; they produce sweet, juicy, colorful, and nutritious meals for animals in the hope that a creature will disperse seed for them. With grapes, berries, and cherries, for instance, if I don't net my crop before they ripen I might as well invite bird-watchers to come over and observe the fruit (and seeds) fly away. The birds do such a thorough job, in fact, I can't recall them ever leaving me dark cherries to enjoy or wine grapes of suitable ripeness. But obviously the same happens in the wild. In the elderberry bush the catbirds are furiously working alongside me; they flap at me aggressively and squawk with perhaps the most annoying voice in the animal kingdom. They want me out.

Berries and most small fruit are their exact size *not* by accident; they were designed (for lack of a better word) to be eaten this way. It's a strategy called endozoochory, and the plant wants to test its seed in as wide a range as possible. Birds just so happen to be best for this purpose. They are the fastest travelers and they are not confined by terrain and water obstacles. But birds are small with small stomachs, so the plants design their fruit accordingly.

The domestic apple is designed differently. It's far too big for a sparrow, or even a crow, and when birds do eat the fruit, which I see them do on occasion, they just focus on the fleshy part outside the core. For all I know, they might not be eating the apple at all but simply looking for bugs to eat inside it. Birds sometimes have the annoying habit of taking a peck, damaging the fruit, and then moving on to the next apple, but squirrels can be even worse—they tend to knock the whole apple to the ground with their play and never even take a bite. And as we know from the old phrase "The apple doesn't fall far from the tree," surely this isn't an opportunistic strategy for transporting seed. So how then does the big, heavy apple become dispersed in faraway lands?

I have heard it said that apples were naturally designed for humans. In some everything-is-for-man view of things (a tradition of thought straight out of Genesis 1:29–30), I can understand why someone would think apples are for humans, but it's simply not true that the fruit is designed for us. In fact, not even nurseryfolks help the apple disperse the seed anymore. Yes, humans are good at *propagating* the tree, but we make very poor seed dispensers. So why do orchard trees produce so many fruits per year, with five times that many seeds per fruit? The answer: because their focus *isn't* on feeding humans.

I know this counters much of the popular folklore circulating around apple trees, but *Malus domestica* never saw much in humankind, except maybe as a decrepit old sugar daddy. We give her the things she needs, but meanwhile she's looking over our shoulder to have her fun. She's looking for some four-legged action: She likes bears, deer, bovines, and equines (but even then, it's not in her nature to pick just one!). This preference is evident in a number of ways. It's not just because the four-leggers are good travelers—they are—but also because they have specially designed stomachs that allow the seed to survive the digestive journey. We can logically assume the tree wants the apple (and seed) to be consumed and then pooped out in faraway lands ("far from the tree"). So ask yourself: Who is better at doing this, humans or the four-leggers? Could a seed even survive our digestive system?

Let's avoid scrutinizing our digestive system and also consider, by comparison, that large four-leggers consume more fruit in a single eating and will therefore have many more seeds to disperse. Have you ever seen a cow under an apple tree when the fruit is dropping? It's like watching in reverse a film featuring a tennis-ball launcher. How many apple seeds would you have in your stomach if you could pass them soundly? And to top it all off, when the four-leggers do "plant the seed," they also happen to drop it within a perfect bed of fertilizer! Seems well designed to me.

I can see you now, anxious and uncomfortable with this news about your trophy wife. "But wait a minute," you say. "Humans like apples, and we're pretty good travelers, too! Plus we have the advantage over four-leggers of being able to climb the trees and get first dibs on fruit." Yes, yes, all that is true. And yet just examine the physical properties of a natural or wild apple, one born from seed (not that one-in-a-million cultivar we've been cloning over and over again). It will become over-whelmingly clear that the fruits are designed to be eaten down where grazing animals can get to them, *not* from the tree. I'm going to tell you this now, but try to remember it when we are talking about cider later: *Malus domestica* was designed to be eaten off the ground.

Again, look at the fruit that comes of the seed: If the tree thought it was a good idea to produce big, soft, juicy fruits with shiny thin skin (like *all* of the fruit you see in stores), then the tree would evolve to produce such apples. But after thousands of years of human cultivation, the tree is still producing "undesirable" seeds that grow up to produce smaller, harder, and bitter-tasting apples. Why would the tree do that if it knows humans prefer big, dumb, and sweet?

Just ask Sir Isaac Newton: The apple is *supposed* to fall. And when it does it needs to withstand the violence and remain on the ground for as long as possible so that as many animals as possible can get to it. Smaller, drier, harder, and thick-skinned (as with russeting) are the traits needed for the drop. Then, to ward off rots, worms, and insects once the fruit is on the ground, it needs preservatives like acids and tannin, whose taste we specifically do not like. And guess what I just described? *Most* wild apples. Maybe when the tree finds out we coat the apples with a chemical wax preservative and store them in gas-controlled storage units for preservative effect it will change its tune and start seeding Fuji-type fruit, but for now four-leggers are her partners of choice.

Maybe it's the word *fruit* that throws us off when we're thinking about apple reproduction strategies. What other trees drop their fruit (and thus seed) straight down from very high up to create the effect of an all-winter-long feeding station? Most other grocery-store fruit is too soft to survive such a drop, and their watery contents are too perishable to remain many months on the ground in freeze-thaw cycles. When you examine the fruit properties of natural apples, you start to realize that they have much more in common with nuts and acorns than with their immediate neighbors in the grocery store. Hickory, walnuts, and oaks (all medium to tall fruiting trees) vary in their external forms, but they all produce fruit that is dry, has a hard outer shell, and is rich in tannin to resist rots and insects.

I previously mentioned that apples are not considered within the realm of forestry, and forestry is not considered in the realm of apple farming, but I hope by now you are questioning this. It's clear the worlds were not intended to be separated; the apple tree *is* a tree, is it not? Forests are not one tree but a community of trees, so perhaps thinking about apples as nuts is a more apt model for our farmers, too. In the end everything about wild fruit tells us the tree belongs in the forest or, in particular, in the community of the forest. We've been fighting nature's intent, not carrying out her will.

Foraging Apples 101

Of all the places I forage, Bill's is one of my favorites. I sometimes come here for the view alone: The Hudson Valley unfolds below like a map until it reaches the Hudson Highlands and Taconics, barely visible 30 miles east. It's stunning. All the stresses that bury me back at my home farm are swept away by the constant wind that rakes across this mountain and swirls around in my ear, creating a soft, subtly fluctuating whistle. After half an hour I'm lost in the noise, and lost in time. It's like stepping into a Fellini movie.

Logically, I try to park downhill from the apples whenever possible —it sucks having to haul them up—but today the cows are in the lower field and I'm forced to approach from the high ground. Parked, I leave my truck in gear and also jam the tire jack under the wheels for safe measure. The parking brake hasn't worked since 2005, and this is one hill you don't want your truck to start rolling on.

I gather my things from the bed and drink as much water as I can, then review my checklist: two tarps, six 5-gallon buckets, two telescoping poles (with hooks fastened at the ends), some clothesline rope, clips, hand pruners, heavy gloves, and a folding saw. The rolled-up tarps, gloves, and clips fit in the buckets (which are stacked in two stacks of three), and I wear the ropes looped around like a scarf. With the pruners and a handsaw in my overall pockets, I can manage all of this paraphernalia in one trip down to the pippin forest.

As I approach the tree line, I can see my target already: bright red apples, up high, and weighing down the ends of the branches. Upon closer inspection I see smaller beige and green apples as well. With this number of apple trees it's often hard to know which boles belong to which apple variety, because the branches intermingle and the trunks are often no more than a couple of feet apart, a dead giveaway they weren't planted by humans. Traditionally farmed trees were planted 25 or 30 feet apart.

My first objective is to pick up the drops—which, as I mentioned earlier, is easy in locations like this because the sloping terrain has gathered them around obstacles like fallen branches or protruding tree roots. There is no grass in this location (it's the woods) and the bulk of the oak and maple leaves have not fallen yet, so the colorful apples stand out well. As I begin to collect, I need to also inspect the apples and identify a discard direction: If the apples are too rotten or too broken by their fall, I toss them far in a predetermined direction so I don't double-inspect them later under another tree.

Filling the buckets and making the heavy haul back to the pickup, I begin to create "clean" conditions under the trees (which is to say there are no more apples to roll my ankle on); then I can begin the work of plucking the high apples. Ideally, I would never harvest fruits hanging firm in the tree—a telltale sign they aren't ready yet—but this isn't my farm and most homeowners don't want me on their land but once or twice a season. At home I just go around every morning and pick up the drops until November, but I don't have time in the short cider-apple season to return to the same site over and over, so I concentrate on the ideal picking times of early October when the apples are approaching 15 Brix. (Brix is the scale that measures sugars in fruits, vegetables, and other plant tissues. There's a direct relationship between the percentage of sugar in the apples and the potential alcohol in fully fermented cider: Higher fruit Brix will equal higher alcohol by volume.)

Now with the ground cleaned up, I can start looking up. The first tree I pluck from I call "Bill's Fence-Line Red." You can guess why. She's a tall redhead, maybe eight times my height, but her trunk is thin enough that I can wrap my arms around it and clasp hands. I have a thing for redheads. This thin characteristic is common with most trees in an even-aged forest, because their energy is concentrated on the race upward. Even so, each apple tree presents a different challenge for setting up and harvesting. No two trees are the same. And I like that.

Out come the tarps. If I could impart one bit of wisdom about apple foraging, it's this: Never rush the tarp setup. Every minute spent draping the tarps effectively will save 10 minutes of bending over later. Plus you will have cleaner, less-damaged fruit in the end. It's for this careful setup that I bring ropes and clips; I need to draw the edges out like a hammock, sometimes over obstacles like rosebushes. I use neighboring trees to tie to, or I can also use the weighted buckets (the ones filled with apples from the initial cleanup) to prevent the tarps from blowing away when wind stirs. Clips can also secure the tarp edges to anything from truck bumpers to thorny bushes. And speaking of thorns, it's always advisable to wear tough overalls and bring heavy gloves. I bring pruners and a handsaw for when I want to eliminate problem vegetation to make it easier to harvest. I even leave a chain saw in the truck for clearing fallen branches or large dead limbs hanging below the tree (but never use a chain saw on poison ivy!). And speaking of poison ivy, Bill's farm is a problem spot. I leave in my truck a 5-gallon carboy of water and some dishwashing soap for when I know my hands have brushed up against the vile weed and they need washing.

When I'm satisfied with the tarp setup, out comes the telescoping pole(s). You can buy these at any hardware store; they are normally used for paint rollers, but I fasten a garden hand rake (or claw) to the threaded end so that I can get the claw's metal fingers around the apple stem and pluck it from the tree. The claw is also handy for hooking the branches for the initial shake. If the apples are ripe they usually all fall with a single tug, but sometimes with apples hanging strong I have to go one by one. (One word about attaching the claw to the end of the telescoping pole: Make sure it's on very securely so it can't fall off in the tree. I use heavy wire to fasten it to the pole, to the point that I could literally hang from the pole when the claw is gripping a high branch.)

My longer telescoping pole reaches 30 feet, plus another 7 feet if you include my reach above my head, but I still can't reach many of the apples in this forest. Bill's Fence-Line Red is no exception—I grab what I can and leave the rest to drop later. I have a code-of-honor rule about leaving a visible amount up there, about 10 percent (this is true regardless of whether I can reach all the apples or not). My reason is I want to give the animals a chance to disperse seed, but I've heard from other foragers (especially of mushrooms) that this sacrifice is the minimum show of respect. Leaving apples for the wild is sort of like pouring the first swig of wine on the floor, "For the homeys."

So now the tarps are drawn, the pole is out, and it's gripping the first loaded branch, ready for the first yank. This is when you need to restrain yourself. Pulling too hard can cause the loaded branch to snap. You need to find finesse in your shaking technique. It's best to start soft and build on the branch's flex-then-recoil action until you are in rhythm with the tree. Build the rocking action to the point that the swing is forceful enough to release the apples.

And here they come! With just the right force, I can release scores of apples from this first branch; they rain down onto the outstretched tarp. I love this noise. It sounds like popcorn. And when the lull dies down I head to the next branch, and then the next, careful never to shake beyond the outreached tarps. In a matter of 20 minutes I am done with this one tree and I can move on. All that's left to do is lift up the tarp edges and roll the apples into a consolidated mass. From there, I can funnel them into buckets or scoop them up. If the six 5-gallon buckets aren't enough for all the apples (which is more likely the case with loaded yard trees, not forest trees), I can also fold the tarp into a hobo sack and fling it over my shoulder like Santa Claus. Apples are heavy, though. If I'm going to hobo-sack it back (not to be confused with the town in New Jersey) to the truck, it's best to visualize no more than four buckets in the tarp. Four 5-gallon buckets is the equivalent of 2 bushels of apples (and a bushel weighs about 40 pounds). If you can haul more than 80 pounds at a time, by all means do, but I'm an old man at this point.

What's in it for the landowner? The deal is: For every truckload of apples I haul from a property, I owe them one case of cider the following summer. That averages out to be a little more than one bottle for every 2 bushels of apples. (A small pickup truck holds about 20 bushels, which, coincidentally, is the same amount as in a commercial orchard bin.) Recently I've taken to buying apples from property owners with wild sources that I know to be exceptional. (Can you believe, they'd rather have money than exchange cider?) In these instances I pay about $150 per truckload when I pick them, and sometimes even more if they help pick that day.

Spending time picking from each tree is important (time together is essential to "acknowledge" the tree), so I don't like to outsource this part of my job as a cider maker. I'd go so far as to say it's the most critical task of the cider maker. A slippery slope exists when buying apples because I believe cider making is a whole life, one that begins with the tree and ends with sharing the drink. And who would want to outsource the best part of the job anyway? Nonetheless, on very big years I have pickers who go on their own, and this requires a very trusting relationship. I pay between $300 and $450 per bin (20 bushels) for truly wild foraged apples, but I need to visit those apple trees first to decide if they are worth the effort. I want to see the tree's relationship to the forest and landscape. Most of all, I need to know the apples have not been sprayed and the soil has not been treated with fertilizers or sprays. (I once had someone try to sell me Roundup-ridden commercial orchard drops as "foraged apples," so I would caution against buying apples without seeing them on the tree first.)

Lady Lazarus

The US Constitution mandates that the federal government collect data from its citizenry every 10 years. You know this annoyance as the US Census, a statistical counting dating back to 1790. It collects more than just simple population numbers; it also probes into your occupational status, your income level, and other none-of-your-beeswax inquiries. Twice, for two separate decennial countings, I worked for the Census Bureau as an enumerator going door-to-door and developing a special love-hate relationship with this constitutional mandate. I love stats and maps, I read almanacs like most people read novels, but once, as a teenager, I had to knock on the door and demand (as an officer of the federal government) that the single mother across from me, 25 years my senior, answer questions about her age and marital status. Uncle Sam sees the forest and not the trees.

Apart from telling the government how to better tax its citizenry, the US Census also has a narrative ambition: It seeks to paint the portrait of American culture as told through numbers in measured time increments. (This narrative thing might just be smoke and mirrors for that tax thing, but nonetheless geeks like me like the numbers.) After 230 years the 23 decennial enumerations have revealed exactly where and how the population has shifted during that span, and you can read (through numbers) how drastically different our lives have become.

In the year 1800, for instance, all but 2 percent of the US population lived in rural areas. We were an *agrarian* society, as Thomas Jefferson had advocated for at that time: "Agriculture is our wisest pursuit, because it will, in the end, contribute most to real wealth, good morals, and happiness." But in a mere 200 years those statistics had exactly flipped: Our US population in 2000 was roughly 98 percent urban, suburban, or exurban in sphere, living dependent on population centers and not off the land. We had become a Modern/industrial people in the course of just two or three life spans. And the 2 percent still living on farms had also been radically changed by industrialization. Farms had become machinery-driven, dependent on chemical and biological technologies, and financed to create economies of scale; their labor and sales markets had gone global. In other words, a look into the recent census numbers shows that by the year 2000 we had become Thomas Jefferson's worst nightmare: "Let our workshops remain in Europe. . . . The mobs of the great cities add just so much to support of pure government as sores to the body." Tell us what you really think, Tom!

But plot twists happen. And these plot twists are readable in the census numbers also. It may go against intuition to link urban development to the benefit of nature, and yet in certain parts of this country that's exactly what it was: good for nature. Whereas by the end of the nineteenth century all but 10 percent of the land in the Northeast had been cleared for pasture or timber farming, after the cultural change nature staged a comeback in these parts.

Try to picture the forests of New York State, for instance, when I tell you that in a mere 100 years, between 1850 and 1950, New York City's population grew 15 times in size, from half a million people to almost eight million, and imagine the impact that had on the rest of the state. As jobs and opportunities consolidated into urbanized areas, the census statistics show that farms were in steep decline and beginning to consolidate as big farms or relocate to other parts of the country. Only in areas with "perfect" soil did farms persist, as elsewhere crop and grazing land went abandoned. The interwoven parts of the rural economies collapsed; entire villages closed up shop. In the Northeast vast sums of acreage went fallow and began to go wild again. In the course of about a century, New York went from 90 percent cleared to 90 percent reforested. And looking down from Google Earth today, the Northeast looks blanketed by trees, making it among the greenest regions in the nation. This might come as a surprise considering that it hosts one-fourth of the total US population (that's one-fourth of the people in just one-seventeenth the total land area, excluding Alaska!). It stands to reason that with this much population, and urban and industrial development (the Northeast also hosts one-third of the total US GDP, by the way), the land would appear from space to be one giant city, but nope: mostly forests.

So what does this all mean for our favorite tree? Forestry and agricultural census statistics have become intertwined with the apple, and a wholly unanticipated side story has the potential to be as glorious as the return of the forests. Or the apple tree could reiterate the depressing history of farms consolidating in favor of mass production (often on faraway lands). Apple history contains both narratives.

When Jefferson was president in the early 1800s, most cultivated apples were grown in small stands around homesteads. An orchard was 8 or 10 trees, and the genetic diversity of those trees was exactly that, 8 or 10 trees (given they were all grown from seed). Even when a tree was grafted, it was still genetically diverse below the ground, but named varieties were not yet done en masse, so apple diversity was still the rule of the nation. In fact, tens of thousands of cultivated varieties existed in the time of Jefferson. And apples were consumed in great numbers as a base ingredient in foods, as America's number one snack food, and of course as alcoholic beverages. But now, over 200 years later, most apple trees are limited in genetic diversity as clones (both above- and belowground); they are grown monoculturally by very few people (and far from the consumer, such as in irrigated deserts), and they are sprayed with an ever-increasing amount of fungicides and insecticides. But to top it all off, Americans don't seem to buy apples anymore! Per-capita consumption is exponentially lower as we've gravitated toward corn- or grain-derived products, as the base of both our foods and our alcoholic drinks.

That's the depressing narrative. But as I said, there's a glorious one, too.

Survival Against the Odds

High up in the fields, nearly 200 years ago, is usually where you would have found Bill's great-grandfather's herd. The cows would either be eating grass or resting, which is pretty much all that cows do. As herd animals, they like to be together; you can sense their anxiety when they get divided. So when it came time to milk the cows down at the barns near the house, it's safe to assume all the cows came down together. This put the herd in close proximity to the backyard orchard. Come September, if Bill's ancestors wanted to use that fruit they'd have to act quickly and get the apples off the ground before the cows did. Even just one horse and a few cows could guarantee that no drops from a 10-tree grove would go uneaten. And if a sudden windfall stirred and the cows didn't get to all the apples at once, surely they would over the next few weeks as the apples started to ferment. Cows love to get drunk.

This pattern went on for decades and decades; they would pack their guts full of fruit and return to the fields to plaster the hillside with apple seed. The following year hundreds—if not thousands—of apple seedlings would spring up in the fields, and yet by the following autumn not a single apple tree could be found. Why? So long as the cows had access back to the same pasture, they would mow the field better than any lawn mower of today. (Interestingly, it's from this heritage that contemporary Americans developed the mowed aesthetic around houses.)

But sometimes a seedling can survive decapitation from grazing animals, and the tree's energy would be refocused underground to its roots (just as the energy returns underground during the dormancy of winter). That energy would be released the following year with even greater vigor, hoping to avoid another run-in with the cows.

The conditions for a pippin storm were brewing. Not only were munched seedling trees building up roots underground with perpetual browsing, but the cows kept adding new seed to the mix, and soon enough these slopes became alive with apple potential. Then came the year of opportunity. Judging by the size of the trees in Bill's pippin forest today, I'm guessing it was about 50 years ago, right around the time the secretary of agriculture under Richard Nixon, and all-around asshole, Earl Butz declared to America's small farmers: *Get big or get out.* The age of large-scale, corporate agriculture was in full blossom, and approaching the end of the twentieth century it was impossible for independent small farmers to make a living. Sure enough, Bill's ancestors were forced to sell off the herd and find employment elsewhere. The fact that they were able to keep living on the home farm and make it part of their income selling hay is a miracle.

Often the first woody material to come back from a clearing, apart from the immediate grasses and wildflowers, are the shrubby thorn-berry bushes. Then, little by little, new trees will make their way in during the open and sunny early stages of reforestation (eventually, of course, the site will go dark beneath tall trees). The design of a tree's seed relates to its place in this cycle. Trees that inhabit the younger stages often have seeds designed to be carried by wind or by birds so that they can pioneer new clearings, often from far away. Aspen, cedar, pin cherry, and other fruit seeds are examples of that. They get dispersed far and wide and set up shop quickly, which is a good thing, because the oaks, hickory, and pines eventually will grab all the light. Nut seeds tend to be dispersed more locally by squirrels and chipmunks.

An interesting thing about this reforestation pattern is that the previous stage of regrowth helps establish the next stage in surprising ways, almost as if the trees were all working together and not in competition! For instance, the thorny bushes that take over during the first stage (the wild rose, the blackberry, and even the invasive Japanese barberry) help to establish cover for the next wave of seeds. Not only do the thornbushes shade the soil and hinder grass growth (enabling the pioneer trees to compete for moisture and nutrients), but these nasty prickers also keep browsing deer from munching the trees. They act like orchard tree guards. Then, once a woody environment is established and a safe habitat is created for nesting squirrels, the small mammals best at stashing nuts help establish favorable conditions for the large trees.

It's assumed that with a diverse set of factors, you would see a diverse set of tree species, both in the upper reaches and in the understory vegetation. The growth habits of specific tree species (including potential height, speed of growth, and seed dispersal methods) are in keeping with particular stages of the forest cycle. They behave accordingly. For example, some trees shoot up sky-high and only later spread out in the upper canopy, while others grow slow and twisted to make the most of the subtle nuances of light down low. If these trees are near a clearing, such as by a roadway, it is common to see the understory growing sideways toward the light.

And an understory tree is what an apple tree is. Everything about the apple tree—its seed dispersal method, potential size, growth speed, and long life expectancy—suggests that apples are happiest in the understory, but will certainly make the most of sunnier forest-edge positioning, too. In fact, upward of 90 percent of the wild apple trees that I've observed are either along roadsides or pasture edges; only rarely are they buried in woods like Bill's forest. With more sun, there can be no doubt these trees produce more fruit, which is why orchard trees are always given maximum sun exposure. But the pippin forest here at Bill's makes me question this assumption. Maybe it's just that the trees had their heyday 20 or 30 years ago and the taller maples and pines will eventually crowd them out, but I think there's something more curious happening. Their unusually tall height suggests some adaptive survival tricks we don't know about. I wouldn't put it past the apple to figure out how to survive in the deep woods, either.

The one thing common with almost all wild apple trees (the ones I see at least), be they in deep woods or along pasture edges, is that they are always in close proximity to a mix of native trees (usually hardwood trees, but also sometimes evergreens). In other words, I rarely see seedling apple trees emerging out of grasslands or open pasture or lawns. Isn't that odd given that 100 percent of the farmed trees are grown in lawn environments? I am convinced, although I don't know the reason, that they need the mix of forest trees in some way—maybe for the soil temperatures or biological composition; maybe for the different bird and insect populations. Or maybe they are communing with the other trees and want to be part of the herd for protective reasons. But whatever the cause, apple trees really do thrive along forest edges. They're trees, after all.

Bill, his sons, and Bill's grandsons are now the fifth, sixth, and seventh generations farming these fields. They have recently taken on cattle again, plus maple syrup production, and sell to a supportive community under the name Mountain Side Farm in Bloomingburg. They are finding that their lifestyle is increasingly similar to the homestead lifestyle of 200 years ago. Bill's cows are living the best life imaginable. They have access to both the grasslands and forests, and it's great (albeit surprising!) to see to see such huge beasts walking through the woods. They do so silently and with grace.

Nationally, there are more farms now than there were in the 1990s. After a century of rapid consolidation, farm sizes are getting smaller again. Thanks largely to customers who do their research, people have reevaluated what a "fair price" for farm goods means; they don't want farmer wages to lag behind society. It seems Jefferson's vision for an agrarian society is making a comeback in health-food stores, farmers

HOW TO TELL IF YOU PROBABLY HAVE A SEEDLING TREE

JOHN BUNKER

↑ LEANING FOR LIGHT!

↑ LIKE AN UMBRELLA

ALONG THE EDGE OF THE WOODS

TALL, WITH <u>NO</u> LARGE LOWER BROKEN LIMBS

~ ALSO: ~

TREE IS GROWING IN A DITCH BY THE SIDE OF THE ROAD; ALONG A STREAM, EDGE OF A POND OR BY THE SEA; ALONG A STONE WALL OR UNDER AN OLD FENCE LINE

MULTIPLE TRUNKS FROM THE BASE: OLD-TIMERS NEVER PRUNED THAT WAY!

MULTIPLE TALL TREES CLOSE TOGETHER AT THE BASE OF AN ANCIENT TREE

Figure 1.1. Clues for distinguishing a seedling (self-seeded) tree by John Bunker of Fedco Trees.

markets, and many restaurants. We have much to thank for that—new knowledge, cultural multiplicity, fortitude, as well as a general will to live. By no accident, these are the exact same qualities on view in wild apples! At Bill's farm the seedling trees have had the fortitude to survive years of grazing; they have the intelligence to read their changing environment; they have the skill to adjust and assimilate; they have the grace to make the best of the situation, even when it's not ideal; and they have the foresight to prepare beyond the immediate conditions. Those are the ingredients for success. Some say it defies the odds that Bill's farm survived, as did the wild apples there. But the oddsmakers, "experts" like Earl Butz, never fully understood their subjects.

TWO

Growing Apples

I'm an apple farmer. It's been almost a quarter century since I started foraging apples, 17 years since I planted my first row of trees, and over a dozen years since I began my homestead orchard, now with hundreds of trees, yet I only recently started calling myself an apple farmer—maybe six or seven years ago. Somehow I felt I hadn't earned it yet.

There are stereotypes our culture assumes of orchard work, and I was equally biased. Today when visitors, particularly journalists, come to the farm I can tell they aren't wowed by what they see: Somehow it doesn't match with my reputation from the cider world. My orchard doesn't fit their preconceptions of a commercial apple farm; my fruit isn't of the same quality or quantity; and my 2005 tractor has less than 1,100 on the hours-meter, which ought to disqualify me as a farmer altogether. But I know what I'm doing, and just as important I know what I'm *not* doing. I *am* a commercial apple farmer.

So I flip the tables and inquire about what they were hoping to see or photograph, and I think I've discovered a common thread aligning their preconceptions. This cultural stereotype of orchard work seems to be emanating from a single source: "the perfect apple." Because we've come to expect flawlessness in a dark red, shiny apple, or in a round, sweet golden apple, we no longer approach the orchard with an open mind. Even people like me, who are okay with imperfections, still instinctively, unflinchingly reinforce this standard when presented with options at the grocery store. No one grabs for the dull-colored apple or the one with scab or insect marks. And after generations of this sort of behavior, stock clerks won't even give us the option. They're tired of throwing out fruit; uglies aren't allowed in their store anymore.

But here's what I discovered about people's insistence on perfect apples that really surprised me: Our cultural standard for apple perfection extends far beyond the fruit to include the places and even the people surrounding the apple! Somewhere, somehow, lay consumers are getting the notion that they know what the apple environment is supposed to look like. But where the heck is this coming from?

Let's look into this. We can fault television and magazine advertising for implanting an orchard fantasy in people's minds, or we can fault consumers for simply not knowing the reality behind where their food comes from these days. Clearly both are culprits, but why aren't we more skeptical of marketing, and why aren't we more inquisitive about something so vital? If my homely-looking orchard and I are victims of agricultural profiling, we can say it's because the dominant players in the apple industry control the narrative and are directing consumers toward what *only they* can produce (and why wouldn't they do this—this is America, isn't it?), but it's also because of the way our culture selects authorities in the first place. We need to believe in experts, which is a much larger cultural vulnerability, easily exploited.

And who are these experts? Well, those who are financially successful in a particular industry are experts, right? Come on, do we *not* give the most profitable automatic authority, particularly over matters that made them rich in the first place? Of course we do! But we also grant automatic authority to scientists and researchers (the academic wing of an industry). And if both the large-scale apple farmer and the pomological researcher promote the same thing, as they do when it comes to "the perfect apple," then the public has heard (with an *a*) all they need to on the subject of apple expertise—no need to challenge it.

Whether these two groups of people, scientists and the most successful, are the right people to be given authority is up for debate, but that's not what I'm calling attention to here. What I'm saying is that my not matching up to expectations isn't a failure on my part; it's the failure of society when it comes to granting authority. As a culture of specialists, we excuse ourselves of firsthand knowledge in many vital fields (most alarmingly health) and champion a system of expertise to guide us.

Authority may be a societal construct to serve over us and protect us, but it's not a foolproof system. And of course, I didn't know I needed to question this when I first started learning about apple growing.

Bought the Farm

The Brown house is not brown. It was a white Colonial-style home when I first laid eyes on it on a steely cold day in January 2006. The original date of the house is unknown, but it appears on tax maps by 1850. It's a small home by today's standards, but for a frontier structure it has a few Federal-style details that suggest the Browns went the extra mile to bring culture to this rough patch of remote land.

Predating all of this, the property was once part of a huge, 2-million-acre land patent that remained unsettled throughout the 1700s. This was the wilderness until after the Revolution, when smaller tracts were divided off and sold to land speculators. From one of these smaller holdings, an additional 130 acres was carved off in 1817 with the help of the New York lawyer Aaron Burr, and sold to homestead farmer William Brown. The Brown family lived here for 150 years, maintaining it as a diversified homestead farm with each generation, until in the 1960s when their eventual poverty forced them to sell. By then highways and cars had made Sullivan County more accessible, and this property twice passed through the hands of city transplants, first in 1962, and then again in 1986. We were to be the third of this ilk to call the Brown house home.

It was my 12th year in New York. Manhattan, then Brooklyn, felt like it had changed in ways that made it hard to stay. It was a gritty city in 1994 when I moved there. For whatever reason, I liked it more as a hard-boiled place, but Mayor Giuliani, and then Mayor Bloomberg, helped file down the rough edges and drop the crime rate, and a drastic uptick in wealth followed. I started to feel like a vagrant being driven out, tarred and feathered. Always there was someone with more money about to move in and change what I liked about the desolate artist neighborhoods. One by one they succumbed: Chelsea, East Village, DUMBO, Williamsburg. Rents climbed and poorer artists were forced to relocate farther and farther into Brooklyn. I was sick of moving. I drew the line at Queens.

You've heard these complaints a million times. It happened before I got there and I'm sure it's still happening now. But really, the city isn't to blame for my eventual flight. I changed just as much as New York did. I moved there to be a painter, and all of a dozen years I tried to make it there as one, sleeping on couches, on the floor of my painting studio, or in shared apartments. Only on rare occasion did my paintings help pay expenses, so I began to rely on gig work in textile design, photography, architectural drafting—just enough to pay for subway fare, cigarettes, and a slice of pizza. I wanted my focus to stay on art, and so long as the city was affordable I could continue believing this was my calling. Until I got older I hadn't considered that another artistic pursuit might be more appropriate for me. That's what changed, not New York.

While living in New York during the 1990s, I'd also return to Maryland for a few months each summer to the fishing cottage along the shores of the Chesapeake Bay that I shared with my longtime friend. At $500 per year, the price was right, and I could just as easily paint down there. Except the cottage was tiny. Split between Steve and me, there wasn't space to sprawl out and paint like in my studio in Brooklyn. Instead I painted on mobile canvases fastened to my backpack easel.

The weather was warm and humid and the sun off the water gave a Venetian glow to the atmosphere. It's the same wet warmth that gives Titian and Tintoretto that sultry quality, distinguishing them from the more illustrative (some might even say "hygienic") Florentine works. But ultimately, for me, the Chesapeake had the advantage of outdoor spaces where I could be alone with my thoughts. And I developed a real love for this. Letting my mind free-associate was satisfaction enough. Nature represented a newfound peace, with things "just the way they are," and this appreciation grew until I didn't even need a canvas anymore. In fact, art, with all its paraphernalia, ritual, and emphasis on the finished product, felt like it was interfering with my direct relationship with the wild. I eventually stopped bringing the paint box with me and just walked in nature, interpreting what I saw.

In a sense, this was a selfish decision. Giving up producing art is a move toward giving up on communication. Or worse, might this be anti-social behavior, or a form of narcissism? Nature, not the canvas, became my mirror. And yes, I fell in love with the gaze. It triggered thoughts in every direction, and I saw giant, cosmic parallels with all of them. I was like a pot smoker without the pot, and I could think of no better use of my time than just observing nature. Leaving communication behind didn't feel selfish; it felt like a calling.

Back in the city, other developments were forcing me to reckon with my identity as an artist, now in my thirties. As I became more exposed to the art world, I began meeting successful artists who were showing in galleries and museums. They offered a comparative model. Being around famous artists had the effect of both filling me with delusions and disillusioning me to my eventual success. I bounced between these possibilities in a manic-depressive state, never knowing which was more likely to happen, until eventually I concluded that I lacked the social skills and the business drive that "showing" artists had. I saw which direction my art career was heading, and I liked my privacy. But then why was I in New York City?

I didn't know anything about the southern Catskills. I had never been here before, Polly had never been here, and we knew no one who had spent time in the Borscht Belt. Geographically, Sullivan County just fell into a cultural blind spot for me during all my years in New York City. But perhaps that was part of the appeal—not a gourmet coffee or craft brewery around.

On paper (or, by this point, online), the near Catskills seemed too good to be true. Images of wild landscapes still resembled the Romantic-era paintings of Thomas Cole or Church, yet Wurtsboro was only 75 miles from the GWB, up New York's nicest artery, the Palisades Parkway. Plus Sullivan County had the cheapest real estate in the tristate area. But the icing on the cake was the Otisville train station. How could it be that a commuter train climbed the Shawangunk Ridge and served an apparent wilderness with a direct link to one of the most populated places on earth? I was working in architecture at the time, and I couldn't resist the thought of leaving the office, boarding at Penn Station, and magically being teleported to a world Thoreau might find familiar.

And so I surfed the real estate websites. *Acreage* and *old houses*: Those were my two main search engine terms. I wanted to live in a house with space and history. The reverse side of this LP, of course, is that I didn't want to live in a neighborhood. I had had enough of that in Brooklyn, thank you. So as I combed the listings I found a few that popped out, and it was time to take action. Coordinating with a realtor, I arranged to spend a day visiting seven homes, starting with the most promising.

It was an easy sell. When I arrived at the Brown house I was instantly picturing Polly and me there. It had history, it had acreage, the land was bucolic, simple, and raw. The place had a gentle past without assertive landscaping gestures or bold architectural transformations. The only problem, apart from the house being close to the road, was that the listing price was more than what we wanted to spend. For a couple of months, our agent tried to find us comparable properties at a lower cost, but the more he showed me, the more my mind fixated on the first one.

Old man Hester was 80 when he put the house up for sale. I liked him, he liked me, and he wasn't keen on letting the realtors do the communicating between us. Hester said that home builders and land developers had come to look at the property—it was a large lot after all, and prime for subdividing. But he was holding out for someone who might save the old farm. I know this sounds like something a realtor would say, but the difference, as I saw it, was the integrity of the messenger. Whereas someone in marketing or sales is known to glorify only favorable elements of the truth and carefully omit parts of the bigger picture, I didn't get this sense from Hester. "I'm 80. I got no kids, nor a wife anymore. Farming can keep you active only for so long, but sooner or later it destroys your back," he said ominously. "I can't do the things I want to do. Still, if farming is about making the right decisions for the land, then properly selling the farm is part of that. I don't want to see it folded up like a piece of trash just because I'm done with it. I'd rather see someone learn the economy of this place just as I did over time."

This was to be the biggest financial decision of my life. Was it wise to tie Polly's and my future to an emotional appeal? Should I have stepped back and let time or fate decide how things went? This pitted acceptance and living within our means against the concept *How are we supposed to live?*—that quintessential American dilemma. I found myself asking over and over again, *What is life if we don't take chances on our aspirations?*

We made an offer. It was countered. We countered his counter. And he accepted. By March we were working on the bank loan, and by April old man Hester was helping us prepare the garden. The rototiller spit up a heavy rock at my foot and I looked down, bewildered, as if to say, *Who planted that there?* Then I looked up to see Hester pointing to the rock walls, the features I most adored about this property. "You see? One stone at a time," he said.

By July Fourth we were in our new home.

The Other Maryland Crab

I didn't just watch *Baby Boom*, with Diane Keaton, and decide to quit my office job, leave New York, and move to the country to start an orchard business. Oh, naïveté played a huge role in it, but don't get me wrong, I also had some experience with what I was getting into. I already had a bit of homeowner experience, and I'd even planted a row of apples in Maryland. As for those trees, they developed with great success, and I figured I could just repeat that on a greater scale in a new location. That latter part is what was naive.

As the previous millennium came to a close, so too did the life of old Neil. Neil was the farmer who owned the lands where Steve and I rented our cottage along the Chesapeake. Following his death, the summer of 2000 proved to be our last season along those western shores of the Bay. Cynicism mounted as the farm switched hands; it was no secret what a California land developer wanted with 200 acres of waterfront property.

For us, the beach didn't seem sunny that last summer; the orchard began to appear tired and the waters had lost their expansive feel. Neil had been a great figure to Steve and me: His patient approach to decisions, particularly regarding the property, had become emblazoned on us. I will remember him as embodying the long view. But just like the waves lapping near our bare feet, the twenty-first century was moving in.

I didn't even get the chance to harvest the fruit before the bulldozers obliterated the secret places where I first fell in love with apple trees. That fall I returned to New York defeated, but also desperate: I needed to find another retreat if I was to survive the draining intensity of the city. I began to search online real estate around the Bay (albeit with the limited funding of an artist in my twenties), and sure enough the Chesapeake provided again: This time, where land was the cheapest, on the opposite coastline in the area of Crisfield, Maryland.

At $34,000, my first house was a fixer-upper. It had been abandoned for years when I closed the deal in May 2001. The structure stood on beams as if on a pier at the edge of a vast marshland. It floated in the company of similar weather-beaten and abandoned houses, giving the overall appearance of ghost ships aligned at port. Only this was a sea of phragmites, a panorama of mudflats with tall grasses in all directions. Yet from the height of the home's widow's walk, I could see above the reeds to where the waters of the Chesapeake swallowed the setting sun. That alone was worth the investment.

Crisfield is the southernmost town in Maryland and it's decidedly "southern" in culture. It's a bit jarring, in fact. I came directly from New York City, and the old storefronts reminded me of Mayberry, or something out of a Wendell Berry novel. But it's not a farming community like the rest of the Delmarva Peninsula. It's an old fishing town, literally built on top of shucked shells from the oyster boom of the late 1800s. Those who stayed in the area after the oyster beds died out became culturally isolated from the rest of America's progressive East Coast. I was equally attracted to that and to its dead-ringer likeness to the Mississippi Delta. The heat often corroborated with this picture. And so, too, did the mosquitos. The people of Crisfield moved slow, talked slow, and they thought slow, a perfect absorption of the natural beauty and challenges.

As a city getaway it was perfect. Except it was six hours south and there was nothing but work, humidity, and bloodthirsty insects waiting for me. Okay, so maybe it wasn't perfect, but it was within my budget. And although I was hoping for privacy, I discovered two or three neighbors in those "abandoned" houses whom I grew to like. Characters straight out of a Popeye cartoon were squatting amid the ruins, and little by little I learned of their tendency to rant to themselves. The mystery of all those empty rum bottles in the drainage ditch: solved.

I grew to see my neighbors as integral to the bucolic landscape. They were warmhearted people without the same judgment I brought to the table. Unwittingly, I had displaced one of their friends when I bought my house, but despite this, and despite the fact I was a city brat, they were friendly with me and didn't treat me as an outsider. Except my immediate neighbor was a little *too* friendly: Dale was what's known as a constant talker. On days when he was home, I couldn't so much as get the mail without finding myself cornered by his opinions on popular news stories, or ex-wives. With his Appalachian drawl, he'd start his rants (ironically), "I'll tell you one thing." Eventually I just had to walk away or drive off in my truck. Naturally, I needed to create separation between our two houses, and that's when I decided on a tall hedgerow. I chose apple trees.

This is the background to my first orchard, if you can call it that. I had developed a love for apple foraging, and as my first summer in Crisfield drew to an end, my thoughts turned to autumn and the thing most missing in my life. I needed apple trees again.

The actual act of planning, planting, growing, and marketing apples is a subject so large that would-be orchardists sequester themselves away in four-year colleges just to get a handle on this. It's worthy of all that focus: Apples have thrice the number of genes as humans, and the act of apple growing touches on every subject, from biology to ethics to economics. But this doesn't mean you can't make it a weekend pastime, either. Apple farming is not regulated by licenses in the same way architecture or medicine is (only when orchardists want to use a controlled substance do they have to be trained and pass tests). Dabbling is allowed.

This is not to say the practice of apple farming has any fewer variables or potential problems than architecture or medicine, just that they haven't successfully boxed out amateurs or the public yet. We ought to honor this permeability. And in fact, we ought to break down barriers with those other less fortunate industries: Children should be encouraged to fantasize and draw pictures of their dream house (and that's architecture), and a babysitter can send a coughing child to bed early after drinking orange juice (and that's medicine), so perhaps there's leeway even within heavily regulated industries? Maybe we can undo reverence for "the experts"? My point being, the joy and the insights offered by dabbling (be it in apple farming or whatever) are too significant to hand over just because we live in a highly specialized era obsessed with efficiency. We have a responsibility *not* to forfeit part of ourselves to trained professionals.

Yes, growing apples is complicated (or it can be), and every location will offer more layers of struggle, but it's important to remember that overcoming challenges is vital to our being. It's important to all beings. And believe it or not, it's fun. Really! Sports offers a good comparison: A game of baseball has all the same challenges (adversity, strategy, struggle), and yet people young and old find satisfaction in it. You don't need to be a master to allow yourself to play. So really, apple growing should be put in this context. Just play ball.

And if you still feel intimidated, or believe apple growing is best left in the hands of professionals, recall that not long ago everyone used to grow them (and in some mountain cultures, everyone still does!). In fact, apple growing was the national pastime 200 years before baseball. It was the orchard, not the diamond, that offered society common experiences. And this is how we arrived with so many common apple idioms that now only baseball can compare. "Being out on a limb," "One bad apple spoils the bunch," "Apple of my eye"; the list numbers in the hundreds. It's just a matter of getting your hands dirty.

I left my home in Brooklyn well before rush hour. There was a chill in the Long Island air, but as I drove the length of the New Jersey Turnpike, and then worked my way down the spine of Delmarva, the heat and humidity began squeezing in like a whole-body blood pressure test. Lest you've never been south of Philadelphia, *September* is just another word for "summer." By 11 AM the cicadas were screaming louder than the whistling from the truck windows. Of course that old Ford had no air conditioning.

Just over an hour before my arrival in Crisfield, I stopped in at an Agway thinking they could help me find some trees. And what did I see next to the register, practically forcing themselves upon me? Eight random ornamental and edible apple varieties in container pots, marked, CLEARANCE, GODDA GO! (*sic*). Well, even I knew it probably wasn't wise to plant trees in this heat, but at $10 a pop it was worth a shot. I laid down four Andrew Jacksons (Delaware is a tax-free state), loaded up my truck with all eight trees, and finished the drive.

Please, God, let Dale be somewhere else today! I thought, and sure enough, I made it from the driveway to the house unmolested. I brought out the hose and a shovel and planned out the locations of the trees by physically putting the pots where the holes would go. The nursery tags gave instructions to plant them 8 to 14 feet apart and expect them to grow about 12 feet tall. That was quite a bit smaller than what I knew apple trees to be, but a 100-by-12-foot wall between the houses was just what I needed.

Digging: The soil in those parts is a 50–50 blend of sand and humus; it's like breaking open a brownie. Best of all, there's not a rock within 100 miles of Crisfield. Digging the eight holes was as easy as saying it. After peeling back the plastic pots from the root balls, I just plopped in the trees and watered. Having lost a quart of blood to the mosquitoes, I went inside to shower. Job done.

The following day I saw Dale ride off on his bicycle and I ran out to water the trees again. This happened again on the third day. On the fourth day I watered the trees one last time and headed over the Bay Bridge to visit my parents in DC. That morning smoke rose from the Pentagon, and as I tuned on the news, just before the towers collapsed, my thoughts quickly turned to Polly, and to all my friends whom I knew traveled near or under the World Trade Center that infamous day.

The lines back home were severed by the wreckage, and the National Guard wasn't allowing anyone to enter the city. I had to wait for calls from borrowed cell phones until I knew everyone was accounted for. By the end of the week, I was able to head back up the New Jersey Turnpike to Exit 13, where the familiar Oz-like skyline had become a foreign cityscape. Summer was now a distant memory.

I had forgotten all about those eight apple trees until, the following May, I returned to my construction project in Crisfield. By then the blossom was long gone and the trees were looking fantastic! In fact, they were looking *too* good; I felt like a parent coming home to find the kids doing their homework. *What's going on that I don't want to know about?* Was it the loose, sandy soil or the salty-humid environment that made these trees thrive in my absence? Was this just what apple farming is?

Another year later and I was already seeing fruit, and on that front I was pleasantly surprised, too: The quality was as good as in grocery stores—not a wormhole, speck of rot, or surface imperfection on the large, colorful apples. And the crab apple trees held on to their tiny red fruit nearly all winter long, brightening the landscape. All of this, without a lick of watering or chemical propping.

I eventually finished my fixer-upper project and sold the house in 2007. Driving out of town on my last day, I felt a huge weight lifting. All the frustrations of second-home ownership—the frozen pipes, worrying about the place while I was gone—were someone else's problems now. But the relief was mixed with nostalgia. I was leaving behind more than just an inanimate object. The trees and the culture were living beings that I grew to appreciate. I was rooting for them. The town in my rearview mirror seemed to embody the end of an era, a way of life that wasn't likely to survive the twenty-first century. I knew when (or if) I ever returned, I'd be sure to find the place better off, as politicians and developers would say—but less colorful to my eyes. Certainly, its uniqueness was in jeopardy.

And Crisfield represented the ending of a personal era. In my late 20s and early 30s everything seemed wide open, much like the Delmarva landscape, and I could take chances and see where fate brought me; now approaching my late 30s, I needed focus. Ahead of me was New York State and another orchard, this time in the mountains. I couldn't just drift around foraging apples and haphazardly planting apple trees all my life—so I thought. The bug of husbandry bit. I needed deliberateness, I needed focus, I needed *intentionality*.

The Back 40

I was a chain saw newbie behind the trigger, felling some 80-foot pines and heavy oak trees on the hillside behind our Wurtsboro barn. Somehow I survived, somehow I didn't flatten any structures, and somehow I rescued 10 old apple trees hiding amid the forest regrowth. By our first winter, 2006–07, I had removed 4 acres of woods; I now had my agricultural blank canvas just as the pioneers did. I was 35 years old, excited by farming, and I had plenty of back to give. By the warmth of the January hearth I fantasized about my future orchard. I pictured rows and rows of healthy, billowing trees just like in Crisfield; I pictured pointed ladders with friendly workers to help collect the fruit; and I pictured field bins loaded with red apples waiting for a tractor to bring them to the barn. In short, I pictured "the perfect orchard" that forever dogs me.

Surely I wasn't the first to be excited by all the possible apple varieties in the nursery catalogs. By the late 1800s there were tens of thousands of documented cultivars in the United States, many of them even illustrated, as if by Audubon himself, in the 1906 classic, *The Apples of New York*. But by the twenty-first century, most of those varieties were extinct, axed when efficiency became the rule of the apple industry. Alas, finding cultivars of interest proved challenging. I had better luck in mail-order catalogs with the likes of Fedco Trees and St. Lawrence Nurseries. I could easily justify the price—just a few dollars more—considering that the common varieties available in common catalogs were already grown en masse in the nearby Hudson Valley and readily available. I craved the rare.

In keeping with our obsession with history, we decided this was to be an orchard devoted to New York heirloom varieties. If we were to create value from a 4-acre orchard, it had to come from a niche market. I ordered: Golden Russet, Newtown Pippin, Northern Spy, and Esopus Spitzenburg for my first 10 plantings. Each variety had a 200-year-plus history, but choosing local varieties (as opposed to, say, a Fuji or Granny Smith) also meant I could be assured they were suitable matches for my climate. And as a buyer interested in local agriculture, I knew these trees to be of interest to like-minded customers. But the icing on the cake (and this is true for most heirloom varieties) is that each of these cultivars was described as "dual-purpose for ciders," meaning that if I couldn't sell the fresh fruits, they had "cider properties," too. I could just ferment the juice and enjoy the apples at my leisure rather than worry about them rotting.

Be prepared to receive the trees "bare-root," said the catalogs. That meant the trees were shipped without soil; their exposed root systems needed immediate planting. This could only be done in a limited window of dormancy, when the tree is not sending energy upward but the ground is unfrozen and workable. April and November are these months in my part of the world. With preparation and an early order, there is as great a chance of bare-root transplant success as there is with potted trees.

And speaking of roots, both of these nurseries explained that their trees were grafted onto "standard rootstocks." I hadn't the foggiest clue what this meant, but the literature went on to describe "standard-sized trees" as fruiting in about eight years, growing tall and stately (often 30 feet tall or higher), and exceptionally long-lived (more than 100 years).

After reading this it now dawned on me that those short Crisfield trees must have not have been on standard rootstocks. No matter, here in Wurtsboro "tall and stately" was just what I was hoping for. But be warned, said the catalogs, standard-sized trees require an enormous distance between them (25 to 30 feet) with rows equally wide or wider. Again, I had no problem with this. There was plenty of space to fill on my freshly denuded hillside. As I mapped out where my mail-order brides would end up, I pictured their fully grown selves shading the slope. By God, this would be a beautiful sight!

That spring my hands were finally getting dirty again. The first 10 trees arrived from St. Lawrence Nurseries, and I immediately set out with a head full of energy to prepare the holes. But waiting out there for me was something entirely not what I expected. The soil in Wurtsboro was exactly opposite from what I had experienced in Crisfield—shallow, heavy, rocky, and lousy with tree roots. (I had just cleared the woods but not the stumps.) Digging proceeded with immense difficultly. Had I had half a brain, I would've aborted the mission at Hole Number One and given those trees to someone else. But I plowed on. I removed more rocks than dirt from the ground; if it weren't for my heist of soil from Polly's vegetable garden, I wouldn't have had enough dirt even to backfill the holes and cover the roots. Finally, adding water, I made a slurry of mud the consistency of toothpaste and reached into the cold, wet mixture to feather the roots outward from the trunk toward the edges of each hole (effectively giving the trees a wide foundation from which to stand on their own). Ten grueling hours later, that was that.

All that was left for me to do was step back at a distance and admire the accomplishment—the harder the struggle, the greater the reward, right? But, wait, what? Viewed from a distance the 10 tiny trees (spaced as recommended, 25 to 30 feet apart) virtually disappeared into the naked hillside. Where was my orchard? This was embarrassing.

That fall, as the window for late-season tree planting neared, I vowed to purchase more trees and reconsider my options. Maybe it wasn't such a good idea to plant standard-sized trees when one of my other goals was to have the hillside appear full now, not 15 years from now. I discovered that there were other rootstock options, ones that fruited more quickly and demanded less space. As it turns out, there are over a dozen rootstock choices that commercial nurseries use to graft their trees onto. They do this for a number of reasons: Some rootstock trees bear fruit more quickly, some create higher yields per acre, some exhibit disease resistance, and most make accessing the fruit far easier without the requirement of being high on a ladder. Above all, the point of these rootstocks is to create a consistent base so that the apple planter can manage the orchard accordingly. Why didn't I know these all-important facts before laying out my orchard?

It's the rootstock that dictates the growing properties of each tree, more than the grafted variety. For instance, if you wanted a McIntosh to grow only to about 15 feet tall (half the size of a standard-sized tree) and fruit quicker—say, in four or five years (also half the requirement of a standard apple tree)—then you can choose a McIntosh grafted onto semi-dwarf rootstock. Planting a greater number of semi-dwarf tress (or fully dwarfing ones) in closer proximity (12 feet or closer) gives the impression of a fuller orchard. And certainly it promises fruit sooner. But was this the look I wanted?

So for my fall planting I chose to compromise between semi-dwarfing trees and full-sized standard trees by planting 30 new "semi-standards" (with the same New York heirlooms grafted on top). Specifically, I chose as my base M111, which was developed in England (and was until recently the predominant rootstock choice of the apple industry). Trees grafted to M111 rootstock begin to fruit sooner (after about six or seven years) and grow to be 75 percent the size of those old-fashioned standard trees (15 to 25 feet, instead of 30 feet or higher). With this particular choice, I was able to space 30 trees closer together and with less space between the rows, fitting three times as many trees in the same amount of space as the 10 standard trees planted earlier in the year. By Thanksgiving 2007 I could say I had an orchard!

Change of Plans

At the start of 2008, I was feeling secure and was excited by where we were as homesteaders, but on a societal level a crisis loomed and the impasse eventually eroded my confidence. By the summer of that year the world economic systems were crashing, our day jobs lay in peril, and our savings were being ravished. Uncertainty permeated everything, even the orchard: The more I read about apples, the more I began second-guessing my decisions. For one, we needed to make money a lot sooner, and my standard and semi-standard rootstock choices were notoriously slow to fruit. I also began lamenting my heirloom variety selections as I discovered more about why they weren't common anymore. They were prone to a number of diseases that could only be subdued with a yearly toxic spray schedule.

No way, for instance, could I grow Spitzenburgs without having also to combat fire blight, so the question arose: What was I going to do when I saw signs of the disease? I wanted to grow apples with little to no spray ("organically," if I must), but fire blight and other killing problems could wipe out my entire orchard in a single season! Would I not employ whatever tool was necessary to prevent this? Scary thoughts and seemingly conclusive science were eroding my idealism, and I wasn't sure which direction to go for a healthy orchard. When push came to shove, what was my orchard management plan? Would I do nothing? Would I use only organic sprays? Or, would I employ every possible intervention (a strategy universally called "conventional orchard management")?

When things are going well, we as a people forget what it's like to worry about paying bills and having enough money to cushion ourselves for life's surprises (like a dental emergency or the car breaking down), but when times are rough and *everyone* is fighting over the same scraps it feels like we're living on the edge. Every little expense is like watching the gas gauge fall further below empty, knowing that we're miles and miles from the nearest station. In October the financial crisis had spread out to an all-out panic on the global markets. Uncertainty was now pandemic. My employment in the field of architecture ran dry as the housing market was hardest hit, and Polly's teaching hours were cut as well. To say the glass was half empty would have been optimistic; it was more like 95 percent empty.

After another growing season my apple trees still looked more like nursery stock than a planted orchard. Was this what my apple dream had come to, a bare hillside with some twigs poking out of the ground? Not even two years in, I already wished I could start the homestead farm all over again—a sentiment, it turned out, that would dominate my orchard decisions for many years to come.

———

Some nights my mind wakes me up and wants to chat, usually around 1 AM. Sometimes I wait it out, but other times I give up and go downstairs to the daybed where I read. During stressful periods this routine becomes a nightly occurrence and I'm likely to be reading until four or five in the morning. The winter of 2008–09, as the world lay stunned by recession, I plowed through a lot of books.

Two stood out for me: The first was eerily fitting for the times, a memoire by Adele Crockett Robertson called *The Orchard*, about a young woman's takeover of the family farm at the onset of the Great Depression. As external conditions worsen around her, we follow her efforts to save the land from foreclosure in the face of blow after blow. I won't spoil the ending, but suffice it to say it's a powerful story about the changing economic landscape and its devastating effect on family orchard businesses. It's a must-read for foodies and the general public alike.

The other book was more of an educational text regarding the how-tos of organic apple growing. *The Apple Grower*, by Michael Phillips, is fact-filled and focused on just apple growing, but because the author takes a holistic perspective you can't help but to read a larger significance between the lines. Both books landed in my hands like divine intervention during a bleak winter, the two books back-to-back seemingly curated by Voltaire: In trying times focus on your apple trees.

I kept planting. I cleared two more half-acre patches from the woodland, and that spring I planted another round of apple trees, this time on a semi-dwarfing rootstock that promised to fruit even sooner, in four or five years. Inspired by Michael Phillips's book, I employed an organic approach in my orchards, keeping my hands dirty and my mind clean. *Try not to worry so much*, I told myself. *Just focus on the trees.*

We were in New Hampshire over the holiday season, near Mount Monadnock, where Polly's parents live. It's an area that has a long New England history, evidenced by the dominance of old colonial homes as well as the numerous graves in the town cemeteries. Unique to America, it's an area where the dead drastically outnumber the living. But it's most famous for its natural history. Anchored by the prominent mountain, a rolling landscape unfurls with "ponds" (which to anyone else were lakes) and forests as far as the eye can see. The natural beauty has long inspired writers such as Thoreau, Emerson, Willa Cather, and Margaret Fuller. But I, personally, would rather focus my attention and time on the towns, which were usually nothing more than a few dozen homes, a meeting-house, a church, and an inn (with a pub). There's something about these villages that seems synonymous with Christmas. The cold climate, the hand-carved details on old wooden buildings, the hilly terrain . . . with or without snow, it all adds up to a storybook holiday. And although I try not to get sucked into the season's hype, I can't help but look forward to my few days there each winter.

My in-laws live 10 minutes up the mountain, but I like to volunteer to pick up groceries to give them "family time" (and I doubt I'm missed). That year, the year after Obama was elected, I remember browsing the shops and working all week on a crossword puzzle at the pub. Maybe it's just an introvert thing, or maybe it's because I live on a farm, but a few days of this each year is all I could ever hope Christmas could be. While walking around I stepped into a health-food store specializing in local New Hampshire produce and discovered Farnum Hill Ciders. It struck me as unusual that a cider would be packaged like a champagne, and that the price was high ($18), making it comparable with wines rather than beers. So I read the back label and learned it was made from English cider varieties—apples I never heard of before, with names like Dabinett, Somerset Redstreak, and Yarlington Mill. This was uncharted territory for me, but I figured I had to try it. This was a good opportunity to represent apples to my in-laws and perhaps shore up faith that their daughter had married into a promising industry.

There is a tradition—God knows when or how it started—that on Christmas Eve you're supposed to eat oysters as an alternative to meat; whatever the reasoning, when I poured the Extra Dry Farnum Hill alongside the mollusks, I had my own Christmas epiphany. Truly, this was a match made in heaven. I knew in an instant what direction my orchard needed to head: My art background, my passion for rare varieties, my need to sell to a niche market—it became glaringly obvious that our farm needed to become a cider orchard.

Cider, of course! What did it matter to a cider farmer that the apples were blotchy, russeted, scabby, or misshapen? Was this not the perfect solution for a no-spray or organic apple farmer? Let the rest of the industry toil for apple perfection, efficiency, and scalability, I'm going to turn our farm into an artist's studio. Warts and all.

Big Bertha

New York has a long apple history and remains the second-largest apple producer in the United States. It's held this position mainly by morphing to meet Modern-era market demands and business structures. Leveraging economies of scale, many smaller orchards were absorbed by big operations consolidating ownership and making it more efficient to manage teams of laborers (temporary foreign workers, mostly) between the lots. Who, exactly, "the farmer" is in this scenario is up for debate: Is it the property or business owner, or is it the people working the fields? Regardless of the answer, this is how the majority of apples hit the market now.

That's one type of orchard, but New York State helps to preserve many small and independent apple farms, too. No doubt, the proximity to a large and wealthy urban population gives New York State a direct-engagement advantage, particularly with consumers who demand to know where their food comes from. The "Buy Local" movement further advantages Hudson Valley growers and even farms as far as New York's Great Lakes region. They might be quite a bit farther away than orchards in New Jersey or Massachusetts, but being in the same state at least guarantees some level of localness.

Furthermore, New York's apple industry has the advantage of comparatively well-funded agricultural programs and pomological research. This manifests itself in a number of ways, but most notably through the Cornell University / New York State Agriculture collaboration. Research stations, like the one in Geneva, New York, are the crowning jewel of pomological development, not just in America, but worldwide. No place on earth has had a bigger impact on *Malus domestica*, and the benefits of this research are available to everyone via a network of Cornell Cooperative Extension offices, local in every county.

Not only do I have access to my Sullivan County Cornell Cooperative Extension where I live, but I'm also only 30 minutes from the Hudson Valley Research Laboratory, where I can meet with people who specialize in apples. Plus I have a number of small and large commercial orchards near me, so I'd say I'm uniquely surrounded by apple culture when and if I need to call on it. These resources are immensely helpful, because to produce apples you need real-world experience and support systems. It's called "produce" for a reason, and any amount of assistance is a good thing, right?

Truth be told, I count my blessings as a New York apple grower. All this support is the market equivalent of being born into an orchard family versus having to buy the land and start from scratch. Polly and I had to do the latter, but we still inherited a tremendous advantage. But if you sense a hint of trepidation or even injustice it's because I know that the current-day support systems are based on an autocratic assuredness about the direction the apple industry needs to head (and all of agriculture, for that matter). There is an institutional decisiveness reflected in trade associations, farm benevolent groups (like nonprofits), and government tax awards and grant money. It's also evident in the academic branch that advises most of these decisions. I admire the confidence and the consensus, but I also have good reason to doubt that direction.

When I set out to learn more about apple farming in 2006–07, one of the first things I did was to consult with my local Cornell Extension. Naturally, the first thing they told me to do was bring them soil samples from my property (both topsoil and subsoil). This would tell them (and me) what I was working with, affecting their recommendations.

So as instructed I brought in jars of dirt, which were then shipped upstate to Cornell for testing. In the meantime the county agents handed me research and reports concerning apple farming in the nearby Hudson Valley. This region-specific information was to counter the glut of unfocused drivel found online, advice that makes no mention of the differences between growing apples in Alaska versus Alabama. Instead, "Read these reports," the agent said. "And talk to some area apple farmers. When we get the soil tests back in a few weeks, we'll both have a better idea of how to proceed."

"That sounds smart," I said.

Over the following weeks I read over the Hudson Valley reports and started talking to area apple farmers, and a very different picture started to emerge from what I naively first assumed. Apple growing was not the set-it-and-forget-it job I thought it was. In fact, their efforts in getting apples to market seemed so Herculean. So epic, actually, that I wondered why anyone would even do it. What's this about herbicides to kill all the grass under the trees? What's this about fungicides and insecticides and a seven-month spray schedule? Did I really need real-time weather monitors and computer programs to tell me, "Quick! Go out and blanket the trees with antibiotics before a contagious disease wipes out the orchard"? What was I getting myself into?

Then I heard how the roundheaded borer beetle lays its eggs in the base of the trunk, and its larvae will slowly kill the tree from the inside. I heard how pine voles, rabbits, and deer will girdle the tree and cut off its cambium, its "blood supply"; and I heard how pathogens like fire blight and collar rot will colonize the orchard and systematically kill all the trees as if they'd been stuck by plague. All this death and destruction, and that's not even mentioning the problems facing the actual fruit! Was this the army I was signing up for? My eyes began to glaze over.

Then came the day my soil test results were in. I went up to meet my extension agent, and we went over the numbers. Displayed in the form of spreadsheets were levels of potassium, boron, nitrogen, pH, and many, many other chemical and biological components that spell the foundation of any agricultural operation. "Yeah, but what does any of this mean to a guy with a shovel?" I asked. So she pulled her chair in closer and broke down each line in layperson's terms, giving me the sensation of being with my eighth-grade math tutor again.

"Comparatively low" is what I heard most often as she paused to sum up each line of the multipage report. This went on for some time. "Comparatively low . . . Comparatively low . . . Not ideal . . . Apple trees require more of this." The complete picture was emerging.

When she finished with Cornell's lab report she referenced another resource, US Geological Survey (USGS) data, which details soil conditions in just about every square inch of land in America. Their maps break down the soil depth, drainage potential, and mineral composition. And then they go on to assign it a soil type, an appellation of sorts, with suggestions about how to best use the land. Guess what the federal government suggested I use my property as? A rock quarry!

The naysayer in me had already made himself at home after talking to a number of professional apple farmers, and now Cornell's soil tests and the USGS recommendations were strikes two and three. As I stared dumbfounded and perhaps in need of a translator for all this information, the extension agent turned to me and decided not to sugarcoat it: "Don't bother trying to grow apples there" was her exact quote.

How does it feel to have your life savings dumped into an orchard dream and then have the world's leading pomological authority tell you it was a giant mistake? But this wasn't the worst of it. The worst of it was their consolatory suggestion: "If you *really* want to grow apples on your property, you should get those numbers up. Start by amending the soil and subsoil. But this could take years, mind you."

She gave me a moment to contemplate what this meant before some further explaining. I was already beyond my threshold of comprehension but I retained a bit about tillers, tractors, and dozens and dozens of trucks. Somehow I had to get ingredients from Florida, Chile, and Canada mixed evenly under several feet of dirt. And this wasn't going to be cheap. The equipment rentals alone would cost tens of thousands of dollars. If I wanted to approach it organically, I could bring in animals, apply wood chips, and plant cover crops to integrate into the soil. This would work, too, and it would be less invasive, but it was likely to take me longer to reach the right nutrient levels at the required soil depth. And only after further testing (and further investment) would they finally say I could start planting. Long story short: With thousands of hours of work, and with massive financial exposure, maybe—just maybe—I could create the conditions for a successful apple orchard.

I'm not one to show emotion publicly. I waited until I got back into my car to sink into total despair. How could I be so stupid? What idiot plunges headlong into a home purchase and orchard dream without making sure it's the best possible option?

During the drive back from the extension office, I kept hearing in my head, *Don't even bother*, over and over again. It sank in. But then a new panic rose: How am I going to tell Polly what a fool mistake choosing this property was? If we didn't already have buyers' remorse, this was going to make it unbearable here!

Hating myself like never before, tears drying on my face, I pulled in off the road and stopped the truck at the base of my driveway. I couldn't go into the house without first composing myself. Cutting the ignition, I sank my head into the steering wheel and closed my eyes.

What's it going to be? I asked myself. *Are you just fooling yourself thinking you can be an orchardist? Are you finally convinced apples should be left to the professionals? How are you going to undo this massive commitment to the wrong property? Think, idiot, think!* I was desperate.

It was then, at one of the lowest moments of my life, I lifted my head and took in a sight I'll never forget: a massive wild apple tree standing before me: Bertha. She was waiting for me along the stone wall like a round old mama welcoming home a sailor. She stood tall and outstretched, glorious in her own way, and it didn't take much imagination to think of this as affection toward me. She said: "*This* is what apple growing looks like." And with her long arms pointing in every which direction, pointing to where nine other seedling trees blended in with the forest landscape on my property, she continued: "*We* are your experts."

The Midcourt

You would have found me in the spring of 2010 busting ground on my New England–inspired from Old England–inspired cider orchard: 200-plus trees with names like Stoke Red, Dabinett, Kingston Black, and Somerset Redstreak, all the varieties mentioned on the Farnum Hill Ciders label grafted on dwarfing rootstocks, ones selected for disease resistance, organic spray penetration, and quicker fruit yields. And with rootstocks developed to be disease-resistant, the job was going to be that much easier.

Ahh, yes, I'd finally figured it all out! Reminded of Bertha and the empirical proof that apple trees do indeed succeed on my property, and after years of gathering information, discovering a niche market in artisan cider, adapting to an organic practice, and choosing to plant a dwarfing bush orchard to see a crop sooner, I could finally say I had a good strategy for lifting Polly and myself out of the Great Recession. But there was a crack in that logic.

There is something about the fresh spring green of May that inspires hope. I'm not sure why the green is lighter, more yellow, compared with the darker hunter green of late summer, but I bet it has something to do with the physics of light and the trees' intelligence. Trees are so damn smart; they've been fueled by solar power for millions of years and we still haven't figured it out! The hue change, I'm guessing, is a chameleon-like adjustment to the sun's "rising" position, but I also bet that somewhere in our shared DNA we do something similar. This must be why late spring is the season of hope, wedding season, and graduation season—in a sense, we wear our own spring green.

The growing season started well. I watered all my new plantings regularly, I hand-weeded to keep the grass competition to a minimum, and when aphids, leaf rollers, and sap-sucking insects appeared to slow down the growth I coated them with neem oil and/or powderized kaolinite clay (organic pest controls). I was out there talking to the trees like passionate apple growers do, every hour of every day, except, of course when the occasional architectural gig reared its head.

I was feeling it, the trees were feeling it; our flock of ducks and even the stock market were excited by May 2010. But something celestial must have happened, something like a solar flare, that in an instant crashed the spring momentum. For me, it became *The Year Without a Summer*. By June we were battling life-threatening ailments in the orchard, within our flock of ducks, and even within our own home. The stock market recovered from its "flash crash" and went on to close up for the year as if nothing had happened, but for us, personally, we were left in a double-dip recession. Now, more than ever, I felt I was living on cursed ground.

What started that year, and became even worse in 2011, was the gradual slow death of my orchard. Whereas in their first few years (2007–09), the trees greened out well, in the subsequent years I was losing more and more of them. Those that survived saw the growing season end just as the sun was reaching the Tropic of Cancer. Fully green trees that were now as high as 12 feet tall were suddenly falling over, as if an evil villain were sawing them in the night. In other instances I watched as death slowly set in and strangled their throats. Over the course of weeks, just as the leaves were turning from spring green to a darker summer shade, they would suddenly fade and turn a pale gray. Oh, I would rush to try to save them: I'd water with compost tea or hand-squeeze any bug threatening to make matters worse. But it was all too late. The tree was already dead and all I needed to do was scratch beneath the surface bark at the base to see that no life was being pumped up from the ground. A brown cambium layer. Not good.

Had Bertha lied to me? Why did she tell me apple trees grew on this cursed land? Was Cornell right? (*Don't even bother.*) Could I finally lay the delusion of being an apple farmer to rest? Combined with more important death threats, this was my resolve. After a year of blows, my youthful persistence had vanished. I took my foot off the gas and simply let nature be nature. This land was destined to become uncultivated.

Agricultural strategy has a good metaphor in tennis. Certain styles of play are more aggressive than others, and conventional agriculture is much like rushing the net. If you rush the tempo, you can eke out a few wins and get the sense you're in control. But a good offense can only cover for a bad defense for so long. Sooner or later the opponent will figure out how to expose your weaknesses. And just like in tennis, you can't withdraw this culture once you commit to its pace. Retreating to the backcourt is impossible because it puts you in no-man's-land, a sort of wilderness that leaves you too vulnerable. There are so many ailments that could kill a young apple tree, from fire blight to the roundheaded apple borer, from collar rot to pine voles, from nutrient deficiency to drought, even boneheaded weed-whacking . . . and I suffered them all. When you take your foot off the gas with a particular type of apple tree, especially in non-ideal soils, things will go wrong. Things will go *very* wrong. To fall back is not an option, and in this sense Cornell was absolutely right: My property is unsuitable for growing *these types of trees*. Some things have evolved to be cultivated. And nothing else.

But what about Bertha? She's a different type of tennis player, one that plays the backcourt and adjusts to her opponent's style of play. She figures it out. Patiently, she survived many losses but knows that there's something to be gained by the struggle. Bertha is not the huge tree she is today because she was force-fed; she's gained that status by absorbing many losses and figuring out ways to continue on. Having done so for decades and decades, she's achieved greatness that no orchard tree of today possibly could. Her reward is longevity and independence, and one wonders how different Bertha would be had she been given agriculture props. Would she even still be alive? There's a great number of other wild things—plants, animals, and mushrooms—that simply *must* be left to their own devices. Some things have evolved to be uncultivated.

THREE

UnGrowing Apples

*A*t some point I should comment on the name of this book. The concept also appears on our product label—"Made from *uncultivated* apples"—so this isn't the first time I've tried to explain what these words mean to me. And it is *to me*, because as a verb the word doesn't make any sense at all. You can't uncultivate anything, in the same way you can't uncook your food. Uncultivation is like trying to get the genie back in the bottle.

The prefix *un* has two meanings: (1) "not"—as in *unwashed*; and (2) "reversed"—as in *undone*. I'm fully aware *uncultivated* is supposed to follow the first definition, but it sounds too much like it's following the latter, as with *undo*. (By the way, the same could be said of a whole slew of tantalizing words: *unlearned, unimproved, unarticulated*, and so on) An easy solution to this problem would be to use the unambiguous *not* or *non* in front of these words instead of *un*, so really what I should have named this book is *Not Cultivating the Cultivated*. Still, there's something intriguing about the two definitions of *un*—an apparent relationship that I can't resist. In the case of *uncultivation*, I think there's some cross-pollinating going on.

Suffer me as I get a little more obsessive on the definitions of *culture, non-cultivated*, and *uncultivated*. I'll admit there are some liberties taken in my title, but I also think the interchangeability between *non-cultivated* and *uncultivated* reflects a popular blind spot to some heady concepts. We really ought to be clear about what we mean, and if the topics of farming, art, civilization, or anything "culture" can be applied to are of interest to you, then maybe this won't be boring.

———

First, we need to talk about *cultivation*. To cultivate is to encourage transformation from one state to another. It's commonly synonymous with *development* or *improvement*, except that *cultivation*, by comparison, seems to offer an extra layer of artistry (making *development* seem lobotomized). The reason for this is its root word: *culture*, which has all kinds of highfalutin overtones, but if I'm not mistaken, *culture* derives from agricultural roots: It simply meant "to tend to the land." But now just about anything can be cultivated. You can cultivate your mind, cultivate relationships, and cultivate bad things, too—bad habits, bad posture, and so on.

The key thing about cultivation, and the reason I'm obsessing on it here, is that *man*ipulation (think *man*kind) plays a part in it, consciously or not, and that's what distinguishes cultivation's transformations from those of evolution. *Evolution* suggests that something bigger (God or Nature) is driving the bus. But there must be some interplay between these concepts of cultural transformation and natural evolution, and this is what intrigues me most about apple trees. Where does that threshold lie?

"In the beginning," things were free and easy, Eden provided everything for Adam and Eve: nourishment, security, peace with our natural form. But after one bite from the apple, God cut the umbilical cord and kicked us out. He chose as our punishment: "Eat by the sweat of your brow." Or in other words: cultivate. We now need to cultivate for our provisions, and that includes apple trees. But isn't it interesting that we found the same type of tree growing east of Eden, too? Does that mean before our cultivation the wild apple was more like the one at the center of Paradise?

Now on to non-cultivated. *Non-cultivated* is that which hasn't yet experienced cultivation. It's the state of that being before humanity's coaxing efforts are made. You might even say non-cultivated is "the natural state." As it is, something highly evolved (a chimpanzee, for example) can still be non-cultivated.

This is a trickier concept than it first appears. Something cultivated is *not* the opposite of something non-cultivated. This is because *cultivation* is a force and *non-cultivation* is simply the lack of that force. The best analogy I can think of to illustrate this point may be lightness versus darkness. Whereas *lightness* is a force or energy, *darkness* is simply the lack of light. You can't darken something, you can only subtract light from it. Likewise, *non-cultivated* is simply the total exclusion of cultivation.

This begs for a third definition: What is "the subtraction of cultivation"? Well, that concept is reserved for Andy's bullshit word, *uncultivation*. They say you can't put the genie back in the bottle. Get ready for some magic.

Uncultivation is an action. To uncultivate is to encourage the transformation from one state to another, just like cultivation, except that it seeks its opposite horizon. It seeks to peel back the layers of cultivation (or, as I said earlier, "Not cultivating the uncultivated.") The key part of this is that without cultivation there would be no uncultivation, only the non-cultivated.

As a concept, it assumes that we are between two points on the horizon. At one end is the thing humanity is progressing toward (be it desirable traits, perfect productivity, greater wealth, or whatever); on the opposite horizon is the non-cultivated (the natural state). Uncultivation tries not to assume the benefits from humankind's cultural trajectory. The goal of reversing course, if we're open to that option, is to reevaluate the steps of our progression, to decide for ourselves if they were truly the best choice. Someone engaged in this act peels away layers of cultivation much the way we might remove light. And what's great about this analogy is that achieving total darkness is *not* the only goal of uncultivation, either. Sometimes you just want it to be less bright.

At least that's not *my* goal. I have no delusions of uncultivating my way back to the Garden of Eden, but I *would* like to see cultivation return to a place that I feel is healthier. I believe that along the path toward greater refinement we repeatedly came to crossroads and we sacrificed unforeseen benefits in order to progress forward. I don't buy that we made all the right choices, and I don't want to inherit the momentum moving forward.

If momentum is our inheritance—and it absolutely is—the first step toward uncultivation is get out of the water. Only away from the dominant stream of agriculture can we discover the benefits we overlooked.

But halting the escalation, I have found, is the hardest part of uncultivation. One reason the train's so hard to stop is that we've achieved great success "sweating from our brow." Now we can't stop messing with things; we're on a roll! But it's a mistake to assume past successes can be repeated or improve our odds. That's not how statistics work: Guessing "heads" correctly doesn't mean you have more than a 50–50 chance of being correct on your next guess. It also happens to be arrogant to use past successes to prove we're right now. Academic science, especially, has been guilty of using its winning streak to prove the correctness of its course. But if the winner does not also absorb the virtues of the loser, I strongly believe that the victory will eventually corrode from the inside out. Even the dominant must acclimate.

As I said, getting out of the river is probably the hardest part, but when we reach this vantage point it's plain to see that in some instances we've chosen an unwise path. I have proof of this regarding apple cultivation. But I've also tried to apply this process to cider making and to my business. Sometimes it's an applicable principle and sometimes not, but for me the tried-and-true ways only guarantee a success that feels mediocre; there were too many compromises along the way. And sure enough, I have come to a place that's better for me by reversing course in those practices, too. Maybe others would disagree, but my point is we have a choice, and in some cases a better choice. We can't know which is better, however, until we rid ourselves of cultivating habits, expectations, and the momentum of authority.

Seeds and Clones

Below a rock ledge, extending out from a steep, rugged, and dreary gray hillside, are thousands of little green sprigs. From a distance this looks just like a woodland patch of spring clover, but as we get closer we see they are actually little tree saplings in an unusually dense cluster. Their thin stems are rusty red, and their little serrated leaflets are a healthy green. As they emerge from under the dead oak leaves, their intense hue adds excitement to the beige hillside. In fact, there are dozens and dozens of seedling patches just like this one bursting from the north face of this slope in early May.

This is what you get when you take the spent apple pomace from a cider press and scatter the dried stuff willy-nilly around a forest clearing. The vast majority of seeds somehow survive the apple grinder, and when you toss this pomace with a shovel from the back of a pickup truck there are tens of thousands of viable apple seeds in the potential forest regrowth.

We can expect overcrowding at first—not just competition from native tree species, but all the apple seedlings crowding one another for space, water, and nutrients. Over the course of the summer at least two-thirds of the seedlings will wither, and their precious green will disappear. By autumn the numbers will have dropped even more significantly. Whereas the initial population per patch was in the thousands, now we are down to a few hundred. They are about 5 inches tall, and their growth has been halted by the frosts of October. The leaves will hang on for another month, but by December these baby trees will look like wiry twigs poking out from the ground. They appear insignificant in the landscape. As the oak leaves fall and snow accumulates, they will be completely invisible for four months.

As the winter settles in, voles, rabbits, and deer find these shoots under the snow and mow nearly every one down to frozen ground. By the spring the patch (down to less than 100 seedlings, but all of them with a good root system from the previous year) have survived the chomping and now have a stronger base for the upcoming year. The combination of good genetics and luck of location have produced a well-conditioned bunch of young trees that are prepared for a second year. Some will be as tall as 12 inches. The stems are slightly thicker and woodier now, but their real accomplishment is in their roots. They have figured out how to navigate around rocks and how to work with the soil biome. To add a little security to the equation, I select about three of these seedling trees from each patch and wrap them with metal mesh so that the rabbits and deer don't eat them over the second winter.

Far away in a flat field, another brood of young apple trees is emerging, also in the thousands, but this is where the similarities end. These young trees are aligned in long, straight rows; they emerge from mounds of sawdust, mulch, and loose dirt; and they have access to full sunlight. A hose drips steady irrigation down on them year-round, resulting in a uniform size that's drastically higher. They can produce shoots over 8 feet long in a single season, and this results in a much, much healthier appearance compared with the slow-growing seedlings described above. But the biggest difference between the two broods is invisible. These trees were not started from seed; they are *all* clones. They've been propagated from the same root system for decades.

We're obviously not in the wild but at a typical tree nursery observing rootstock propagation. This operation provides conventional apple growers with their preferred variety of trees and, even more important, with their preferred root base. These root bases, or rootstocks, have been chosen for size, speed of growth, disease resistance, and above all else consistency. Farmers don't want to adjust for every tree in a 10,000-tree orchard; they want it the other way around: All those trees must adjust to the one farmer. They must follow the prescribed harvest times, pruning methods, marketing standards, and spray requirements. In our economy of scale, efficiency is king. The trees, therefore, must all be uniform.

This isn't new. Cloning rootstocks has been a common industry tool for some time, and by the mid-twentieth century it was standard practice. In fact, if you didn't use them you couldn't compete in the market —they were that much better and faster. But that was a different time in terms of acceptance; "the American century" could also be described as "the chemical century," because both farmers and mainstream culture mythologized radical and progressive science. Back then apple farmers could proudly, albeit perhaps naively, announce the marvel of sprays, breeding, and cloning and boast to their customers: "We've got 5,000 apple trees, five apple varieties, and they're all growing on just one root system!" Today that would sound more like a horror story! *Diversity*, and particularly *genetic diversity*, have become buzzwords in the food world and beyond. Warnings from agricultural theorists about having all our eggs in one basket have hit the mainstream, and now no apple farmers would quickly disclose what they actually have out in the orchard— certainly not underground. You hear words like *crisp*, *juicy*, or *honeycrunch*, but you never hear the word *clone*.

Yet at this point, the world's apple supply is nearly 100 percent dependent on a remarkably few genes. In chapter 1 I mentioned that the apple was naturally designed to be transported and dispersed by four-leggers, and that the seeds were designed to be extremely diverse so that they can test out a multiplicity of environments. But I didn't mention the magnitude of this diversity, and it's jaw-dropping: An apple tree has on its palette nearly 60,000 genes (three times the number that humans have), and the potential genetic combinations are practically infinite via pollination. Successful pollination will produce in an apple 5 seeds (sometimes 10). Those five seeds are not only unique from the parent just as a human child is unique from its parent, but they are genetically unique from one another, too. (All five seeds are different!) So if a tree produces 1,000 apples per year, it has the potential of creating 5,000 new varieties each year—all of which are apples this planet has never seen before. At that rate it would take just 10 years for 10 apple trees to create half a million new apple varieties!

There have never been two humans on this planet exactly alike. Why, then, does the North American apple industry brag about "hundreds of apple varieties" when it has billions of trees? Shouldn't we be talking about an equal number of varieties? The reason for the discrepancy, of course, is cloning. But I'm not just talking about grafting (taking a piece of a tree and splicing it onto the roots of another tree). The other form of apple cloning, root tissue propagation, equally limits diversity and is hardly ever seen or discussed. In fact, rootstock cloning is now fully integrated into the apple industry, and there's even less genetic diversity underground than aboveground. At this point, nearly all orchard trees are clones on clones.

But this isn't an exposé of apple farmers or tree nurseries. What I intend to challenge is the *dignity* of apple cloning. The fact is, outrage at anyone other than ourselves is wholly unjustified. This all came to be via the economies of scale that the customer rewards via buying greater quantities of the cheapest produce. I don't know of a single orchardist who wouldn't rather grow big, beautiful real trees instead of short-lived clonal dwarfs. (That's like blaming apple farmers for spraying pesticides; do you honestly think anyone *wants* to spend money and spray chemicals on their land if they don't have to?) We, the customers, are agriculture's upper management, not the farmers, so it should be on us to do something about it. Maybe we pay more for apples from real trees (trees from seed), or maybe we grow them in our front yard where we can have direct control. Either way, we need to come to terms with food cloning and consider if it's a serious enough matter for action.

Because cloning, let's face it, is a sensitive subject. Inevitably we will start thinking about human cloning and we're going to put our foot down. "Absolutely not!" we say. It doesn't matter if your religion is a religion or your religion is science, it doesn't matter if you vote liberal or conservative; cloning humans feels icky to us because it directly confronts the ultimate question: Is there dignity in life? Though we think we know the answer to this, we've never been able to actually prove it, and this makes us *very* insecure. Just as the death-penalty and abortion debates stirred this anxiety, so, too, will human cloning when science narrows in on its ability to perform it. There's no escaping it. Sooner or later we are going to have to address the topic of dignity again and come up with a working definition.

Yes, I know some people are okay with small amounts of human cloning, but no one—and I mean no one—thinks that creating a vast population of genetically identical people is a good idea. But why not? Why not do to humans what we have done with apple trees? Let me play devil's advocate here for a second. After all, let's face it: Some people are designed better than others for certain tasks. These include very important tasks, such as saving human lives. Michael Phelps, the Olympic athlete, for example, is a naturally strong swimmer because of his build. Even before his training, his God-given body shape and size gave him an advantage in the water, so why not clone him to staff our Coast Guard or to watch over beaches and pools as lifeguard? Why rely on the local gene pool to fill these all-important jobs when we can be selecting only the best? Why *don't* we do this? Because we sense something's amiss, that's why. Mass-producing humans would somehow erode the barriers we set up to protect *our* humanity, which is just our species-specific word for "dignity of life." But we're going to have to do better than "something's amiss"; we're going to need some hard definitions.

This may sound like it's only a conceptual topic, but a number of horrific examples prove its existence: instances of slavery, genocide, bio-logical and chemical warfare, to name just a few. Even when the logic of the day rationalizes these terrible measures, the defense of dignity proves to be a greater cause. The ends don't justify the means.

But equally vexing is why the dignity of the plant kingdom—and most animals—is fair game for cloning. This points to a slippery-slope argument that will someday be applied to humans, too, if we don't hunker down and define the term. In particular we need to define the exact point at which we feel life has dignity. (Why do some creatures warrant protection and not others?) It's icky, I know, but it's just a matter of time before we broach The Phelps Argument, so looking at our treatment of apple trees, for instance, prepares a road map for what's to come. And I can tell you one thing, as someone who knows apple trees: We've selected for "superior" genes before and we'll do it again—whether that *we* is the experts or just blind popular consensus. But compare that selective decision against the decision to defend the tree's dignity and I'm confident you will see that the ends don't justify the means here, either.

Is apple dignity too abstract for you? If you saw a group of 13-year-old boys senselessly kicking a dog or a homeless person, you'd be sickened and outraged. But what if you saw the same group of boys whipping an old apple tree with chains? Chances are you'd be outraged, too! Instinctually, you'd want them to show that tree respect, am I right? Gloriously, the slippery slope can work both ways; dignity can be strengthened, not just eroded. We are not *that* evolved yet that we can't regain sympathy for non-humans. Not only can we look back, we still have the power to go back, too.

Don't believe me, believe Einstein: "Our task must be to free ourselves . . . by widening our circle of compassion to embrace all living creatures and the whole of nature and its beauty." I'd like to offer the apple tree as the place to start. People do not grow real apple trees anymore. Every apple you've ever bought in your life is from a clone (and probably a clone of a clone of a clone). The same is true with other fruits. The question is: Does that bother you? Or: Does that bother you *enough*?

Art and Wild Apples

What seemed exciting at the time now seems a stupid thing to boast about: In 2011 we became the first modern cider makers to produce a

Table 3.1. Cultivated Versus Non-Cultivated Apple Trees

	Cultivated	Non-Cultivated
REPRODUCTION		
Propagation	Tissue culture, vegetative cloning (rootstock cuttings, grafting) from tested, hybridized, or engineered sources.	By seed (or in rare instances natural root divisions) from native or once-cultivated sources.
Varietals/ selections	Human-directed (for taste, appearance, disease resistance, ease of farming, ease of shipping, storage, branding, etc.).	By chance (often theorized to be evolutionary selections—adaptations, "testing the waters," survival of the fittest, etc.).
Breeding, pollination	Natural and artificial crosses usually from limited or controlled sources. (Still rare: genetic engineering.)	Crosses with any available compatible pollen (via natural pollinators).
GROWTH		
Companion plantings / population	Monoculture / greatest population per acre (economy-of-scale layouts—high-density bush orchards, including spindling, trellising, etc.).	Diverse / limited or unlimited in scale according to locational conditions.
Soil (and inputs)	Usually amended for optimization. Sometimes irrigated or drained, and frequently fertilized with foreign inputs (including natural and artificial nutrients).	Watered by rainfall, seasonal flooding, or proximity to water source only. Natural soil fertility from wild plant, animal, climate, and geological inputs only.
Habitats	Introduced to new habitats that are usually zoned compatible. Common habitat props include deer fence, wind machines, netting, etc.	Grows in its natural habitat or grows feral in a similar habitat (wherever the seed may grow unassisted).
Training	Pruned and trained for optimal light access, airflow, and spray penetrations. Usually stunted or dwarfed, often staked (modern rootstocks often require support).	Grows to full height and shape according to local conditions and genetic growth traits (may even include dwarfism).
Flowering	Blossom and fruit thinning to induce annual production (includes use of chemical thinners or is machine- or hand-thinned).	Naturally biennial or longer. Flowers in tandem with local climate factors, insect pressures, and/or forest mast-year cycles.
Immune response / pest susceptibility	Varieties are often selected for genetic resistance, but artificial protectors are still sprayed (and supplant the trees' immune response.)	Learned immunity (antibody buildup) and communally triggered immune response.

Protection	Pesticides, fungicides, herbicides, antibiotics, animal poisons (rodent control), animal guards, etc.—*all* are commonly used on both conventional and organic farms.	Whatever it's lucky enough to get. (Seedling trees are sometimes protected by rocks, thornbushes, and fallen branches.)
FRUIT		
Fruit appearance	Generally large, round, thin-skinned, with intense color, often shiny. (Sprayed for uniformity.)	Smaller fruit with less flesh. Thicker-skinned, hard (dry), multicolored, and sometimes russeted (often deformed by bugs or bacteria during the growing season).
Fruit taste	Crisp, juicy/watery. Selected for sweet taste with variations of acidity and aroma.	Dry, tart, and often tannic. Often aromatic. (The more subtle variations are too great to list here.)
Fruit content	Generally low in fiber, vitamins, and minerals, and often very low in probiotics and phytonutrients.	Comparatively high but can be extremely high in some categories.*
HARVESTING		
Harvest method	Hand- and machine-harvested from trees (but includes mechanical drop sweepers at cider operations).	Mainly eaten from the ground (though some animals occasionally eat from the tree, too).
Storage	Washed, graded, waxed, and fumigated—sometimes pasteurized—put into cold storage or CA gas units.	Waits on and under the tree. Certain varieties last for many months and are built to survive bruising, rots, pests, and freezes.
Distribution	Divided into unit size and sold locally; distributed globally in refrigerated units; or are drummed as apple concentrate.	Only the seed is distributed (via the four-legged friends).

Note: The Cultivated column represents, for all intents and purposes, 100 percent of the apple trees on commercial apple farms (with the exception of crab apples). The degree to which people maintain the tree will vary greatly, but the information does accurately represent the intent of most farms. The Non-Cultivated column represents apples in their most wild state. There are 40-plus *Malus* species, each at home in different environments, but as for *M. domestica* the example of feral apples in the United States is given for its similarities to the wild apple forests of Central Asia. Also bear in mind that a similar chart could be drafted to show differences for all cultivated and uncultivated plants and animals. While you read along, consider where your garden crops and even pets land between cultivated and non-cultivated!

* Phytonutrient studies on various wild foods by author Jo Robinson ("Breeding the Nutrition Out of Food," *New York Times*, May 26, 2013) show that most popular apples varieties contain only a fraction (as low as 2 percent) of the nutrient content of other wild species of *Malus* (and some are even thought to have a nutrition-depleting effect).

commercial wild apple cider. First of all, in communities with an *integrated* apple or cider culture (and by that I mean areas where residents typically have apple trees, as opposed to commercial orchard communities where the trees are concentrated on farms), the use of similarly neglected wild fruit in cider has *always* been very common, if not the norm. With or without Prohibition or the government's approval, a culture for cider has persisted in backyards and rural communities, and it's well documented that wild apples have been the unanimous favorite for hundreds of years. Furthermore, there is no real definition of the word *wild*, and the apples growing wild in my area are mostly a version of *Malus domestica*, an apple that owes its entire existence to human cultivation. There are no truly native species of apples in my region for *M. domestica* to even cross-pollinate with, so how can I call it wild when the term should be *feral?*

When we commonly call something wild, we are (without really thinking about it) assuming humankind isn't a factor. But humankind has influenced or changed almost everything on the planet; we'd be hard-pressed to find anything that hasn't, in some way, been affected by our cultivations. After further consideration we understand *wild* not to be a pure state of non-cultivated things, but more like the concept *uncultivation*, which also incorporates things with a "MANipulated" past. *Wild* just refers to that which is currently free of our cultivations and can include the once-cultivated and the never-cultivated. A wild bird can still be considered wild even when it goes into the suburbs and eats seed from a feeder. And on the other end, something that is cultivated, like a pig, can become feral and eventually achieve "wild" status (like a wild boar). The important point is, *wild* does not take direction from human cultivations; it faces the other direction. And that's a big difference.

If something cultivated can become wild via feralization, an interesting question arises: At what point does this happen? Is it after so-many generations? Is it after it becomes integral to the ecosystem? There are many thresholds in the go-between stages that leave the status of *wild* to subjective interpretation. Nonetheless, it's important to explore the dichotomy because we can learn more about ourselves by determining where we, personally, feel *wild* begins. In the case of cultivated and non-cultivated apple trees, I've tried to present a full list of comparisons.

I can't stress enough that this chart represents a *gradient* dichotomy that all agricultural practices are in between. For instance, there's always been a strong counterculture of apple growers, such as permaculturalists and organic orchardists, who seek to preserve some of the wild's better traits while also absorbing the market pressures that force them to produce standardized fruit. This chart merely shows the two horizons that every apple grower stands between. That said, do note that nearly all orchards lean toward (if they're not 100 percent in keeping with) the "Cultivated" column on the left.

Indian Orchards

My county is named in honor of the man responsible for starving the Iroquois nation to death and for killing more apple trees than anyone in human history. The Sullivan Expedition was launched as a scorched-earth campaign in 1779 by none other than George Washington to rid central New York of its native population. This goal pivoted around the strategy of rendering the Indian homelands uninhabitable by means of crop destruction, and the timing of the campaign was most vicious: just before harvest and the winter. As Sullivan's army advanced from the south into the Seneca heartlands, they were maniacal about girdling every fruit tree along the way, rendering the trees lifeless aboveground. That which survived needed to send up root suckers and start anew—fruit would not return to these homelands until many years later.

The demoralizing effects of this campaign saw the permanent retreat of the Iroquois into Canada, but not until they suffered monumental losses at the hands of starvation and winter exposure. The campaign was a sweeping success for the new United States: It opened the door for white settlement in central New York and the upper Ohio regions (including, ironically, Johnny Appleseed). This expedition survives as John Sullivan's legacy (despite other accomplishments) and it begs this question: Today, as southern states now consider removing monuments to Confederate soldiers, why do New Yorkers—progressives, as they claim—still proudly honor the name most synonymous with the 1779 atrocities?

As an apple lover I can at least take perverse pleasure in the fact that hundreds of thousands of wild apple trees survive in Sullivan County and that "Indian Orchard Road" is the very first road a driver comes to when leaving the heavily cultivated Hudson Valley upon arriving in this wild Catskill region. I even suspect a few trees remain from the so-named Indian Orchard, either as the original trees or having grown indirectly from the seeds of them.

Indian Orchard Road is a quiet residential lane in the Mamakating Hollow that winds along the creek and open wetlands parallel with the Shawangunk Ridge towering above just east. I drove by the road sign dozens of times on my way up to the train station and never once thought about the name until Bob, a 95-year-old cider maker in Wurtsboro who's been growing cider fruit since the 1970s, handed me his copy of S. A. Beach's *The Apples of New York*. Beach's book, famous among apple enthusiasts, was written at the turn of the twentieth century and serves as a catalog of hundreds of pre-Modern and early-Modern apple varieties. In his lead-up to apple descriptions, Beach has a small essay about "Indian Orchards," hinting at another history of apple agriculture in America. He doesn't go into great detail (Beach was most focused on apple varieties), but his brief essay was enough to wet my whistle. I've been fantasizing ever since about what Indian apple cultivation may have looked like. (By the way, the whole of the S. A. Beach book is available to read for free online.)

I believe accurate information about Native American apple agriculture is inconclusive because the people who reported on it (people like the soldiers in Sullivan's army) were looking at it through the eyes of Western cultivation. They focused on how the trees measured up to Western orchards, including the number of trees, the size of the trees, and their apparent health (all apparently very impressive by the way), but they failed to flesh out the few peculiarities they stumbled across (things like companion plantings) and couldn't imagine the thinking behind the larger form of plant cultivation. Being of two different cultures, I am certain Sullivan's soldiers would have looked at Indian orchards in the same way a caveman would view a cell phone and assume it's nothing more than a fragile shiny rock. So I don't believe that we have evidence enough to form conclusions, and I'm unsatisfied with the base-level understanding of this history. I believe the history is still open for speculation, albeit without the satisfaction of assurance, and there is still greater significance it can play to apple agriculturalists today. Needless to say, I'll offer my opinion on key considerations.

But first we need to back up a little. How was it that Sullivan's army, people of European descent, found Native American people cultivating a fruit of Asian descent in the first place? It's a history that starts sometime in the early to mid-1600s in the province of the New Netherlands (which included present-day New York State). By 1640 orchards grown from seeds brought over from Europe were already becoming established in Dutch settlements along the Hudson River, including the town of New Amsterdam (now New York City). Soon fruits born on American soil were producing new stocks of seed to disseminate further. And the Dutch were unlike the Puritan settlers of New England in that they were out-ward-seeking: Rather than keeping things to themselves, they were known to be eager and open traders (it's what made New York what it is today). So it was that in the mid-1600s they were trading with the local Indians for such things as furs, tools, and handmade items—and of course exchanging seeds (including apple and peach) from their respective agricultures.

In 1671 the first Indian orchards were reported "found" in Ulster County in the Central Valley region of the Hudson Valley, but by then the English had taken over control of the state and a return to isola-tionist culture dominated the slow advance of settlement in rural New York. This means the Iroquois people had between 100 and 125 years to test apple seeds in their homelands before the Revolution and western expansion began in earnest. By then the genie was out of the bottle: 125 years is a lot of time to devise a strategy for how to acclimate the trees to this continent, especially drawing as they did on the wisdom of their own cultivation practices. It's safe to assume this was time enough to devise a competing form of apple agriculture that was (and is) the only true form of American apple farming.

What was the apple culture that Sullivan erased? When considering Indian orchards, I think the most telling clues would come *not* from historical accounts but from considering Indian culture versus Western culture in general. This, of course, would trickle down to agriculture. To begin, Native Americans lived a fully or partially nomadic existence, traveling to where the food was plentiful seasonally (and yearly), which is in stark contrast with Western cultivators, who fussed over one plot of land all year round. Native people would fish the Hudson River when the striped bass ran in spring; in the summer they would live along the cooler ocean shores and harvest clams and oysters; and they would likely be hunting and trapping in the forests during the winter. In other words, any form of agriculture would need to be developed in lieu of a roaming lifestyle at the mercy of nature. This is not to say the native people didn't have villages, nor set up land to cultivate, but they saw their cultivations in a monumentally different way: They needed crops to be independent. Or, in the case of apple trees, they needed their "crop" to fend for itself for large periods of time.

Another extreme difference derives from the fact that native people didn't "own" the land they ate from—the rivers, forests, and oceans. This set up a peculiar relationship with the local environment that must have been (and still is) hard for Western minds to comprehend: Why cultivate the land if you don't own it? Some oddities of this sort were documented, but again the conclusions we make are contained within Western knowledge of nature and of agriculture. For instance, Native Americans were known to have abandoned cultivated fields for many years at a time, and our conclusions as to why are based on *our* understanding of agriculture. We might think this was to allow the land to recover so that it could be more productive in the future, but to the native way of thinking they may have been giving "borrowed land" back to nature, returning it to the original owner. A seemingly subtle shift in perception can change agricultural practice, including apple cultivation, astronomically.

Again, I'm not saying I know any of this. I'm merely pointing out that previously recorded information about Indian agriculture is fundamentally biased. I have read, for instance, that tree fruits were not a major part of the native people's diet, but even though I have no archaeological evidence to prove otherwise, I can't help thinking this is a falsity based on our own flavor biases. Did the native people *really* not utilize pawpaw (*Asimina triloba*), American plum (*Prunus americana*), or chokecherry (*P. virginiana*)? That seems highly unlikely to me. It's more likely that the Western historical account says these things because no one found evidence of those trees being "farmed" as we would expect to see them—growing in monocrop orchards. But it's well known that the Iroquois made frequent use of nuts and acorns (the latter can be made into flour) without having to farm those trees in isolation, so why the double standard? And in actuality, many fruit trees grow their best as understory trees and in a mixed polyculture. *Theobroma cacao* (the chocolate tree) is one famous example.

When the Iroquois planted apple seeds, it seems likely they would have planted apples to mirror similar fruit trees growing in the wild, most notably the native *Crataegus* (hawthorn). This is botanically one of the apple's closest relatives, and it, too, likes sweeter, well-drained soils but can thrive in a huge host of environments. It's an understory tree, sometimes growing in stands where the dense hawthorn populations literally support one another, but it also appears as isolated specimens and can be seen hanging around with the likes of tall cherry, maple, ivies, and thornbushes, as well as in tall grasses. In other words, it's diverse. But as an understory tree, when it is located along forest edge / meadow edge the hawthorn definitely fruits more with the opportunity of full sun. If the tree served as a role model for Indian orchards, chances are apple trees were also planted along meadow edges.

What else was unique about Indian orchards compared with Western apple farming? The Iroquois did not keep livestock, so there would never have been mowed grass, meaning that the trees didn't appear naked in grass-only meadows like Western trees. The apple trees were probably not spaced evenly, nor were the trees designed to form straight rows as in Western orchards. And the trees probably grew to their natural shape (or were shaped by deer browse) since it's unlikely the native people pruned or trained their trees. Finally, it's unlikely that the native apple growers were concerned with grafted varieties. I suspect they preferred "undesirable" apples because they were higher in nutrition value. Last but not least, they most certainly weren't growing them for alcohol like the European settlers. (Although next to today's cider orchards, I would bet you *anything* their apples made an infinitely greater drink.)

I'll say one last time, lest I offend historians, archaeologists, or cultural sensitivities: I don't know if any of this actually applies to Indian orchards. But I'm sure as hell not going to concede the narrative to anyone who doesn't grow apple trees from seed and their trees in the wild (at the mercy of all of nature's elements). And given the huge diversity of micro-environments that exist, knowing truths about one location doesn't allow us to derive conclusions about any others, much less about a whole system of agriculture. As someone who grows apple seeds in various uncultivated locations, I, too, need my trees to be self-sufficient because I rarely visit the vast majority of them. I know of only one universal strategy: Plant as many seeds as possible and do it *everywhere*. Actually, it's not a "strategy" at all, it's just the way it was intended to be when God or Nature designed the apple tree. Whether Native Americans were growing apples this way or not, the fact is the tree knows best how to cultivate itself. I suspect Indian orchards were more attuned to this.

My reason for speculation and my fascination with Indian orchards isn't a historian's interest. I don't have a we-need-to-honor-them agenda, either. What I do have is interest in independent trees and a commercial cider-apple farmer's objective of making the best cider possible. I'm sure that others interested in cider, human nutrition, and environmentally sustainable agriculture are also particularly fascinated with the subject. Plus, a different form of apple agriculture could benefit our economy— by expanding into new fields, we can allocate new resources rather than perpetually resupply the same old ones.

Brice's Orchard

Right in the dead center of the Hudson Valley's apple belt, in the premier soils of the open lowlands, is Walden, New York. It started as a small hub for farmers moving to the area in the 1700s, but a mill was established and the town grew. Later in the 1800s a rail line was added, and jobs gravitated toward light manufacturing. A familiar fate befell the population when in the twentieth century larger-scale manufacturing drifted elsewhere and the town remained stagnant. Growth was relegated to the outskirts of the village, where suburban development began eating away at agricultural land. The town buildings began to look as though they had inadequate funding for upkeep, while outside of town the Hudson Valley apple industry barely survived the darkest days of farming, the late twentieth century.

Apple cultivation in the Central Valley began in the late seventeenth century, and it has remained a constant. Although most every crop is grown in this region, the apple industry emerged dominant at a time when the fruit was profoundly more popular than it is today. With many orchards already established, they utilized their strength in numbers to build an identity and survive even after it was cheaper for faraway mega-farms to supply the East Coast population centers. Today you can still drive 30 minutes in any direction from Walden and find many medium and large orchards, most of them in operation throughout the 1900s. As the apple-world itself has shifted, and trends came and went over the past 150 years, the Hudson Valley orchard industry has done well to keep pace.

Depending on who you ask, it now faces either a new challenge or an ally in industrial cider. Business entrepreneurs near and far are strategically setting up bases in the region, no doubt for the benefit of proximity to New York City, just 75 minutes south. But equally strategic, they want to appear orchard-based and integrated within an apple community—they might even throw in some Hudson Valley apples to boost the "local" claim. Smoke and mirrors is what it's called in magic shows. One such company chose Walden for their this-is-where-our-cider-is-made location, specifically building in the center of a preexisting orchard just a few miles from town. They erected a beautiful new tasting room that faces the Shawangunk Ridge to the west: The white cliffs, famous among rock climbers, spread out like a movie backdrop, cutting a light ribbon between the sky and the tops of tens of thousands of apple trees. No one can argue it's not beautiful.

I used to drive by this orchard before the change in ownership and think to myself how well maintained those trees looked. I even asked the lady in the house if I could glean the drops, but she said the land was now leased by one of the Hudson Valley's big farm companies; they maintain the orchard as a satellite. Those apples were theirs to do with (or not do with) what they wanted. I don't know what she got out of the deal, but when the national brand moved in they chose a particularly good location. Even if less than 1 percent of their product is made from the local apples (an extension that includes all of the Hudson Valley), everyone from Walden's Main Street to Oxford Street in London seems to believe this relatively small orchard (and relatively small apple region) supplies a global product. But that was the goal.

———

Anyway, that's what's happening on the other side of the Shawangunk Ridge. I started to tell you about Walden not to get all pissy about authenticity or smoke and mirrors in the food and beverage industry but to tell you about a defunct 75-acre orchard that I once tried to maintain on the edge of town there. This is about those trees.

Brice was a local businessman and avid fly fisherman, but he also loved the company of apple trees. How could he not, growing up in the Hudson Valley? So despite knowing little about farming, he bought an old orchard in the 1990s when the previous farmer couldn't keep up with the market (and I don't mean *the farmer* couldn't keep up with the market, I mean *his orchard* couldn't). This was the darkest time to be a local orchardist. Scale economics, globalized trade, and 100 years of toxic agriculture had caught up with the farmers. Even with a sizable 75 acres, there just wasn't enough profit in the commodity market to counter increased regulation, taxes, the chemical bill, and labor costs. Over the course of the twentieth century, the USDA kept upping the minimum size recommendations for a sustainable apple farm operation: 20 acres, 50 acres, 75 acres, 100 acres. By the 1990s many farms had been left behind and very little in the way of support systems, or even sympathy, remained. As a result, many agricultural properties transitioned to residential development. It appeared that this orchard was on track to do the same.

Brice had different goals, though. With the exception of building one house, his own home, Brice wanted to preserve the thousands of apple trees and old barns just where they were. And although the farm around his new home progressively fell into disrepair, there was an aesthetic to that, too: It added an air of nostalgia. Still, it came at great financial expense, since the Hudson Valley had evolved into a high-tax district. Only by actively farming the land is there any relief.

Then, after nearly two decades of decline, Brice heard about a local cider maker who preferred wild apples over farmed apples and man-oh-man did he have a lot of apples. When he contacted me in 2012, his hope was that I could breathe new life back into the farm without the use of chemical sprays. We met, and we saw eye-to-eye on these points. I, of course, was excited by the sheer number of uncultivated trees to experiment with, but the virtual jungle of overgrowth posed a significant

obstacle. My biggest concern was not the thorny rosebushes, not the stinging nettles, not even the poison ivy blanketing the tops of the trees, but the residual effect of decades and decades of toxic sprays—both in the soil and systemically within the trees. Even though it had been 20 years since the last spray application, the previous century had been notorious for its widespread use of chemicals that only scores and scores of years could detoxify. (By the way, only time will tell if today's "approved" sprays are any less detrimental to the environment. Many chemicals, including some that will blind a person, are all still commonly used.)

It quickly became apparent that Brice's orchard was far too big for me to manage on a shoestring budget, and I wasn't about to invest my scarce savings into another venture without knowing more about the land. I needed to give it a test season and devise a plan over the winter. I set my sights on the best part of the orchard and discovered the south block—a unit of about 200 trees that were slightly lower and younger (only about 30 years old). My first-year plan was to clear this section of competitive growth, clear out the dead branches, and begin grafting them over to cider varieties. Then, by gauging how difficult this might be, I could later reflect and decide how the other 1,000-plus trees would go.

That February I collected grafting wood from my home orchard, robbing my young trees of 2012's growth. Wood from Dabinett, Stoke Red, Reine de Pomme, and Golden Russet lay waiting in my refrigerator until the snows melted, when I could get over to Brice's. By mid-March I started in on my plan, clearing the dead branches and identifying healthy limbs and trunks to be grafted over, thus forming the basis for future cider-apple trees. Tree by tree, I was starting to become intimate with the orchard. And as I got up close and personal with individual trees, I started to notice the details of my challenge. Evidence of cankers and fire blight was present, forcing me to proceed with extreme caution. I had to constantly wipe down my secateurs with rubbing alcohol and dunk my pruning saw and chain saw in a bucket of bleach-water after each cut, lest I spread the disease from tree to tree as I worked. I burned the removed wood for added security.

Spring returned, and the blossom was sizable in 2013. Elsewhere in the Hudson Valley, farmers were busy with their spray schedules, but I sat back and paid only occasional visits, touring the orchard to check

on progress. By early June the south block was looking promising. The grafts were taking (always a few weeks behind the other shoots, but nonetheless greening out as they should), and I was able to drive my truck down some of the rows, which were now passable for the first time in years. Brice was getting hopeful about the orchard, too. He'd fire up his antique tractor equipped with a swinging-arm mower that got between the trees and create that golf-course look. You could almost hear the trees breathing in fresh air as though they'd been cooped up for years.

I checked back again around the summer solstice, and a damn fine fruit-set was emerging. Tiny little green balls formed in clusters of four and five. The trees were definitely compensating for the previous frost year, but now I was worried about there being too much fruit! Did I need to buy more equipment and larger tanks and build an addition to my barn now that I had a sizable orchard with readily accessible fruit? I combed my financial options, thinking scaling up was in my future.

Another seven weeks went by before my next tour, but by this time a new picture had emerged. In August things had turned in a bad way: After two months of summer heat, my grafts were facing an orchardist's worse nightmare, fire blight. This foul plaque can wipe out an entire orchard in just one season, and by the time you see it the disease is already systemic. The growth shoots (the most vulnerable part of the tree) had peaked at about 10 inches sometime in early July before they turned black and curled up like a shepherd's crook. One hundred percent of my grafts were infected, resulting in their death, and I had a hard time imagining how I could go forward from there. Restoring the vigor in this orchard without awakening this disease presented a catch-22; I didn't know if it was even possible without the artillery of costly orchard sprays.

But I saw an even more curious problem emerge that August. The fruits, which had grown to baseball-sized by late August, showing also good color development, were falling off the trees prematurely. Varieties like Macs and Romes that shouldn't have been ready for another five weeks were dropping en masse with the gentlest sways of wind. What in the world was happening?

"Brice," I said, "I can understand how fire blight would be a problem, but what's with the apples falling already?"

"Oh yeah, they do that every year," he told me. "They used to spray these trees with something that helped the fruit connect to the tree longer. It was some hormone that forced the stem to hang on longer so that they developed a deeper color. What can I tell you? People like red apples! I think the trees just got used to that assistance because when we stopped spraying it the trees didn't know how to hold on to the fruit on their own."

Everyone at some point in their career realizes the core beliefs that form the basis of their "style." Artists, farmers, doctors, lawyers—even scientists and administrative workers—everyone brings their beliefs to work with them, whether they know it or not. This causes you to adapt a personal approach to your work, or it will cause you to gravitate toward the areas of your practice that most excite these beliefs. Either way, inevitably bias penetrates the practice and people naturally form styles. If allowed, these styles can even guide the practice. By 2012 I had enough apple wisdom to navigate my way around orchard management, but I couldn't say that I had developed a personal style or even a base belief that could birth one. But when Brice told me that his trees had turned spray-dependent I realized, lo and behold, I had already formed a belief system that was largely incompatible with agriculture. Although I wanted to be an agriculturalist, this non-congruity was destined to cause me numerous failures in my early years farming.

Nearly two decades of apple foraging had formed in my mind the idea that apple trees are part of nature, not part of the human world. I had the impression orcharding was simply about making it easier for the trees to fruit while simultaneously making it easier for us to collect, as though the trees magically exist on their own and all we have to do is plant them in straight rows and run around collecting like squirrels. This is what 18 years of foraging in various Edens did for me.

But what an insult to apple farmers it is to think this! Actual agriculturalists have as their core belief an agenda to form mutual reliance with the trees, not independence. They make certain demands of the tree and in return offer it protection. Call it marriage or call it a co-dependency; the more extensive farmers are with their demands, the more they need to provide extensive protections. In fact, the history of Modern orcharding has been an abrupt evolution toward the point where the tree's independence actually poses a threat to today's farmers. Having now succeeded in subverting the tree's natural survival instincts, and having replaced them with our own protections, we ask the tree to sacrifice a self-made identity. From the appearance of the fruit to their grafted tips, from rootstock breeding to the young age at which trees are forced into sexual reproduction (fruit)—everything must now be propped up by humans. Now at least I understood why I couldn't achieve the appearance of apple agriculture on my own land. It wasn't my soils to blame, it wasn't the diseases and pests to blame, it wasn't necessarily the rootstock choices or even something I was doing wrong. The reason I failed at being that type of apple farmer is that I have a different vision for the trees. Perhaps naively, I want them to exist in nature, a place I imagine to be independent of me.

PART II

Between Art and Nature

FOUR

Cider

*C*ider does not begin at fermentation, it does not begin with the milling of the apples, and it does not begin in the orchard either. To that effect, cider does not end when it is bottled, cider does not end when it is sold, and cider does not end when it is drunk. This is because there is no beginning or end with cider. It's a loop, not a target. There are no isolated stages or participants. The death of cider (and there almost was one) is when that loop is broken.

Sweating

It's late September, and it's a plentiful apple year in the Northeast. Returning from the hills west of town, our two pickup trucks are weighted with 800 pounds of fruit each. We have a lot more picking to do this afternoon, but first we must unload. In the courtyard next to the cider barn is an incline where I park my truck front-end up so that I can position empty barrels behind the tailgate. All I need to do is drop the hatch, and the apples cascade out and fill the barrels. Most roll out of the truck on their own, but I use a snow shovel to scoop out the rest. Inevitably, though, some apples miss their intended target and bounce off the barrel rims onto the ground. Not to worry: Hammy and Schlemmy, our two border collies, have come to expect this and have been waiting with eyes the size of silver dollars. Dogs love apples. They will pounce on any escapees like a grizzly waiting by the edge of the river during a salmon run.

Blue plastic barrels are not very romantic, but they are light and cheap and there's a nod to tradition about them. Old photographs of orchard harvests from the very early 1900s feature barrels, albeit oak, as the principal container for apple storage and field collection. A standard photographic composition emerges when you see enough of these vintage images: The barrels overflow with apples in the foreground, the workers are positioned behind the barrels in the middle ground (staring into the camera with that creepy dead-face expression that predates "cheese"), and the apple trees and ladders occupy the top of the image in the background. I simply pretend my blue plastic barrels are oak and I'm right there with them.

Next, we unload Benford's truck and fill another three and a half barrels, seven in total. One by one we secure the lids, tilt them on edge, and roll their weight (about 250 pounds each) into the cold storage closet in my barn. The "cave"—what I call it—is an artificially cold room I built myself according to the instructions on the CoolBot website. What's a CoolBot? It's some gadget invented to fool your average wall-mounted air conditioner into thinking it's never cold enough. With this invention, a $350 air conditioner, and enough insulation, I was able to convert a 16-by-8-foot room (the cave) into a cold storage unit for less than $1,000. I bring the ambient temperature to 34°F, which I find perfect for storing apples. With the apples secured, and the trucks now empty, we are able to go out picking again this afternoon—but first, lunch.

Lunch at The Cidery has become the number one attraction for workers during the bottling and picking season. Pizza monopolizes the food options in the Wurtsboro area, but I'll take the trade-off over not having franchised fast-food chains around. I call in two pies and dash into town to pick them up. Polly has prepared the picnic table and brought out plates and hard cider, while Benford has foraged some greens from the lawn and arugula from the garden. Ambika and Carlos have also just arrived with more apples from the Summitville area, and now they join us for lunch. All of us at the picnic table in the sun, a couple of bottles of cider, and what we got here is, at least in my mind, a real sophisticated midday break. Too nice, in fact. It's hard to get going again once the pizza kicks in. The afternoon shift starts as a slog.

But we are out to a new location this afternoon, this time along the Neversink River, where we meet up with more volunteer pickers. This location is particularly overgrown, and despite the added help it takes four hours to fill our trucks again. Plus the late-afternoon temperature has climbed into the 80s, making it extra-sweaty work. But when we are finally loaded with apples again, we have a river beside us and a chance to cool off. Rivers, I've found, are a godsend when you're foraging far from home and you find yourself standing in poison ivy. After an active hot day, the water does more than wash off dirt, sweat, and poison ivy oil; it changes the vibe from agitated to serene. It's a mood cleanser and gives the day a punctuation mark. Tomorrow we'll do it all over again. As fun and appealing as it is, harvesting is serious work and there's no time to waste this time of year.

Traditionally, early apples (apples that ripen in August through mid-September) are baked, sauced, cooked, or canned—but you *don't* use them for cider. When a landowner calls me in early September to tell me to rush over because the apples are dropping, I tell them to call a pie or jam producer instead. I can't use them. Or, if the site has many apple trees and the early drops are in the way of the later cider harvest, then I know a pig farmer who's happy to take them. In fact, a traditional cider orchard is not without farm animals to help with this situation.

It's only the late apples I'm looking for. They are drier inside and out, which is what I want. The late-summer air is still too humid and the nights too warm to promote this condition, so I don't start to collect until around the equinox because (1) the fermentation temperatures are too warm, (2) their sugars are lackluster, and (3) the heavy early apples tend not to store well. I look for the maple trees to turn color and tell me when cider season is starting.

I have only four or five weeks, late September and October, to collect all my apples, which are scattered on wild "uncultivated" trees all over the county. I need to focus on fruit collecting and nothing else over this short span of time, so it's for this reason I built the cold storage unit, to keep the apples until pressing season (which ideally starts immediately after harvest season and not during). But in England's West Country, they discovered a brilliant way of forestalling the press during the fruit rush. They lump the fruit into massive heaps in the grass, where the apples naturally lose some of their water. It's thought that vapors from the grass help preserve the apples and promote a drying process, called sweating, that helps create a richer liquid, albeit at the sacrifice of volume. Consumers who find "light and refreshing" ciders to be dull are rewarded with a drink that's richer and carries a higher alcohol percentage.

I, however, am foraging in rougher conditions than British cider farmers, and my apples don't fall into soft grass. Whereas in England they have mechanical harvesters to sweep the apples off the orchard floor, we have to pick our apples up one by one in a diversity of wild terrains. There is, however, an advantage to individually scanning the apples as we harvest: We can keep out the rots. You know what they say about one bad apple spoiling the bunch—and I found this to be true in our storage unit, too. I need to be vigilant about inspection before all the apples get heaped together and stashed until we're ready to press.

Crushing, Grinding, Pressing

Definitions can be problematic for Americans. We seem to thrive in ambiguity and tend to morph words toward the subjective, often for personal gain. Normally, I like this about our language (in fact, I'm one of the worst offenders), but in the case of *cider* we've inherited a shit-show of definitions that obliges me to preface my remarks. Whereas in the rest of the world, *cider* simply refers to fermented apple juice, Americans have replaced this definition: The word now signifies farm-fresh (unfermented) apple juice. Those still making real cider after Prohibition clung to the word *hard* to specify the alcoholic drink, despite *cider*'s etymology: The word is from the Hebrew language and simply meant "strong drink" (it also was applied to wine, by the way). *Hard* compounded the problem tenfold in America because it, too, morphed and has taken on all kinds of associations. *Hard times*, *hard luck*, *hardheaded*—these are not terms one wants to associate with a sophisticated drink, so now we must combat the residual effects of *hard cider*, which sounds like a drink teenagers throw up.

Prohibition and industrial food production both had a hand in this. Understandably, Modern apple farmers wanted to distinguish their delicious fresh-pressed juice from grocery-store "apple juice," which is mostly water and made from apple concentrate. But their success in commandeering the word *cider* created a problem for the reemergence of real cider. To this day, the industry is coming up with still more terms and definitions to distinguish itself. So be it. But let's just remember that cider is a simple thing: fermented apple juice. Cider is to apples what wine is to grapes. Period.

One other thing I must preface before going further in this chapter is that I, personally, make only regular ol' cider and will not be talking about fanciful alterations. Perhaps this is arrogance on my part, but I feel that cider making has a base method in the same way that the word *cider* should have one base definition. There are many traditional and modern twists to the craft, technologies and strategies such as keeving, macerating, or freeze-concentrating. All heighten the artistry of cider—however, I have nothing to offer on those subjects other than what has already been written in informative books by authors such as Andrew Lea, Ben Watson, and Claude Jolicoeur. I recommend all of their books for cider makers, and I still frequently look up things in their texts. But as far as my approach is concerned, I try to keep it as pure and simple as I can. People at the farmers market claim I'm stubborn this way, that I'm only making cider the way I like it (which is true), but in my defense I come from the art world, where it's uncommon to have many different styles. "Real artists" don't usually bounce between cubism, surrealism, pop art, and classical, so why should a wine or cider maker be expected to offer different styles?

In really big apple years, my cold storage unit fills quickly. In years like this I have no choice but to devote every fourth day of harvesting to juicing apples—it frees up space. In terms of volume: One barrel of apples makes about a quarter barrel of juice, so I can consolidate space quickly by staying on top of the pressing. And as an FYI: 1 bushel of conventional apples usually makes about 3 to 4 gallons of juice, but it's much less with small, dry cider apples—closer to 2 gallons per bushel.

Historically, it used to be that when you wanted to make cider you simply squashed the apples with a heavy weight and either fermented the result just like that, or transferred it to a press capable of separating the liquid from the solids. It wasn't even that long ago that people used a giant club like a mortar-and-pestle setup, as if cider makers were cavemen. But in more advanced cider regions, it was more common to use a heavy stone or giant wooden wheel to crush the apples, rolling over them repeatedly in a circular trough. It was usually the job of a horse or mule to push the wheel around, but human power was utilized, too. The cider maker would then scoop up the pulverized apple mix and apply it like paste between layers of straw to give it substance so that it could be stacked. These layers of straw-and-apple stood about 2 or 3 feet high underneath a wooden screw press that brought down a plate to squish it all. The straw acted as a filter, keeping back the solids and allowing the juice to flow freely. People waited nearby with buckets, and the fresh cider was immediately poured into oak barrels. You can go to the Metropolitan Museum of Art in New York (or just go online) to see a painting by William Sidney Mount that illustrates this process. Interestingly, the Mount painting was commissioned as political marketing in the 1840 presidential race to represent good-ol'-country-values candidate William Henry Harrison versus fat-cat city-slicker Martin Van Buren. A flood of cider seemed to wash Harrison into office, but he died only a month after his inauguration (of un-cider-related causes).

In practice, much is the same with apple pressing today, except that electric and hydraulic force now powers the operation. The biggest advances are in apple pulverizing (before the press): Rather than smashing the apples to a pulp, now grinders are designed with teeth to tear the apples to shreds, but the degree to which the teeth do this has become a secret art in cider making. Depending on the grinder, you can end up with something wet like applesauce; you can end up with something creamy, like toothpaste; you can end up with drier, coarser chunks of apples; or you can end up with a combination of the three. These can all be pressed in a conventional rack-and-cloth press, but the grind creates different juice traits and clarity. Creamy pomace can lead to a hazy drink and encourages pectic enzyme colonies (sometimes that's wanted), while coarser pomace is the goal for those who want to macerate (let it sit for a while) before pressing. People employ all sorts of stylistic variations at every stage of cider making, but traditionally the goal during the grinding and pressing stage is simply to get as much juice out of the apple as easily as possible.

As mentioned, the old method of squeezing the apples is hardly any different today except in the use of hydraulic power: Today's cider makers still stack "cheeses" of pomace between two plates (now we use linen cloths instead of straw to contain the wet mush and build upward), and the pressure is delivered by squeezing. This rack-and-cloth-style press, as it's known, is hard to improve upon when it comes to pressure, but it can get messy and it's only practical as an all-day affair with large quantities of apples. The prep work and the cleanup are both extensive. For small batches and for micro-cideries that can't afford such investments, other press options have been developed. I use one based on the familiar center-screw press associated with winemaking. Known as a bladder press, it inflates a rubber tube inside the core of the machine and presses the pomace outward against the perforated cylinder shell—only the juice can escape. I use these presses because they are small, cheap, and easy to clean, but they are also weaker and slower than the rack-and-cloth method.

The environment where the pressing occurs is also an important consideration to anyone making cider regularly. William Sydney Mount depicted apple pressing as an outdoor activity, and that, no doubt, is part of the romance of apple pressing, but today almost all modern operations are located indoors because of regulations and to avoid weather disruptions. The mill room must be designed to accommodate the flow of bulky apple bins and juice barrels—at least two-thirds of the room must be designed as clear space so that the perpetual movement of bulk containers is not obstructed. Ideally the mill room would be all of the following: oversized, well lit, well powered (most machines run on high-voltage three-phase electricity), and clad with wash-down surfaces, leading toward a large floor drain.

But that particular setup is nothing like what I have. I have a tiny barn with exposed walls. Nonetheless, I've found a good system with a small Oesco grinder and two Lancman bladder presses. (I use two presses because while one is pressing out the juice, I can load the other one. This way the grinder is never waiting for the press to catch up.) These machines are light enough to move outside on pressing days, making pressing more enjoyable and also leaving room inside the barn for the movement of barrels. I can fit both grinder and press—they weigh less than 300 pounds combined—in the back of my Subaru and take the show on the road, pressing on location. This adds further appeal to foraging in faraway locations.

But no equipment is the best if it doesn't fit within the whole of the farm operation. This, of course, means buying a grinder and press designed to accommodate the volume and type of apples you'll be using. The latter, unfortunately, is not something most manufacturers consider. This is because almost all equipment, especially at the large scale, is designed to handle large culinary fruit, which is heavy and wet, not small dry cider apples. The reason they do this is obvious: Well over 99.9 percent of the apples in America are eating apples, and the US cider industry has evolved as a value-added benefit to those farmers. Smaller cider apples and crab apples, for instance, literally fall between the cracks of the automatic apple conveyers used to feed the grinder. (This was a problem we found at my friend Fabio's place, Westwind Orchards, in Accord, New York, where they had just purchased equipment from Orchard Equipment Supply Co. Immediately we discovered the equipment was struggling with some of the smaller apples coming out of the Catskills. Luckily, Oesco is one of those companies that takes responsibility for their work, and they were able to fabricate changes to the system. Few, if any, other companies will do that!)

My grinder is also made by Oesco but it's designed for home-scale or micro-cidery operations. It has small teeth that work beautifully on smaller apples and crab apples, but they struggle with larger, softer fruit. That's a trade-off I'm personally willing to take. And although toothed grinders like mine tend to sauce the apples more than blade grinders or hammer mills do (grinders that slice or whip apart apples), mine works well with my bladder press because of its weaker extraction pressure. My only grievance is in processing pears. Even my dry little "choke pears" tend to cause blowouts in the press (blowouts are what it's called when the pomace squeezes through the weave and squirts like a quahog all over the place). But appearently (*sic*) everyone with every kind of setup has trouble pressing pears.

One day in early October, years before we were licensed, two old men stopped in off the road. They were curious about Bertha, our largest apple tree and the nearest to the road. Having nosed into our driveway, perhaps to help themselves to her apples, they saw something of greater interest by the barn and they continued to drive up.

Peter and I were pressing apples in front with my new bladder press when I heard their car door slam. Looking up, I saw the two old-timers excitedly coming toward us: Faded overalls, short stocky bodies, white curly hair bulging out from faded caps, both with round, bulbous noses. As they approached I heard them speaking in a foreign language that I couldn't quite recognize, though I gathered they were Eastern European. So focused were they on my apple press that they forgot to introduce themselves or even make eye contact as they moved in next to Peter and me to complete a circle around the flowing juice.

"Uh, hello?" I said.

"This machine you have, eez for apple vine, no?" one asked, obviously intending to say apple *wine*.

"Yes. We're making cider," I said.

"We have country house near here, many years now, we make vine in basement too."

They introduced themselves and told us they were from Slovenia (or possibly they said Slovakia, and I misheard them). They also told me they were brothers, which I should have gathered from the resemblance they bore to one another.

"Do you see this juice here?" one brother said while bending over. He pointed at the downspout below my press, not concerned about the fact his finger was touching the flowing liquid. "Do you know good apples? Do you know how make good vine?"

I knew what he meant. In most world cultures cider is the same as wine, just made with different fruit. It's only in America, with its strange reverence for wine, that people consider cider to be "less than." So I tried to translate *vine* to *cider* for Peter who, at 15 years old, I had assumed was new to all these traditions. But Peter was a local boy, and I thought wrong.

"No. How do you know it's good wine?" I asked the man, playing along.

"You zee how it pour in bucket? Do you hear sound it make?"

"No. I don't hear a sound," I said.

"*Exactly!*" the other brother chimed in. "Good apple vine makes no sound! Bad vine splashes in bucket like vater. Good apples pour like oil, no splash."

It was nice to know I had good apple vine.

A few years later I learned what the two brothers meant. In 2012 there were no wild apples for me to forage. A killing frost had decimated all but a few micro-climates in lower New York, but at this point we had our winery license and I felt compelled to make cider anyway. Eventually, Polly and I tracked down a commercial orchard along the river that had survived the frost, and they allowed us to pick up the drops underneath their trees for a nominal fee. We filled our truck with dented and bruised Cortlands, Macouns, and Golden Delicious apples, all fairly ripe, and returned to Wurtsboro to turn them into cider. Sure enough, we heard a splash. Conclusively, the brothers were onto something.

Live Cider

I hear this a lot at the farmers markets: "How do you make cider?"

If I were to answer that question honestly, I'd sound like a smart-ass. "You're asking the wrong question," I'd tell them. "You don't make cider, cider makes itself." Other organisms, yeasts, are responsible for converting apple juice into cider, so technically *they* are the cider makers. My job is just to allow for the conditions where yeasts can do their job, which isn't all that difficult because yeasts are everywhere and pretty self-sufficient.

Sometimes I get a follow-up to that question: "No, what I meant was, how do you make *good* cider?" And to that, I have another smart-ass response: "It's not about making good cider, it's about *not* making bad cider." You can't improve on silence, either, but you might think of the accomplishments of great musicians like Mozart or Beethoven as improvements. That's the wrong way of looking at things, though, and when cider makers obsess on an end result they actually fail to see how most great artworks evolved from silence. With cider that silence is the drink's natural state. Unfortunately we have an industry that pays no mind to this process; it looks immediately to bypass it and improve on Mozart. This is a recipe for noise, and it's not an environment that will foster future artists or art enthusiasts.

Sweetness, for instance, is not the natural state of cider; it must be achieved by combating the life responsible for it (yeasts don't just stop eating the sugars on their own; you have to force them to quit). So if you want to make good cider, the better choice would be to honor the pure process rather than assume it's bad, or worth fighting. Maybe then an appreciation for humble cider can emerge among drinkers, too.

Along the same lines, it's incorrect to think of *the cider maker* as a chef-like title similar to *master brewer*. In actuality, cider makers are just those who help the apple's natural progression from fruit to drink, simply providing the necessary assistance in this realization. Beer makers, on the other hand, are responsible for imagining recipes, mastering the ingredients, and cooking it up ("brewing" it, with heat). In other words, their fingerprints are all over the product and they are deserving of the accolades if the drink is sublime. Meanwhile, on the opposite spectrum, cider making is just an extension of agriculture; it's the artist's job to continue that life. It's the cow that tastes good, not the butcher's handiwork.

Because the goal of cider is to allow life on the farm to blossom in the bottle, a weird distinction arises that beer consumers will forever have a hard time with: The "product" is not the physical drink inside the bottle—or even the taste of the cider itself—but the *appreciation* of the life itself. Admittedly, this creates a bit of a chicken-and-egg situation, but it's an important distinction: Though the appreciation is linked to the physical object (specifically the taste), the satisfaction exists with or without the need of this physical evidence. An even better way to think of the cider maker's role is the example of the schoolteacher: Being a teacher is not about producing something physical but about fostering something that can become physical. Einstein's mentors can't take credit for producing his discoveries, but they can be proud that they helped foster his ability to discover them. So, too, Einstein's fans should appreciate their work.

As a cider maker I want to support a living being that I (and hopefully customers) can sit back and marvel at for its own success. But if customers are focused on what I've achieved, or if they think my ciders are good because of me, then they aren't seeing natural cider correctly. When cider ceases to become agriculture, when cider becomes about the industry that takes credit for it, we, as a culture, have lost our way.

Yeasts start to colonize fruit juice immediately after pressing, and it doesn't take but a day or two for the liquid to become a frenzied pot of microorganisms. This is known as the primary fermentation stage. Not that I know what's going on the microscopic level, but my guess is that yeast cells are finding the environment to their liking and responding by reproducing. They do so by dividing (I think): One becomes two; two becomes four; four becomes eight; and so forth. But yeasts need energy to divide, and they are finding their fuel in the sugars of the apple juice. They eat the sugars and convert them into alcohol and CO_2. The foam that we see on the surface of the cider during this first stage is a by-product of this energy. Carbon dioxide (CO_2), a gas heavier than air, is expelled from the liquid and sits above it while pushing oxygen out of the vessel. This is why you see air locks on modern wine tanks and carboys: The air lock traps in the CO_2 and keeps oxygen from getting back inside, potentially bringing spoilage microbes along with it. Carefully managed, this natural CO_2 by-product of yeast fermentation will act like a shield on the surface of the cider, even when the vessel is wide open.

When we first started learning about cider, we made all our batches in 5-gallon carboys (glass containers with narrow necks the shape of a Red Stripe bottle). Carboys are the standard vessel for home wine and cider production, largely because when they are full of liquid they weigh less than 50 pounds. which is about the maximum weight an average adult can move around. We learned early on that a good place to let the carboys ferment was in our bathtub upstairs. This is for two reasons: (1) The indoor temperature in early November (plus or minus 67°F) was perfect for getting the yeast activity started, and (2) once the yeast activity began, it tended to get a little too active and bubble out of the container for a few days before it settled down. As the yeast took the party to the streets, the tub made for easy cleanup.

In 2009 we needed to up our game. By this point in our careers we had already conceived of our cider business, and 5-gallon batches weren't going to cut it anymore. I needed to learn how to make barrel cider, a standard of 55 gallons liquid volume. Barrels, of course, are made of wood, but nowadays wineries more often use stainless steel or plastic barrels for their primary fermentations. Plastic is especially light and cheap, and compared with wood it is easily cleaned, so it made the perfect vessel for my first attempts at scaling up cider production. Always a spendthrift, I found hand-me-down plastic barrels from a local winery at $10 each.

The bathtub option was out. And there's no way of moving a barrel of cider once it's full of liquid (close to 500 pounds). Planning was key. Knowing how messy things can get, I would have liked to ferment the cider outside, but certain yeasts (particularly wine yeasts) require stable, relatively warm temperatures and that's *not* what you'll find in October. In fact the nighttime-to-daytime temperatures can swing 50°F or more. Ultimately, I determined the cider needed to start indoors where I'd had much success at the 5-gallon level. And this is how our dining room became our first cidery. The plan was to start the barrel fermentation behind a Japanese screen in the corner so we could maintain the illusion of domesticity; later we would draw a hose down the steps to the basement so as to eventually siphon the liquid into an aging barrel (a used oak barrel, also a winery leftover). I prepared the floor with towels in case the fermentation got too rowdy. After 11 trips to the dining room with 5-gallon buckets, I was able to fill the blue plastic barrel in the corner, and within a day the liquid assimilated to the indoor temperature of around 65°F. Perfect.

The good part about having cider as your house guest is that you can check it often and monitor the progress more acutely. It wasn't until the third day that a small amount of bubbles found their way around the edge of the surface like river foam. Each day I spooned out a sample to taste; my experience was that the sweetness faded over the coming days, giving way to a more chalky experience. The foam edge grew until the fifth day, at which point the entire surface was submerged under a light yellow crud dancing with tiny bubbles. And the crud was growing. By Day 6 it was 4 inches thick and approaching the rim of the barrel. I closed the lid to keep tiny flakes of apple scum from leaping out onto the floor. And on Day 7 I woke to find the foam oozing down the outer surface of the barrel. I quickly lifted the lid to scoop out bubbles with a strainer and wiped up the mess. Now our house guest was wearing out its welcome.

And another unforeseen issue made itself known. Living under the same roof as a fermenting 55-gallon barrel of cider is like being under the bedcovers after a bean dinner. I would describe a healthy fermentation as smelling "meaty" or "bready." Camembert also comes to mind. It's an acquired taste. If what you are used to is deodorant and fastidiously sanitized people, then a human's natural smell can seem offensive, but after being in Europe for a little while you get used to these odors and may even miss it once you've returned home. But I'll admit I wasn't a Camembert fan at first, either.

After two weeks the foam had finally subsided and returned to the surface of the liquid. It was at this point I started to worry about air contamination. My curious opening and closing of the lid had likely blown off the natural CO_2 that had formed invisibly on the surface, so I took one last sip before letting it rest another week before racking. Twenty-one days in my dining room, and the cider still had a touch of sweetness, but it was definitely alcoholic. And there was a briny quality that I now know is common at this stage, reminding me of hand soap (unscented Dial, specifically). This note now serves to let me know things are progressing as they should.

Racking Brains

After a few weeks of fermenting, the yeast population in most ciders has expanded so greatly that the available food (sugars) becomes scarce and the activity dies down. It's at this point that a cider or winemaker usually racks the liquid and leaves behind the solid deposits that form at the bottom of the barrel, known as lees. (*Racking* is the term used for the transfer of wine.) There's nothing special about it except that you want to be careful to leave the lees layer behind and not stir up the sediment. Traditionally this was done with a siphoning hose, but today it's mostly done with pumps.

I rack my ciders twice: Once after about 15 days or whenever the yeast settles, and once again a month later (usually in early December). But there are many strategic variations you can adopt, each producing multiple effects in the final product. That aside, what's conceptually important about this step is that you're preparing the cider for winter. Living cider, like everything else in nature, needs to slow down in tandem with the seasons, and this is one way to prepare the microorganisms for hibernation.

Racking isn't just a way of removing some of the stinky solid deposits after fermentation settles; it's also a tactical assault on the remaining yeast population. Every time you move the cider, huge numbers of yeast cells get left behind, and any yeast that is transferred becomes stressed or is killed by the turmoil. Surviving yeast must rebuild the colonies all over again. For that reason some people rack early and often to inhibit the yeast from eating the sugars too quickly. Their goal is to preserve the initial fruity character before the yeasts eat it all. This is also one of the few ways to naturally preserve some of the perceived sweetness, but even so, time will eventually finish the cider to complete dryness. This effect helps bridge the gap for consumers who mistakenly think cider is naturally sweet—in actuality it requires a fair degree of manipulation and artistic skill. In the end, wine does not taste like grape juice, so why should cider taste like apple juice?

It's been 10 days since Thanksgiving and the upstate sky is lit by a low, weak sun that's doing very little in terms of warmth. Swirling gusts of wind usher in-and-out clouds. The fallen leaves stripped of living moisture rustle like tin cans against the side of the barn. For a brief second it's sprinkling and then it's sunny again (or sort of sunny). This goes on all day long, and although the temperature is just above freezing, the cold is deep in my bones, like the way San Francisco somehow can feel colder than Minneapolis.

I'm in my heavy overalls with insulated rubber boots working over the gravel crush pad in the front of the cidery. It's in this same spot that in October, open to the orchard air, we grind and press the apples in a colorful and bucolic setting. But this late into the season, the landscape is monochromatic (shades of a gray-brown) and my job is to clean barrels. And this job sucks. This is the behind-the-scenes job that few winery workers volunteer to do. During racking season it's just me, the cold water, the cold wind, and cold hands.

The hoses have lost their flexibility, and because my goal was to rack and clean six barrels today, I'm falling behind. The sun only makes a brief spin across the sky each day, and I have to make the most of it. I try to steady the nozzle with one hand while attempting to angle the plastic drum with my other. I have it on edge so that I can lean my whole body inside to examine for sediment stuck to the blue walls. I don't want to scratch the drum and create little bacteria foxholes in the lining. Close scrutiny and a hard blast of water is my best cleaning strategy.

The next step is to sanitize the barrel. I use a water and sulfur dioxide solution (the same stuff people add to wine), which is toxic enough to kill whatever life is still colonizing the barrel (including mine, if I keep my head in there too long!). After pouring the solution in, I seal the lid back on and roll it around my driveway to make sure every surface is touched by the sulfite. Then I've got to pump it out of the barrel back into its designated 5-gallon bucket, and thoroughly rinse the barrel with water again.

With my pumps clean, the hoses clean, the barrels clean, and "the wand" clean (the pipe for racking), I can begin the task of pumping cider from one barrel to the next. It takes only five minutes, but after the first barrel is empty I need to clean it and all the above-listed equipment again, then sanitize them, then rinse them, same as before. I don't want to move from one batch to the next without doing all this, because I'm worried that if one cider has a malady it will infect the rest. But first I've got to collect the lees.

After draining the barrel with the wand submerged all but 1 inch from the bottom of the barrel, there will be a 1-inch-thick layer of sludge waiting for me. This is the lees—the settled yeast mixed with any other solids from the fruit. It has the color and consistency of toothpaste. There's not much market value in this by-product, but I found that if you collect the sludge from all the batches and then mix them together in a big container, it will settle out and the top half will eventually become drinkable clear cider with great texture. (This is what poor cider makers drink, rather than their "fine product.") To harvest this thick sludge, I pour 1 gallon of clear cider back into the barrel and agitate the container so that the paste mixes with the liquid and can ooze out when I tilt it upside down. I position a 5-gallon bucket under the rim of the barrel to catch the lees as it slowly drips out, and I usually end up with about 2½ gallons per container.

We used to sell the lees to the local plumber, who'd use it to pour down septic systems at various job sites because yeasts are great for cleaning cesspools. Assuming the systems have not been shocked (killed) from bleach, soaps, and chemical cleaners, the added yeasts will build populations in the cesspools and act in the same way probiotics do in our stomachs: helping with digestion. A homeowner may conceivably never have to pump out their septic system if the culture is alive and well drained.

Unfortunately our plumber friend retired and moved to Florida, and for a while we weren't able to find interest in the lees. I started reading about how the French use it in recipes, such as salad dressing and soup stocks. Around this time I also read Dan Barber's book *The Third Plate*, and passages about wasted food inspired me to reach out to him at the famous Stone Barns restaurant (about 45 miles from us). Sure enough, he was interested in experimenting with using lees in food recipes, and he and his staff created a braising sauce used on pork. I had the pleasure of breaking my vegetarian vows of 20 years on this dish and as a result I'm eating meat again! (Assuming I know the animal's backstory.)

Barreling

Let's face it, cider and winemakers are just glorified canners. We preserve our crop in a container, that's all. Why we are celebrated more than the gardener who pickles cucumbers or cans heirloom tomatoes, I cannot say. Maybe it has something to do with scale or the fragility of our egos? Probably the latter. But we aren't just glorified canners, we're also glorified dishwashers, and any occupational pretense should be curbed then and there, because for every 10 minutes spent working with the precious liquid we spend two hours cleaning and sanitizing. This happens all year long, too—at pressing, racking, and bottling—the dishwasher job is part of our being, whether our glamorous marketing speaks of this or does not. It's the least pleasurable part of the cider lifestyle but it's as important to the *whole* as anything else. To remove this from our self-image would be to undermine the whole of the being. I wouldn't go so far as to say I have *no* respect for cider makers who pass the dirty work over to someone else, but it is one of those signs that tells me who's for real and who's just trying to industrialize the process. *Who, exactly, is the cider maker?* is a lot like asking *Who's the farmer?* Call me too dogmatic if you must, but I don't accept excuses: Cider making is a whole existence.

In my experience, new oak barrels will overwhelm ciders with musk aromas, a dry mouthfeel, and inky tannins (which are very different from the "good" tannins in fruit). Unlike red wine, cider is more easily abducted by these flavor infusions (and make no mistake about it: Oak is a flavor infusion no less so than spices or other foreign flavorings). These imparted notes might be appealing at first sip, or they might be used to mask something hideous, but additions become salacious really quickly—they are not what any true cider maker hopes to create. To avoid this, all the cider maker needs to do is use good apples, keep things clean (or at least keep them from getting out of control), and give the cider time to develop.

One solution for wintering barrels, and the universal cheap solution, is to buy hand-me-down oak barrels from wineries. This is because after one or two uses (a couple of vintages of use), an old oak barrel becomes stripped and neutral in terms of its flavor. And that's a good thing for cider. That means the oak bomb won't dominate. The round shape of a barrel is also perfect for whatever slow convection might occur in the vessel; the tapered top at the bunghole allows for minimum headspace contact (the surface area at the top of the barrel). That said, working with oak is a pain in the ass. It's heavy, it's hard to clean, it can breathe and allow in oxygen. And it can leak, too! I don't use oak much anymore, but when I do I have to really talk myself into showing up to work that day. But who am I kidding?—even plastic and stainless steel tanks are a pain in the ass when washing and sanitizing is done outside in December. I will always have to psych myself up on racking days, and I do so by pretending that the cider batches are like children in need of tucking in before winter: I must wash their faces, brush their teeth, and read them a bedtime story. Come Christmas, I want all the batches dreaming of sugarplum fairies.

But pep-talk words only mean so much to a glorified dishwasher. In the end I start feeling sorry for myself. I ask myself why I'm breaking my back while wealthy industrialists press a button and get this all done from their cell phone! They just pay someone else to do the dirty work and take the credit like the white-collar farmer. And man oh man, this gets to me sometimes. I become the Willy Loman of the cider industry. Does anyone else value the ugly, the painful, or the untouted? Am I just imagining this thing called *whole*? Am I just stupid for not figuring out how to take my farm to the next level and hire people to do the dirty work? Why am *I* the one cleaning barrels?

Inevitably, this is when the hose stream bounces off the bottom of the barrel and blasts my face. The freezing winds amplify the shock and I'm in utter disgust. I drop the hose and look up, trying not to yell.

As I plow on with my chores, I curse my bad luck, my lack of money, my lack of business sense, and all those decisions that led me into this miserable existence. Most of all, I curse my own vision for cider. Why does it have to be this way? Why can't I just accept progress? What's wrong with me?

A word of caution: If dark thoughts bother you, if you need to avoid deep pits of despair or feelings of futility, then farming and cider may not be good life choices. Somehow I've persevered, I know the sun eventually comes out, but I might have my art background to thank for that. Tolerance for dejection can only come when you give up hope—in this case, for wealth. Seasons come and go, the world dies and comes back. Nothing is complete without its opposite. When I look at the ads for popular wines and ciders, I see pretty girls on warm summer days, or I see sophisticated lumberjacks in front of fall foliage studying their cider glass as if it were a Degas sculpture. That's marketing. What you'll never see is a depressed artist, poor and worried farmers, or the cold and tired cellar rats trying to clean barrels. But let me tell you, if you don't want those sour notes in your glass then I can't recommend real, seasonal cider. For you, there's another product the French call *cidre industrielle*. As for me, I know of only one way to make cider, and it's got the winter in it as much as it does the summer. Real wine and real cider—it's just part of the circle of life.

Overwintering

December 21, one of the two great calendar dates. People throughout the Northern Hemisphere celebrate this benchmark in different ways, usually with religious overtones, but the one thing our various cultures have in common is that we recognize this as a time for introspection, celebration, and rest.

Rest is understandable, given that we as humans are (or were) an agrarian sort and the winter caps our busy time. In the colder climates especially, we have a shortened growing season, so the prep work is particularly frantic the farther north you go. Then, when the ground freezes and the snows come, there's not much to do but rest. Rest.

Celebration is also understandable (assuming that we've done all the work to prepare for winter). Yes, it's true that the modern economy never slows down anymore—we have lightbulbs and fossil fuel to blast our way through winter, we have food shipped from the other side of the world where crops are in season—but modern people still recognize the lack of daylight and the cold temperatures. We've injected seasonality wherever possible and use this to escape the day-to-day routine. If nothing else, we'll celebrate that.

Introspection and celebration are surprisingly similar; one is simply the extroverted response to the other. Both activities pivot around the passing of time—be it the accomplishment of the recent past or the beginning of something new. But introspection is especially what winter's all about. It is therefore no coincidence that our society encourages resolutions (New Year's), sacrifices (Lent), and allocations (tax season) during winter. It's as though we have no choice but to follow nature and incorporate dormancy into human-made structures. We take ourselves out of the game for the moment, take inventory of our personal and cultural lives, and assess the best way forward. And although a week of holiday parties is sometimes needed to prompt this response, in the end winter is a three-month period pre-mandated for introspection.

The apple tree is the perfect symbol of seasonal response, and its progeny, cider, follows suit. In spring the apple tree pushes its energy up from the ground into its extremities to form new leaves and flower blossoms. Its outward gaze is so strong then that it blasts beyond the individual specimen and sends forth pollen. In summer the tree basks in the sun and incubates its seed, and in fall that seed is dispersed along with the dropping of leaves. Now, in winter, the tree's energy returns underground where it concentrates. Bears do this, trees do this, and cider does it, too. Winter offers living things the chance to bottom out after a wild ride—through the growing season to the harvest, through a grinder to fermentation, the apple (and then cider) has been through a lot this year and it needs a chance to collect itself. Inside the winter barrels, that's exactly what's happening. Living cider has a mind, body, and soul that respond just as all living things do to the position of our planet.

———

The physical protection of insulation is all-important for the wintering cider, but there is mythic significance to having the barrels in an environment that keeps pace with the ground temperatures. It's the memory of the tree's energy that signals the cider to hit dormancy in December and not wake until March or April. Think of the barrels as bears: It's best for all parties just to let sleeping bears be.

I've built a long, narrow closet extending only 4 feet from the back of my barn, but it runs the full 30-foot length. With multiple exterior double-door openings (6 feet wide each), I have full access to everything inside. The depth of the closet interior is 42 inches and the height is 9 feet. The walls and doors are padded with 6 inches of soft batting and it's sheathed with ½-inch foil-faced rigid insulation (and taped at the seams to prevent air gaps and vapor loss). The goal of all this is to provide a home for my barrels, to mirror the environment of my home cellar. This includes the darkness, the temperature, and the insulation from atmospheric energies (including motion and sound). Stacked three layers high, I can get all 30 of my barrels, 1,500 gallons, in a relatively small space and out of the way, undisturbed.

The heavy insulation is good both in the winter and summer, when it's hot out (closets stay cool), but it's equally important that the insulation adds stability of temperature during the spring and fall when highs and lows might fluctuate 40° to 60°F in a single day. The closet interiors do not perceptibly change with the exterior volatility, which is vital for preserving the protective CO_2 gas layer inside the barrels. At their peak in August, the inside temps might reach 70°F, and in early March the room might be as low as 35°, but that difference between the high and low temperatures takes place very gradually.

The nights are clearest in January and February, and I sometimes get bundled up and head to a clearing in the woods. Without warmth or humidity blanketing the earth's atmosphere, I can explore the nighttime sky free from the sheltering dome. It feels like there's direct access to outer space and this planet is nothing more than just a rock, another asteroid. It feels like I can just float messages through the weightless abyss and connect with whatever sits on those other rocks up there.

I lie against the frozen slope of ground so I don't have to crane my neck, and because I have so many layers on I can't feel the cold through my clothes. Only my nose and eyes are exposed, leaving my muffled breath under the hood to further lend to the astronaut illusion. I came prepared to travel the expanses of space and have in my coat pocket my copilot: a 500 ml bottle of cider with a champagne cork.

I like that our ciders are accessible without a corkscrew or a bottle opener. In 0°F temperatures I barely have the finger dexterity to get the wire hood untwisted, but the cork is an easy pop. I sip from the rim in ½-ounce increments: a zany blend of puckering *Malus baccata* crab apples, now aged for four years. This is definitely a winter drink. Its tart acidity and extreme tannin create a sensation in the mouth akin to the heat of whiskey, and I'm forced to slow to ¼-ounce increments—tiny gulps compared with the average cider.

Making cider means drinking cider. It means it's in your hands nearly every night. This quality is shared by every cider maker I know, even the industrial producers with whom you'd think we have nothing in common. Those who prefer beer or mixed drinks simply don't end up becoming intuitive cider makers, in the same way steak restaurants are not run by vegetarian chefs. Our brother- and sisterhood revolves around the acceptance of this lifestyle.

To outsiders this might appear like alcoholism, but we are actually quite moderate. I wouldn't say we're drunk or tipsy any more than your average person, and yet we do intentionally try to incorporate cider into every aspect of our lives. We may not physically have it with us, but it's a relationship that we don't put down. When we let it in, the drink becomes part of our memory, which supports the intuition needed for cider making. Would the customer want anything less from a cider maker?

Spring Blending

True to the saying, March came in like a lion this year with repeated snows. But as the equinox approached, the sun wore through the white to expose many areas of thawing, dark brown earth. The start of mud season. Already robins are combing this calico landscape in search of worms. After a long introspection period, the previous year's vintage is approaching the age when it starts to express itself as the cellar temperatures reach their annual lowest. The yeast activity has dropped over the winter, and the liquid is left clear and without atmosphere. It is the ideal time to sample the cider because it has had time in a barrel, the unifying component that young ciders lack.

My goal with sampling and blending is to get to know the barrels before the bottling season. For me, that means April, May, and June. I want my ciders in pressurized bottles when they wake up, which they do in earnest just before the summer solstice. Perhaps more skilled cider makers could get a jump-start on me and blend their ciders earlier, maybe even do their blending before the apples are pressed, but I lack this skill. I have to wait until after March 21 to judge the components and know what I'm working with.

They say time heals all wounds, and I find that to be true for cider, too. Time gives the drink holism. Instead of the broken stages, like the rises and runs of a staircase, the drinker of an aged cider experiences the ups and downs like the unfolding of rolling hills. In the mouth the beginning, middle, and end stages echo like the color tabs strategically scattered in a Cézanne composition. This is all assuming the cider is made from a diversity of desirable cider apples—rich in life, with good genes and with personable characteristics—but it takes more than just that to make a good cider. It takes time. Without time, young ciders are like a bad comedian, devoid of tempo and bombing in front of a squirming audience.

My way of celebrating the spring equinox is to go through my barrels and collect samples with a thief. (*Thief*, humorously, is the winemaker's name for the glass tube that you dip in the bunghole to extract samples. It's just a large straw, really, capable of trapping 2 or 3 ounces at a time with the suction of your thumb. But a turkey baster works fine, too.) My thieving mission is to fill dozens of 8-ounce Mason jars, each one to represent a barrel. I will return the samples to my house refrigerator so that I can study them over the next few weeks. I take sips from each jar and gradually get to know the ciders the way you might start to know your classmates at the start of the semester. The character of each batch discloses itself slowly. First impressions can be very deceiving; it would be a fool's mistake to make decisions based on objective analysis alone. It's one thing to identify the drink's physical properties (*Is it tart? Is it tannic? Does it have the perception of sweetness?*), but it's another thing entirely to assess the cider's true character. Personable traits dazzle gradually, never immediately.

Back in the house, I line up all the glass jars in front of the sunny window and first note (without sipping) the color, clarity, and aroma of each cider. Then I take tiny sips and focus my first descriptions on just the objective traits (the specs), including the acidity, tannin, and sugars. Then I do another round and comment on the notes (the subjective traits) in search of metaphors to describe both the good and bad qualities. Does it have vanilla, banana, or tropical notes? Or does it have horse manure, nail polish, and egg breath? I try to allow myself license to write down nonsensical images that pop into my head—"marshland," "carpentry shop," "after a heavy rain," et cetera.

Inevitably I will run across something wine people call flaws. Sometimes an issue of this nature can be remedied with more time or with more racking. The egg-breath smell, for instance, can quickly be solved by racking, especially through a copper wand. Sometimes it works and sometimes it doesn't. Late bloomers will find a home eventually, maybe in another vintage, and crappy cider will end up as vinegar or brandy. It's just the way it's always been, and who am I to buck tradition? I try to remember I'm not the one leading this dance. Of the 1,500 gallons that I make each year, only an average of 1,200 gallons end up with a label on them.

The note taking and the sampling process continue for about a month. As April drags on and anxiety builds about early blossom or late frost, I want to feel like I've got a good grip on what's going on in each barrel. I want to identify the barrels in a blind taste test and look upon them with anthropomorphic eyes. I want to have a good sense of who I'm dealing with.

When I was a kid, I used to play with Matchbox cars. My friends and I would assign personalities, family positions, and occupational titles to the cars as we'd enact races, smash-'em-up derbies, or dramatic scenes involving crashes. Intuitively, we'd know how each car would respond to the drama as it unfolded unpredictably. We were like improvisational actors and directors having to deal with plot twists the other kids would throw out in lieu of our own.

Every adult still has this intuition in them. Adults usually structure their day for practical functions, but at night, while they sleep, the improv playwright takes over and their subconscious mind proves that even the most by-the-book people have wild imaginations. I don't know the function of dreams, but David Lynch would have some serious competition if the waking world were to value subconscious creativity like it does cerebral intentionality.

Blending cider is an art, not a recipe. Yes, you must be formally skilled in the craft, and yes, you need to master your palate (by fully grasping the barrel samples), but even so, the final decisions during the act of blending are entirely dependent on intuition. *Talent* is what they call this in the fine arts. You can deem this snobbery if you must, but the fact is some people allow themselves greater sensitivity than others. There is no way to teach this, either. But for those who show a talent for cider (and I'm talking those who don't approach it as a recipe), time and practice are all that's necessary.

Luckily, there are many, many kinds of artists in this world, and there is *no* hierarchy to them. You don't need to be Rembrandt; in fact self-taught folk artists are no less artists than he was. I would go so far as to say that in the wine world, folk artists are at the very top of the pyramid. Frankly, I could give a rat's ass what Mondavi and Rothschild are up to. Generally, the better funded an operation is, the more detoured the winemakers are from the immediacy of artistic intuition. No amount of marketing can make up for that. Fake art is fake art. Meanwhile, if you want to find cider's purest forms of artistic expression, take a look at what the hillbillies on the other side of the mountain are drinking. Good or bad, I guarantee you it's noteworthy. And I can tell you another thing: They aren't following a recipe. They are making cider the way they want to and have total creative license to experiment, fail, or rise to unforeseen heights that the play-it-safe crowd will never see.

The goal of blending, of course, is to make a complete cider—one that stands alone, without the need of another product for reference.

Is it only because I know what one painting looks like that I can appreciate another? That's not how art works, and cider should be no different. Completeness in cider is about crafting a world unto itself, making it seem simple. I want the cider to feel like it was destined to be, like there were no other possibilities. But "simple," it turns out, is anything but simple. Yeats once wrote: "Yet if it does not seem a moment's thought / Our stitching and unstitching has been naught." And what he means by that, of course, is that there's plenty of grunt work behind clean, immediate communication. So for that I need to roll up my sleeves and start experimenting. I break out the pen and paper and my measuring beakers, an eyedropper and Mason jars full of barrel samples, and I become like a Poindexter lab technician for a few weeks each spring. I want to experiment with blends at the micro-level before making major decisions, and I need to keep records because the variables become exponentially more complex once you start combining percentages from various batches.

This isn't a Lego set we're assembling. Again, the goal is to complete the cider, but by that I mean make it whole, not done. If completeness were a matter of incorporating all the physical notes, then a cider maker could just borrow components from other batches and blend the three primary notes of acidity, perceived sweetness, and tannin like a painter would use primary colors. But how interesting would a painting be that looks like a flag of red, yellow, and blue stripes? Cider artists need to do more than just complete the components; they need to maintain the vision of the landscape from which the cider originates. I'll say it again: The world we create with cider is the world the apple trees live in.

Even though you can theoretically make every color from the three primary colors, artists know that this isn't true when it comes to painting. That's also why Winsor and Newton, Sennelier, and other paint brands produce so many colors, because artists usually want as broad a palette as possible. As a cider maker I certainly don't want a limited palette, either, and that's one reason why wild apples (which live in very diverse worlds) are so important. But I've also found that the more diverse the apple environment, the more diverse the color palette becomes, and I'm often overwhelmed with aromas, potential yeast notes, mouthfeel, viscosity, carbonation, clarity, and other "objective" components that add up to a labyrinth of options (and that's before blending the subjective notes even begins!). So I'm not exaggerating when I say the possibilities are endless. Ultimately, blending is as much about subtraction as it is about adding. Think, as an example, about blending two barrels that have competing characteristics that arrive at the same time—for instance, the front note. One of those barrels might start with a flowery nose while the other starts on a woodsy/musty note. Both want to be leadoff batters, but only one can have the job. We might hope a merger will be complementary, but often the merger detracts from the favorable characteristics of each. So what's a blender to do except reduce the chaos?

Another example I find quite common is when a cider ferments out to be thin and lemony. This is almost always the case with early to midseason apples (and why I don't use them). I can hope to find a complementary cider that will balance it, pinning my hopes on other barrels that are earthy, bitter, or sweet-like, exhibiting signs of malolactic fermentation (butterscotch notes) or minerality. But adding those components won't always work to complete the first cider. It might still be thin and lemony even after those components, but now there's just a bunch of white noise that obscures the core of the drink. Talk about a muddied picture! The better solution would have been to embrace the soul of the drink and use other components as passing secondary features. Again, keep it simple.

And speaking of keeping it simple, I'm not going to belabor talk of blending any longer. It's either the easiest thing in the world or the hardest thing depending on how well you understand the environment from which the apples come. Plus you need experience, talent, and intense familiarity with your palate—and for that, I can't stress enough the getting-to-know-the-barrel stage. I will just add faith and patience to that list: In the end, the stitching and unstitching *will* add up to a moment's thought.

Bottle Season

For years we kept finding old lawn mowers mysteriously placed outside what's now our cider barn. We couldn't figure out what the hell was going on. Maybe some high school kids were playing some drawn-out prank on us? But then where were the kids getting all these mowers? Eventually we learned that the guy who lived in the house before us ran an unadvertised small-engine machine shop from the barn, and finally it all made sense. Locals used to "donate" their old equipment to him for parts and they just didn't know he'd moved away.

I told this story to Al the carpenter, whom I hired to make an addition to the barn. Al didn't bat an eye in returning: "Well, then you're lucky the guy who lived here wasn't the town coroner."

Al helped us make a few upgrades to the barn, including a concrete floor, a storage shed, and water connections, and now the small building is the scene of the two great cider activities of our year: pressing and bottling. What makes them great, especially the bottling (since we do things the old-fashioned way, manually), is that they are the two jobs that Polly and I can't do ourselves; we need to coordinate work parties.

But I hate being an employer. I feel that, in the time it takes me to explain something I could've just completed the job myself. Plus, as an introvert, I find social interaction to be a slow trickle of my energy. Solitude was largely my reason for moving to a farm in the first place! But when cider and orcharding overlap in the spring and fall, the work overwhelms me. So there are times when I need to shelve my aversion to specialized roles, I need to shelve my shyness and frustration with communication and just become a boss. And every time I do this, when I put my protective shield aside, I always surprise myself: People aren't so bad after all! In fact, bottling days have become my favorite on the farm, not because we make progress (although it can be frustrating when we don't), but because the community effort is so rewarding.

Conceptually, I need to think of the objective differently. I know that as the boss (or the guy shelling out the money), I should expect an exchange of service. But after organizing enough work parties I'm not so keen on this dynamic. What I want to cultivate is something similar to what the Amish have during their barn raisings or akin to a community theatrical performance: I want helpers *wanting* to play their part. My job, if my role is in any way exceptional, is to promote this; I'm less the director and more the producer. I need to do all the prep work (starting a day ahead of time) so that the community chemistry can then cultivate itself.

I need a minimum of five helpers to make a go of bottling day. Seven would be even better. I need one bottle filler, two corkers, and two wire cagers to complete a 265-gallon tank (my maximum size), but if I'm lucky enough to get seven people that day, I'll have a third corker to speed things along and I become like a bar backer to the whole operation. I bounce around supplying corks, boxes, and bottles to everyone, then stacking full cases on the pallet and taking them away.

It's essentially factory work: Everyone is assigned a simple task and we just buckle down and knock it out. We start at 8:30 AM, after I've had a couple of hours to pump up the cider and sanitize the equipment, and we go until about 4 PM (although I spend an additional two hours cleaning up).

The cider starts in the large mixing tank on the second floor of the barn and flows via gravity down a hose to the bottle filler. The filler is a stainless steel machine that resembles Rome's Capitoline She-Wolf with four legs and six spouts to affix the empty glass bottles. It sits on the counter so that the filler-person does not have to bend over. We call it the cow, for obvious reasons. It takes 12 seconds to fill each bottle. Six spouts, each filling at staggered intervals, means the bottler filler is constantly draining and the person operating it must be moving fast.

Once the bottles are filled, he or she hands them over to the corker people, who, one by one, insert the bottles into the lower half of the corker machine. We use what is known as a floor-corker, which is a simple, manual contraption available for $150. The corker person puts a cork into the jaws of the machine, steps on the base for stabilization, and pulls down on the upper lever using all their might to compress the internal jaws around the cork. Simultaneously, the upper lever plunges the cork halfway into the neck of the bottle, and when the person releases the lever, it snaps back, releasing the now-corked bottle, which is handed over to the next person, the wire cager.

The wire-cage machine is a plastic beer capper that I rigged with a rubber hood so it doesn't crush the champagne wire cage when the lever pressure is brought down on it. This, too, requires a bit of strength. With one hand the person pulls down on the lever and with the other hand they tighten the wire cage. First, the thin wire hood must be placed over the cork so that when the lever pressure is achieved they can use the hand tool to manually twist the wire flange, creating a tight fit around the neck of the bottle. This keeps the cork from popping off when carbonation later builds in the bottle. (Also, the pressure of the cork trying to press out of the bottle helps form the mushroom shape commonly associated with champagne corks.)

The bottles are now fully assembled except for the labeling, which can be done on a rainy day sometime before the summer, and they are inserted into the empty cases on a pallet near the double doors. When the pallet reaches four layers high (40 full cases), it represents the maximum weight my tractor forks can lift. I drive around to the open double doors and lift the pallet, bringing it to the insulated storage shed (the one Al the carpenter built).

So now you know how our bottling operation works. Memorize this in case you show up to help one day. A simple diagram could have just as easily explained it.

There were six small-engine machine shops in the Wurtsboro area when we moved here. In the twelve years since, five of those six have gone out of business. The reason is simple: It's just as cheap to buy a new mower or chain saw at the Home Depot as it is to make a simple repair. Score another one for the economy of scale. The only repair shop left is owned by Rich, who isn't bending over backward to find new customers, either. He's mostly retired and his garage serves the dual purpose of being the local men's hangout. If people would rather drive out to the box store, at least his shop is still integral to the community.

I stumble in on five men drinking beer. They've formed a standing circle around the room's only heat source, a home-welded cast-iron stove. A thick layer of cigarette smoke hovers between my shoulders and the low acoustical-tile ceiling. The conversation pauses mid-sentence as the orator freezes his jaw in the open position and shifts his eyes toward me without moving his head, then resumes his monologue—something about the "take-down strength" of various hunting rifles. I wait for him to finish, or I hope someone from the klatch will break away and tell me where Rich is, but this is like a Parisian restaurant: I am to acclimate to

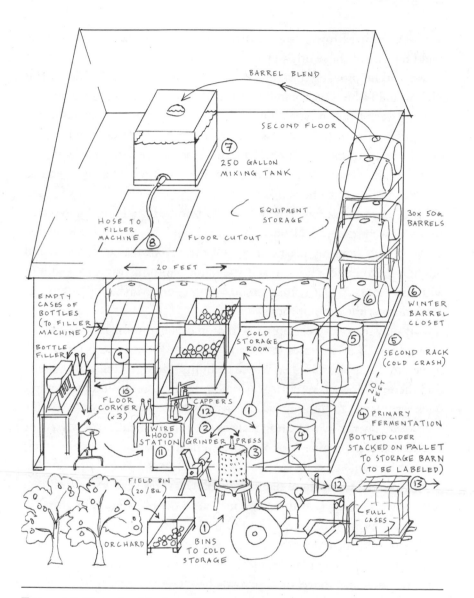

Figure 4.1. How the cider barn functions.

this environment, not the other way around. I pray I don't say something stupid in my nervousness, like, *Winchester rifles, are they from England?*

Then I spot Rich through the back window, tinkering with a snowblower. I smile at the indifferent group as I slide by and make my way out the rear door.

"Hey, Farmer Brown, how are the trees doing this year?" Rich asks. He could top any of those other guys for the part of the hillbilly in a horror movie, and he probably has more guns than all of them combined. But Rich would rather talk about gardening. It used to be that growing and hunting went hand in hand, but fewer men these days garden, adhering to Modern gender stereotypes, so my occasional visit is a chance for Rich to talk about his green thumb. And he's especially excited to do so this time of year: It's early May, and he's buzzing about what he's going to do different in the raised beds this year.

The forecast calls for 31°F on Friday night, and I tell him I'm worried about blossom damage. "I hope not," Rich says, "I already transplanted my seed starts, and my plastic cover got torn up by the wind last year. I might have to build a bonfire and spend all night misting the seedlings with the hose. Actually, that sounds kinda fun. Maybe I'll catch the groundhog while I'm out there!"

My only reason for coming was to drop off chains for sharpening, but I found myself 30 minutes into a conversation about flowers. Then talk turned to the apple trees near where he hunts. He won't tell me where to find them, he doesn't want me scaring off his deer, but he likes that apple trees serve for both hunting and gathering.

Eventually the conversation feels as though it's winding down. As he ratchets on some engine-mount bolts, a reflective tone consumes the rest of what he wants to say.

"I've seen a lot of these damn snowblowers this year. I guess all that soft snow was rough on them. I don't care how old I get, I'm going to stick with my shovel. I have good memories with a shovel."

He paused for a deep breath, or what could have been a sigh, and then continued, "I remember during big snows the whole town used to form brigades and shovel out the roads first, then the driveways, starting with the old folks' homes. You never know if they are going to need some emergency attention. We got out of school on a snow day, just like kids today, but instead of meeting your friends to sled or play video games we'd meet and make ourselves useful. It was just as fun."

Was this one of those in-my-day Andy Rooney speeches? I worried.

"I used to run groceries for my neighbors and check to make sure they had power after a storm. Folks looked out for one another. And they still do around here," he went on, pausing for a few seconds between each sentence . . .

"I don't think city people understand this. I guess it's because they have more money than we do; they're used to paying for services like plowing and deliveries, or even the fire rescue. After a while that's just how things work: You have money, and you pay your taxes, and you expect something in return. That money substitutes for the negotiation, or it relieves you of physically pitching in, and after a while no one equates services with being part of a community. I'd sure hate to see that change now that the suburbs are coming."

Knowing I was new to the area, I wondered if that was a shot intended for me, like an invitation into a secret society.

Conditioning and Acclimation

Polly and I don't put sulfites in our wines or ciders, so they end up developing a layer of yeast sediment that, when the bottle is flipped, resembles Sea-Monkeys in a snow globe. Over the past half century, wine customers have increasingly been sheltered from this sight as sterile filtration and additions of sulfite have become the industry standard. At a high-enough dosage, sulfur kills the existing life and ensures that nothing can come back and colonize the finished product. This is important for shelf stability in today's marketplace given the likelihood of gross neglect in the retail environment or in the customer's care. Wine, regardless of its sterility, should never be exposed to excessive movement, shaking, daily temperature changes, light, or loud noises. (And yet I've even seen $2,000 Bordeauxs displayed in the bright window of a wine store on Park Avenue!)

It's not just for the cosmetic clarity that sulfites are added to wine; they also protect against the influence from microorganisms. Today, those "alive" notes, even the ones that are tasty, are classified as flaws. The chemical addition of sulfur dioxide (SO_2) kills these life-forms in the liquid, but it also creates a poisonous gas that hovers in the air of the sealed bottle. It's probably unwise to quickly sniff the neck of most bottles after they've just been uncorked without first allowing this gas to dissipate. Although "research shows" that low-enough sulfur additions don't harm human health, Polly and I doubt this. To us, it sounds like the guarantees the oil companies gave that their offshore drilling wouldn't leak.

I've learned that naturally produced CO_2, by way of bottle conditioning, can also add a similar layer of protection inside the bottle. When unkilled cider enters the bottle with a tiny amount of residual sweetness (I use a SüssReserve to bring the specific gravity to 1.002 to 1.004, for all you wine geeks) and then it is capped or corked, the yeast will eat those sugars and go dry; a trace carbonation is produced. And since CO_2 is heavier than air, it will hover over the liquid surface and protect it against airborne microbial influences just like SO_2 does.

I feel better about this because I, too, worry about airborne bad guys, particularly acetobacter, the microorganism that turns wine into vinegar. But really, I just enjoy the properties of CO_2 in the cider. I like the tiny bubbles. Bubbles add an early high note in the mouth as floral esters are prolonged on the hard palate. Sooner or later the symphony of flavors will march things down the tongue (assuming, of course, the properties of the cider are there for this to happen) but not without a moment of pause, like stopping to smell the roses. This means carbonation in wine was originally meant as an artistic tool. The perfect analogy is the sustaining floor pedal on a piano, the way it prolongs the chord. In the right hands and with the right mix of apples, carbonation can be a powerful tool for building compositions. But it can create an undesirable staggering effect, too, if instead the cider calls for a velvet-like slide front to finish.

By the way, carbonation can be achieved naturally or artificially. Today most producers simply force-carbonate with canned CO_2—as with a SodaStream—but this produces a different effect than natural carbonation, which is what champagne is famous for. And speaking of champagne, another lesser-known fact is that bottle-conditioned cider predated carbonated wines by many decades. Cider had been bottled this way in the glass-producing regions of England since the 1600s, long before Champagne producers followed suit.

All the stages of bottling take place in close proximity to one another; it is only natural that it's a very social activity. I like observing the buzz, particularly how the energy rises and fades at various points in the day. Sometimes there are even prolonged stretches without conversation while the rhythm of the machines takes over and becomes like a marching beat: the empty glass bottles clanking against the stainless steel shelf of the filler machine; the metallic creak of the floor-corker spring as the lever is tugged down and then cracks back into place; and always a *squink-squink-squink* emanating from the spinning wire-hood hand tool.

I had the benefit of learning how this all works two years before it was my turn to "run the show," to be the boss. My first experience bottling was as a volunteer at the Paul's winery, just a mile east of me on the opposite slope of the Mamakating Hollow. I showed up for work thinking it was going to be a slog when instead I found myself in the middle of a party. The whole town was there, music was playing, people brought food, kids were running around, dogs were eating out of the garbage—it was like walking into a tent at Oktoberfest. I had to fight to get in on the bottling line, which flew at a caffeinated pace because of the party energy. The moment anyone got tired at one of the stations they were tapped on the shoulder and someone was there to jump in and take their place.

Paul, who is my age, started the small winery right as the world stock markets were crashing: Watching the Great Recession roll in was like watching a fog approach from across the water. Investing in a new business weighed more heavily on an entrepreneur because customers didn't feel confident parting with money. But Paul was cash-strapped even before the hard times. Nonetheless, he still managed to survive and even thrive in the economic environment, and it took me a long time to see how this happened. Paul's success says a lot about him, but it says just as much about the people of the Mamakating Hollow.

Just as Rich, the small-engine repairman, had predicted, the people around here descended on Paul to support him in any way possible. They brought food for when he was open, they helped him clean up, and they volunteered to help with big chores, like harvest or bottling. No one had much money to spend and Paul wasn't able to spend on labor, either, but this type of economy in Wurtsboro was thriving as the world financial economy was reeling. We had our own secret bull market, a gleeful rebuke to paper money.

The work parties were an opportunity to build sweat equity in the community. You could argue, as a politician would, that spending public money on a private enterprise benefits the whole of the community with jobs. Or it could help prop up neighboring real estate, as would spending on a golf course or winery. But that's not what I saw happening at Paul's, and frankly, it seems jaded to think humanity requires this oversight. What I saw when I joined the work party was a community-wide reassurance that we were all there for one another. I remind you, these were scary times for everyone, but in the Mamakating Hollow no one's struggles are invisible. The teamwork is done in service to a secret economy, one that only strengthens as financial economies weaken.

Drinking Cider

Traditionally, when a cider emerged from winter (and the penultimate vintage has just about run out), farmers would go down to the cellar and tap a new barrel from the previous vintage. This is what's known as young cider, only five or six months old. They would stand the barrel on end and use a conical auger to drill a hole in the flat side, then pound in a matching tapered spigot before returning the barrel to its side. The tight, freshly sawn wood would swell from the cider's moisture, further sealing the pounded-in connection; the only leak thereafter would come from the tap end when farmers stuck their heads under and twisted the handle. This, of course, would happen a lot.

That's simple Barrel Drinking 101, and that's what our country was founded on. A careful re-reading of American history and you'll see I'm not exaggerating much. But other cultures still make a big ado of this ritual. In the regions stretching along the mountainous north coast of Spain, between Portugal and France, there evolved the world's greatest cider tradition involving the cider's spring awakening. In Asturias they celebrate the cider with elaborate dinners below the casks (literally). The people hold out their glasses or large decanters as the barrels are tapped and cider streams down from the mezzanine, creating a hefty splash. Presumably this "long pour" opens up the cider much the way natural carbonation does, but certainly the fall creates bubbles capable of blowing off funky gases that overwintering has been known to trap. (The splashing might also soften the volatile acidity or sour notes that these cider regions are known for.)

It's by no coincidence that some of the best restaurants in the world are located along the north coast of Spain. Cider and food evolved hand in hand in view of the Bay of Biscay because nothing (and I mean *nothing*) goes better with seafood or the region's famous cheeses than tart-tannic ciders. Apples are rich in malic acid, which can be described as *bright* or *tart*. Tart foods, like tart cherries, make your mouth secrete saliva—the mouth's natural response to the threat of acids. This dilutes the acids and protects the enamel of your teeth. When a drink of this nature is paired with the taffy-mouth feeling of rich, buttery foods (like cheese or oily, fatty fish), it is as if the clouds have opened up and the heavens are shining through. Someday, when the rest of the world finds out about these food pairings, cider will deservedly replace fine wine in many regions, particularly those that aren't conducive to wine-grape growing in the first place.

Polly and I discovered this on a tiny island 40 minutes off the coast of Maine. In 2012 we went to Isle au Haut to forage wild apples because the ocean temperatures kept the crop-ending freeze from settling on the coastal blossoms (elsewhere that year all the inland orchards were zapped with three consecutive 22°F nights during blossom). On a Thursday in late September, we packed up our grinder and press and decided to make a long weekend of it. On Friday morning the boat dropped us off at the town dock, and before we even made it off the planks the closest tree, an apple tree, was rolling fruit at our feet.

After two days collecting, and one day grinding and pressing, we stashed 50 gallons of cider in an abandoned outhouse and returned to our lives in New York. Only after the fall chores settled down did we make it back to Maine on the long Thanksgiving weekend. We bottled our outhouse cider and brought it back home with us, where it aged in our cool cellar.

The following year we returned to the scene of the crime, on a glorious Maine summer evening, to try the cider with lobster (from the shores of Isle au Haut, of course). We served it with steamed beach peas, a buttery chanterelle sauce, and topped with blueberries, all of which were foraged on-island earlier that day. Maybe I'm biased, maybe it's because we had invested so much of ourselves in the drink and dinner, but I'm telling you this was a holy matrimony. And if it's because of bias that this food pairing was the best ever, then who cares?—I would rather the earth be swallowed by the sun than be deprived of the story behind food.

Wine is fantastic with the cuisines it evolved with. French, Italian, Lebanese—with them, give me the fermented grape any day. But if there is such a thing as traditional American food, guess what's missing from the equation? The picture of "the Thanksgiving dinner" may not be completely authentic to what the Pilgrims ate, but if you are celebrating a local agrarian harvest meal in the northern two-thirds of the United States (eating squash, oysters, wild turkey, and corn), and you decide to pair these dishes with wine or beer?—then I say skip the apple pie and have some chocolate tiramisu for dessert because you don't get it. The overlooking of cider must surely be America's greatest culinary blunder during the past century (and that was the century Cheez Whiz was invented!). Even today, many of the great northern restaurants and staff sommeliers are pushing wine when one of the world's best apple regions reigns right outside their windows.

We can blame the apple industry for not supplying cider-worthy fruit, but it's a bogus excuse focused on the effect, not the cause. Our larger culture just fell asleep and let globalized food take over our food traditions. If we were not lazy, if we were not gullible, then it never would have happened. Learning the true story behind what we eat and the connection we make to the land is nobody else's responsibility but our own.

Summer

It's after 9 PM and there's still enough light in the sky that the ducks don't want to go in. I have to herd them up the ramp and close the door to their duck-house behind Miss Wobbles, always the last one. And now my workday is officially ended, 17 hours from when it started. I raid my personal stash and walk the orchard with a cider bottle, taking inventory of this season's progress. I have one season in my hand and another in my sight.

It's a magical time. Fireflies dance along the edge of the meadow as the forest darkens beyond. Everything just feels alive: In my eyes, on my skin, in my mouth and my lungs. From the woods comes the haunting flute of the hermit thrush, its distant sounds echoing among the trees, giving the forest depth. I feel as if the wilderness goes on forever.

This is one of those moments that reassures me that cider is timeless. No matter what agricultural horrors lie behind modern cider, no matter how new and innovative the marketing of that type of cider is, I know that real farm cider predates all modernity and will live on unchanged for another millennium. I'm honored to be making a drink in this tradition. I am just a little blip in time—this current moment—and somehow that fulfills me.

The year in cider does not end when everything is bottled, labeled, and conditioned. Yes, I can take a break from cider making and orchard work during July and August, but that doesn't mean it's a downtime in the life of cider. The summer is just as important to the whole cider process as any other season; in fact, it's arguably the most important, because it's market season. This is the time of year I must devote to bridging my existence with the lives of my fellow citizens.

In rural areas we see an increased number of second-homers and tourists. Thankfully, they want to engage with the local farmers. They, too, recognize the season as important, and they escape their daily routines to venture into the unfamiliar, meet new people. I sell most of my cider in farmers markets because we don't have a tasting room (as an introvert it's important for me to keep my home off-limits to visitors), but connecting to the people in my county is all-important for my model of business. For one thing, I seek unknown apple trees and permission to collect from people's land, but just as often I find that people are excited by cider and they end up seeking me instead. At the farmers markets we exchange contact info, maps, and setup dates for the fall. They sometimes even help pick the apples, which I think makes those apple trees feel that the property owner is invested in them.

The bridges among people, their land, the fruit, and the miller—this interconnected topic is so hugely part of cider that I won't do it the disservice of condensing it into this chapter. Instead I will devote the third section of this book to this significance of cider culture. I will just say for now we are the third species of the cider trinity, equal to the apple and the yeast, and we have a responsibility to participate if we want to drink whole cider.

FIVE

Cider Apples

*H*ow could I not? I like this tree so much, a tree the property owner calls Denniston Red, that I'm willing to drive 25 minutes, park the truck by the side of the road, and trek another 25 minutes through knee-high snow with secateurs and a 12-foot tripod ladder in hand, so that when I finally arrive at my destination I'm sweating through my long underwear on a 19°F day. My legs have started shaking from the muscle strain, and before even setting up the ladder I'm worried that I might not have the energy to make it back when this is done. My goal is to collect graft wood for another cider maker in California and to visit Denniston Red, a favorite tree of mine, to see how she's holding up this long, cold winter. If an emotional bond can exist between a human and a tree, honestly, how could I not visit?

Although I would classify her as a wild tree, she may have been part of the Dennistons' home orchard when they pioneered this farmstead near the strategically important shallows of the Neversink River. Known as Denniston Ford, this was where horses and wagons crossed before New York's first covered bridge was built downstream in 1807 (at the town not-so-imaginatively called Bridgeville). The ford was the original gateway west from Ulster County—soon to be Sullivan County, which divided off from Ulster two years later in 1809—hence many westbound settlers made their way through this area. Whether or not the famed Johnny Appleseed was one of those crossing here during his 1792 migration from western Massachusetts to western Pennsylvania, or whether he passed by my farm along the Old Mine Road (now Route 209), is unknown, but either way he must have sprung a hole in his bag when crossing the lower Catskills.

John is also the name of the current-day owner of the Denniston Farm. He's no less eccentric and excited by the discovery of apple trees on his property. There are close to 50 large old specimens scattered on his land, but we've recently found 14 grouped suspiciously on the far side of the field. I say suspicious because as John and I have started to clear around these trees, we've noticed a pattern to them: They seem to form two rows and are all spaced approximately 50 feet apart. This suggests that it was once a cultivated orchard. And Denniston Red, the tree of my cider dreams, is among them.

My home orchard has been through many theme changes when it comes to apple varieties. It started as a New York heirloom variety orchard, but then I switched focus and started planting European cider varieties. Then I switched focus again and one by one began grafting all those named varieties over with scionwood that I've collected from mysterious old trees around my county. My orchard has become like a zoo of specimens that I've collected from the wild, not necessarily for cider reasons but also for the preservation of ancient trees that may have local cultural significance.

Another John, North America's preeminent apple explorer, John Bunker, planted this bug in my head, and he's encouraged me to ask landowners questions about human history and the possible origins of these trees. He's taught me clues to look for when identifying wild trees versus once-cultivated, planted, and grafted trees (see John Bunker's illustration, figure 1.1 on page 37). Although my sympathies are more for the wild ones, and introversion rules my way in this world, John's outreach to the community as an agricultural history detective has proven to be so enchanting to Polly and me that it's inspired us to bring scionwood from several hundred mysterious locals into our home orchard. And anyway, I'm glad to have started clone wood from so many of them, because many of the parent trees, especially the ancient ones, have since died.

When a tree becomes of reproductive age, its energy shifts from vegetative growth toward reproductive growth: the setting up of fruitwood (including fruit spurs and, eventually, flowers and fruit). Farmers obviously have an incentive to see the trees turn sexually active sooner rather than later, but interestingly, farmers also spend massive amounts of energy in calming or rationing a tree's urge to fruit. A farmer wants annual consistency while the tree itself wants the opposite.

This is very apparent in the wild when native fruit and nut trees get on forest-wide cycles known as mast years. You might notice, for instance, that acorns and pinecones often produce in abundance one year and hardly drop anything for the deer or squirrels in other years. Nature requires this unpredictability; it keeps the animals guessing (or struggling), and without unpredictability the system is unhealthy. This might seem counterintuitive to us, that struggle is actually a healthy thing, but we have examples of self-automated irregularity within our own culture, too, and it defies our reason. Tons of fluctuating dichotomies can be cited for their creation of balance: honoring both extroversion and introspect, "appetite" versus "withholding," or—most notably—progressive versus conservative politics. Just when we think one way is better than the other, some cosmic order steps in and finds a natural balance that we couldn't predict on our own.

Apples are deeply in touch with their connection to forest mast cycles, and this is a major bane to farmers who are dominated by market pressures and financial quotas. These worlds collide. So farmers have devised effective ways of seducing regular fruit production by virtue of controlling the trees' urge to fruit overabundantly during on-years. When farmers thin the fruit, they're asking the trees to withhold themselves and put some of that year's energy into setting up fruit buds for the following year (a year in which the tree would naturally bear little to no fruit). Some varieties are more cooperative than others, and it's no coincidence that the commonly known varieties are the ones most easily controlled, while forgotten heirlooms that tend to go biennial have fallen out of favor. Again, it's all about consistency.

Obviously market pressures mandate that farmers cultivate regularity into the trees: Customers have lost their patience and understanding for years-at-a-time cycles in nature (and in fact, annual seasonality is invisible to us in the modern marketplace). But there is another reason for cultivating regularity: Once a tree has decided to concentrate on growing fruiting wood (branches heavy with fruit spurs), it develops older wood that can become a safe haven or home base for disease colonies. In contrast, a younger tree given only to vegetative growth is constantly changing shape, and the farmer's saw can easily influence the way the tree forms. In much the same way that a balance between conservative and progressive actions is needed in a healthy culture, so, too, a farmer wants to cultivate a balance in the tree between reproductive and vegetative growth. New shoots will form the basis for future fruitwood, thus allowing the farmer to take out the older wood, which also helps thwart the tendency toward biennial fruit bearing. On a visual level this balance is instantly noticeable. It lies at the root of why wild trees look the way they do versus cultivated trees: A good mix of vigorous growth and well-spaced fruit makes farmed trees look "healthy," while wild trees look hardened and defensive. But like I said earlier, struggle may counter intuitively be more healthy.

I tell you all this because as I'm repeatedly grafting my orchard over and over, I'm essentially setting my trees back to a young age with new shoot-wood. Trees that could have been producing New York heirlooms or European cider-variety apples six or seven years ago are now devoted to growing mysterious-origin apple trees instead; and in turn, I'm constantly sabotaging my hopes for any home fruit production. My orchard is essentially an orphanage of vegetative wood with little age balance, but it serves to counteract the imbalance of the same variety in the wild. Only when property owners give me permission to prune the original tree on-site do I get the chance to restore some of that balance, subsequently giving me the chance to see that apple produced as if under the "ideal" conditions of a conventional orchard. But frankly, I'm no longer sure my concept (or anyone's concept) of a healthier-looking tree is best for the tree. And besides, for cider I prefer the mangled apples from older wood.

Only about 4 percent of the apples I use in my Homestead line of ciders come from my orchard; the rest come from trees like the ones adjacent to the old Denniston Ford. Denniston Red is only 1 of 14 trees in this newly discovered "orchard," and there are about 30 other wild trees on this one property alone. I don't know what percentage of them were grafted, but the overwhelming majority are straight seedlings trees allowed to grow in unusual ways (only a few seem trained). Up in the Neversink Highlands, before the river crashes 1,000 feet in elevation through the gorge, there are thousands of similarly uncultivated trees. I try not to favor any one of them, but as a cider maker it was hard not to get attached to Red. I know that no one variety represents the best characteristics of a cider apple, but if I were to pick one that best sums up *my* type of cider I would pick this one: Denniston Red.

Good Cider Apples

Sometime around 2014 we rounded the corner as a nation and we don't have to call it hard cider anymore, but now my frustration is given to another cause: the new definition of the ancient term *cider apple*. To me and to most cultures around the world—as well as to apple growers during the first 350 years of our Western history in America—a cider apple is just an apple that makes something known as good cider. I can't define this—you know it when you see it—but one reads these words *good cider* over and over again in every apple text dating back centuries.

There are no specifications as to which varieties to use and what the correct growing practices are, but anyone who's discovered which apples make good cider will have firm opinions about what is and what isn't a cider apple. It's how the apples got that way, and how the right apples for good cider are grown, that have always been the hottest topics in the field of cider making.

You'd think we would have given up by now and just say *It all depends*, but that's not the nature of farmers, cider makers, the market, and especially academics. We want to discover that universal conclusion. Diversity is still the rule in nature, however, and if Western farmers were not self-limiting, contained landowners, if they cultivated trees in many different locations like the Native Americans did, it's likely we'd abandon the quest for the decisive answer. Determined nonetheless, these days we're looking to cider varieties to provide the conclusions we seem to need.

To be clear though, a cider variety is *not* the same as a cider apple (the mix-up is at the core of my frustrations). Cider apples have been around for hundreds and hundreds of years, while the grafting of whole orchards is a relatively brand-spanking-new preference in the overall history of cider making. And even newer still is the cider industry's preference for "bitter-sweet" apples (starting around 1900). While we still haven't addressed how to specifically grow them for cider, either. Technically a cider variety, like a Harrison or Dabinett, is *not* a cider apple unless it's grown uniquely as one. In fact they could be good eating apples if grown conventionally on eating-apple farms. The opposite can be said of eating apple varieties if they are grown as cider fruit: I personally know of culinary varieties on certain trees (especially old, uncultivated trees) that make a superior drink compared with cider varieties that I've tested from conventional orchards. The key to *good* cider, in my opinion, is *how* it's grown.

But let's not get ahead of ourselves—is it nature or is it nurture?—when over 99 percent of the world's commercial orchards still staunchly promote a third, thoroughly unhelpful definition of *cider apple*, given as a grade of conventional fruit. This now makes three camps of theory, each of which promotes a different definition of *cider apple*, and they don't see eye to eye given that there are other interests involved beyond taste. Two of those camps are dominated by either commercial growers or commercial cider makers, while the third is largely made up of home cider makers and rural growers considered outsiders to modern agriculture. Of the two commercial definitions of *cider apple*, one is supported mainly by cider makers and academia, while the other is supported mainly by conventional apple growers supplying nearly 100 percent of the commodity fruit.

Definition 1: A cider apple is any apple that ends up in cider.
Supporting this definition (the unhelpful definition) are the existing commercial apple growers. Each year their orchards produce billions upon billions of culinary apples, and often they can't sell the majority of what their trees produce, thanks to hail damage, discoloration, a glut in the market, or what have you. Of course they want to sell the apples, duh, even if just for pennies on the dollar. But the term *cider apples* would seem a misnomer if it weren't for the fact that most commercial cider makers—particularly the producers who leverage the advantage of scale—conspire in this definition by using these apples almost exclusively (although few openly admit this in their marketing).

Adding further weight to this definition is the influence those commercial apple growers exert over misinformed government lackeys. In *The New Cider Maker's Handbook*, Claude Jolicoeur tells the story of Canadian legislation essentially ensuring that only leftover commodity apples can be used in cider making. Maybe on a certain level we can understand the good intentions behind this rule: The socially conscious society was simply trying to use its existing resources efficiently, not see them go to waste. But to place limits on creativity and place their blind faith in *what's advantageous for certain growers is best for everyone* is shocking! (A similar abuse of good intentions happened in Nova Scotia's Annapolis Valley when commercial growers convinced the Canadian government to sanction the roundup and removal of "unkempt" homeowner apple trees. They believed, and probably accurately, that the uncultivated trees were harboring diseases capable of spreading to farms, but the decision to concentrate trees to commercial orchards only further exacerbates the problem of tree immune response!)

Actually, the United States has a policy that seems to suggest that leftover culinary apples are synonymous with cider apples, too. The USDA divides the fruit by grades: Extra Fancy, Fancy, No. 1, and Utility—a grading system that was created to set standards for apples in the marketplace. Obviously the Extra Fancy apples get carried off in a gold chariot, but guess where the Utility apples end up? Cider apples, by this definition, are the same apples as the ones in the grocery store: They are the same varieties, they are grown on the same farms, and they are grown in the same way. So even though farmers explicitly worked their asses off *not* to grow Utility apples, in the end the inspector stepped in and deemed them to be cider apples. Both in Canada and in the United States, 99 percent of all "cider apples" are apples of last resort.

Definition 2: A cider apple is one specifically grown for cider and possesses genetically advantageous cider properties (a cider variety)

I like this definition, but by now you can guess my protest. Who but someone with something to gain gets to christen certain varieties as cider apples? If an apple makes good cider on your land but makes shitty cider on my land, what does that get me when the market begins to favor particular varieties? It gets me strategically boxed out is what it gets me. I'm not only opposed to this definition for reasons of sharkishness, but also morally opposed to this definition because the apple tree itself is opposed to it. The last thing I or the *Malus* genus wants is to see another market pinched to a few specimens like the culinary apple market has been.

Nonetheless, I'll admit there are some great varieties for cider out there. On my land, for instance, Porter's Perfection, an apple grown in England, creates the properties that I like in cider: It's tart, it's little, it ripens mid- to late season (having higher sugars), and it's exceptionally tannic. I have this apple growing on five trees in five different locations and it's more or less a good cider apple on each (with some quality variations because of its high fungal susceptibility). I would hate to see cider follow New World wine into the varietal obsession (a scheme to favor mass-scale growers), but I should think an apple like Porter's Perfection could serve those interested in sophisticated cider while still being amenable to macro-market pressures and the rules of efficiency. Even so, it's unwise to pin cider down to select or limited diversity. In fact, most cider varieties were originally selected as complements for their properties (usually bitterness) and are rarely appreciated as stand-alone varieties. In other words, cider varieties were initially conceived as blend components rather than for single-variety ciders.

It is thought that every apple can be classified as one of four types arranged like a Four-Square court pattern: above are two squares, the sweets and the sharps, and below are the bittersweets and bittersharps. It's also thought that good cider is made from a balance of the four components (with personal variations the result of a bias toward one of the four directions). When the cider varieties began to emerge, they were selected for their lean toward the bitter range, because by the 1800s sweet eating apples and sharp cooking apples were being mass-grafted on increasingly big farms. But just like today those apples had their gluts, and the excesses of sweet and sharp apples overwhelmed stocks of bitter fruit grown in smaller, diverse cider orchards. So to complete the Four-Square balance at the mass scale, cider varieties emerged for their monopolies of tannin. They are cider apples in the sense that they are grown specifically for cider, but they are *good* cider apples because the tannin gives them depth and character, and can assist in bringing other flavor notes together. Most of all, tannin helps the cider to age, which is *absolutely* crucial for good cider.

Definition 3: A cider apple is any apple that makes good cider

This, of course, is a value judgment, but the same discriminating tastes that are behind Definition 2 apply here, too. The game of Four Square (or, in particular, balancing in tannic apples) is done with these apples, but two key differences arise: (1) It's *not* assumed that genetic variety is why cider apples possess favorable traits, and (2) the apple itself doesn't have to be grafted or farmed; it could be left to its own devices to grow. I obviously like this definition because it includes wild apples, but even though it's more inclusive than Definition 2, it still excludes 99 percent of the apples grown on farms today because they lack the spectrum of traits needed for good cider. I'm not likely to win any friends in the existing farming community with this stance.

It excludes those apples on grounds of a judgment call (that's the nature of the word *good*), but other growers and cider makers are free to exclude me, too. I, however, vehemently disagree that *my* definition of a cider apple is exclusive in the sense that commercial orchards are likely to provide cider makers with the best cider fruit. To the contrary, it's the commercial growers in well-established agricultural areas (the ones that survived the twentieth century) that are exclusive, for not everyone lives near these lands nor are they able to recreate similar growing conditions with their own soils or small lots. Meanwhile with apples, beggars *can* be choosers, and people living on poor soils can also be privy to the best fruit, so it's no wonder cider never disappeared in non-agricultural regions of the United States where wild apples remain. In those parts there was never a need to put a name to those apples (apart from names like *spitters*, *chokers*, or just *wild*), and it was with wise opposition that the people in those cultures rejected the new narrative of cider, particularly as it revolves around European scionwood. Such a definition of *cider apples* not only overlooks their long-established cider culture, but actually seeks to erase it.

What conclusions can we make about growing good cider apples? I hope by now we all agree that there is no universal conclusion. In fact, the answer we're looking for is *exactly* opposite from the universal: Look to every single location and every single variety. Pomophiles have been saying something similar throughout American history when they've claimed (as they always have) that wild apples are superior for cider. Even as large grafted orchards began to dominate in the 1800s, they *all* agreed on this—from John Chapman, to William Coxe, to Andrew Downing, to H. D. Thoreau, to S. A. Beach—all the way up through recent accounts in cider country where mill operators claim wild apples are simply synonymous with cider apples; so needless to say, wild apples ought to serve as the greatest models on how cider apples should be *grown* as well. That means: no one type of soil, no one type of agriculture, no one type of variety; diversity, diversity, diversity—that's your cider apple.

Denniston Red, Part 1

Denniston Red rises from a fallen trunk by a trickle of a stream that carves a steep 3-foot bank along the outer edge of "the orchard," a 5-acre patch of woodlands that looks *nothing* like an orchard. There are 14 ancient apple trees hidden among towering native species, and this patch of woods functions as an island in the flats, which are hayed twice a year. Massive grapevines extend to the tops of the 70-foot cherry and maple trees; from a distance the orchard looks like a circus tent emerging from the open floodplain. The apples were well concealed under this tent until September 2013 when John and I first noticed brightly colored fruit extending from beneath the cloak of dense grape leaves. Mike the hunter knew about these apples all along. He strapped a perch about 16 feet up overlooking the north end of the woods, where he had a clear but well-concealed shot at the deer who came for the fruit each year. While Hendrix played at Woodstock, while Valley girls leaned against Pac-Man machines, through the dot-com bubble, and even after Osama bin Laden was captured and killed—all that time these trees were fruiting without human use.

When we first noticed the apple trees, the ground was your typical shaded forest floor: covered by leaf mulch, decomposing branches, ferns, thorny bushes, and ivy. Draping grapevines and large broken tree branches hung about, making it hard to see through the woods, and they obscured the pattern of apple trees that might have given us an earlier clue that this was indeed an intentional planting site. Four apple trees, including Denniston Red, emerge from fallen trunks, suggesting that a flood or high winds tore through many, many years ago and knocked parts of the orchard over. The soils here are sandy and deep, out of reach of bedrock, so it's feasible that if the ground were soaked from heavy rains or a spring thaw the trees could have lost their anchorage in high wind. And in fact, it may have been this event that triggered the farmer to give up on the orchard. But four of the overturned trees survived this hardship (other trees may not have survived though no trace of them exists today), and judging by the size of their now-righted growth I'm guessing this event took place in the mid-twentieth century.

Reading a tree is like reading a history book. Denniston Red's brush with death 50 or 60 years ago is evident not only from the sideways trunk but in the decisions she's made since then. The sideways trunk is about 24 inches in diameter and rises only slightly from the ground at a 20-degree angle for the length of about 12 feet. The original top half of the tree continued at that angle when it fell over, but a few leaders took over and she invested her energy upward while allowing the old part to die off (we eventually cut this part off to make it easier to get around). There are three strong shoots along the sideways trunk that vie upward for the position of the new leader. Starting where the trunk leaves the ground, there's contestant number one at the 4-foot mark, contestant number two at the 8-foot mark, and the eventual winner around the 12-foot mark. This is now the main trunk, but all three are still alive and all climb about 30 feet. Only the leader climbs higher, and it's obvious that Red is most invested here because 90 percent of the fruit traces from the main leader.

The dominant axis of the new leader reaches to about 45 feet at its peak and has long airy branches that measure as long as 20 feet. Her overall footprint covers a span of more than 50 feet. Her style of growth is similar to that of a Northern Spy, which is famous for branching deliberately upward, making it a hard tree to spread. It's the eventual weight of the fruit that bows the branches outward, and in the case of Red this process is ancient history. By no means is her scaffold crowded, except with grapevines (which we since have severed at ground level). And her fruit spurs are spaced well, too, making for your classic stately tree, even if the angled trunk suggests a troubled past. Her fruit spurs are out of the reach of browsing deer, and neither Bambi nor I can reach the fruit without a ladder or an extension pole. In fact, even with my 12-foot tripod ladder and a 30-foot extension pole (plus my own height with my arm extended), I still can't reach all the apples in fruit years. Only the crows, porcupines, and wind can.

A tree of this size, and age, and character can only be a standard tree. I wonder if the farmer laying out this orchard could have envisioned this outcome. They used to say, "Plant a pear for your heir," a dictum from a time when fruit trees were grown from seed rather than from quick fruiting clonal rootstocks. Given that it's been 50-plus years since these trees were abandoned, and given that they are prime for cider today, I wonder if the farmer wasn't also planting this orchard for future generations? I'm sure the trees served the farmer in his or her lifetime, but I'll also bet you they considered that their touch would be felt for decades, possibly centuries, to come. I think their larger culture was more conscious of an era-spanning form of agriculture, and although there is no way to empirically tie that thought to the physical properties of the apple, I believe their consideration is partly why this is the perfect cider orchard today.

Our modern alternative, the dwarfing tree, speaks volumes of our present culture, particularly the consumer culture that favors disposable products. Dwarfing trees might produce higher yields in a shorter time than standard trees, but they're dependent on constant human intervention as well as famously short-lived—about 20 years. We have taken a species capable of living for centuries and surviving independently for generations, and reduced it to a crop that's rotated almost like an annual, like a vegetable garden. The message this sends is vicious, not just to the tree, but to ourselves. Do we not have children? Rather than make a commitment to the tree or to the land, we've been creating fruit gardens to serve our most immediate needs only. And frankly, I'd rather not eat from this culture of agriculture, just like I would rather not accept blood money if I don't have to. I'd rather not eat the "fruit of the poisoned tree," to use a legal metaphor.

But please don't take that to be an attack on farmers. I'm specifically trying to engage you, the reader, because nearly everyone alive participates in this larger culture. It's much too easy to say we're divorced from agriculture (which we are); there's also a direct relationship that we still have from afar. Modern agriculture is basically a consumer mandate. We have constructed a reality filled with plastic water bottles, cheap clothing, disposable cars, and shoddy home construction materials; our foods (even gourmet foods) are basted in this same marinade. We don't build things to stand the test of time, and we have created a sort of purgatory for ourselves: Do we commit to something or not commit knowing that in 20 years' time whatever we do today will be deemed too unfashionable, too small, or too inefficient to serve the future economy? Dwarfing apple trees might be ideal for tiny urban spaces, but as a culture of agriculture, in my mind we're investing heavily in plastic water bottles. But that's us—almost no one plants pears for their heirs anymore.

Bridezilla

Small apple growers and cider makers have been saying for many years now that to develop a sustainable cider industry, we need to focus on growing cider apples. Nothing lasting could come of cider's resurgence unless the horse was in front of the cart, prompting a number of small cider farmers to join or form activist groups to champion a "new old" form of agriculture. Its mission: Grow cider apples to grow a cider industry. I joined this cause, too, in the earlier stages of my career and was a witness to the formation of several trade associations that have since grown in power. Now they have lobbying muscle. But when I was a member, they weren't official trade associations yet; it was more of a think-tank group trying to prioritize the steps to take. We agreed on most points but particularly that if cider was to have good standing in our larger society, we needed good cider, thus good cider apples. Unanimously, we agreed that America needed a new form of apple agriculture.

To review some key points about cider apples that distinguish them from the familiar grocery-store fruit:

- The apple is never seen so the appearance of the fruit doesn't matter.
- The large size, juiciness, and the nitrogenous content commonly associated with conventionally farmed apples are bad for cider.
- Residual chemicals and fungicides in the fruit are bad for fermentation, thus bad for cider.
- The limited number of commercial apple varieties is bad for cider.
- Early and midseason apples are generally bad for cider.
- Apples with thick skins (such as from scab or russeting) are good in cider, whereas apples with a tiny overall fraction of skin (large apples with paper-thin skin) tend not to be good for cider.
- The exclusion of tannin and bright acidity is bad for cider.
- And last but definitely not least, the consolidation of apple trees to a few farms capable of dominating the market price (and away from the people and away from the forests) is bad, bad, bad for cider.

This last point unfolds into a huge topic, but getting apples out from conventional farms and assimilating them into unconventional environments (be it communities, multiuse lands, new or old diversified farmsteads, and so on, and so forth) was *not* the mission of me alone in the early stages of the trade associations. In fact, the majority of the small producers wholeheartedly endorsed these priorities; I merely raised my hand and said, *Yes, I agree.* A stated list of related goals emerged and included: growing apples more healthfully, shifting production to new farms, and educating customers about the huge distinctions between cider and culinary fruit (as a crop, but also as a farming practice). These goals sounded ambitious, but it was based on a simple premise: Just let cider apples lead the way.

Then around 2012 or 2013 cider as an industry left the runway, and for four years it did nothing but climb exponentially. As sales skyrocketed the number of new producers expanded tenfold and then tenfold again. With scores of new association members, the focus on cider apples quickly got lost in the commotion. Something exciting was happening for trade advocates, and attention was now devoted toward sustaining and expanding market growth. Whatever petty issues individual members or subgroups had prior to the explosion were repressed, as we were encouraged to promote "all cider." Increasing sales, it was now expressly stated, was the common goal of the trade association, because it was assumed that money would cure those other ills. The rising tide lifts all boats.

It's a great argument for other industries, but dogging cider's growth is the fact that it's based on a scarce commodity. What was going to fuel all this growth? You can't just hashtag cider apples into existence, you have to actually grow them, and it would take decades before cider apples were available. So how did the cart get ahead the horse? How did cider suddenly find huge quantities of apples in such a short time? The answer, of course, is by not growing cider apples at all, but by using the culinary fruit already described as Utility Grade.

By 2016 it was a done deal. It took only four years for trade association priorities to shift 180 degrees, and many grower/producers were tearing their hair out protesting it. Most decided to return to the hills and just do what they always did: make cider. But speculation about what cider could be (or could have been) to American culture still intrigues me. It also intrigues me to think that I was a witness to a tidal wave, a political wind that shifted course and carried us off into a wholly unexpected land. And I've come to conclude that *both* missions—growing cider apples and growing the cider market—were simply small boats in a much larger ocean that pre-fated where we ended up. In other words, the trade associations and all the internal activism were unnecessary. American culture wanted something, and it demanded we make it. Success was simply a matter of filling the void.

My personal feeling is that America's romance with apples was behind the mission shift, not some evil scheme perpetrated by big beer companies (now reaping three-quarters of all "cider" sales in America). I don't credit or fault any producer, grower, or politician for what's become of this industry; I think cider's resurgence was fated by a cultural need for something nostalgic, and it was just unfortunate that few cider apples were there to take part. We, as a people, love apples so damn much that we are willing to ignore a lackluster performance. It doesn't matter that today's cider is the artistic equivalent of a bride's rambling, drunken wedding-day speech—the people in the audience love her and are willing to overlook clumsy and pointless blabber. At the reception we are all on the same side. That is, unless the ex-girlfriend is present, and then you've got a real critic. I obviously have not moved on.

Denniston Red, Part 2

I wake up in Jeffersonville and my forehead is throbbing. I'm still holding my pole saw, but the ladder is folded in an awkward position beside me. As I climb out of the bed of snow I survey what's going on, including the round depression where my head was resting. The bowl is stained red like a cherry Icee.

I couldn't have been out for long. Ryan, who's helping me prune this homeowner's orchard, is still sawing away on another tree; he would've noticed had I been out for more than a few seconds. But as I lift myself my right eye fills with blood and I get a little freaked out. In the past I've broken my arm and dislocated my elbow, so I'm aware of the harm from falling and that shock can mask some serious damage. Today, though, I'm lucky. I pad down my body in search of internal damage, but after a minute I conclude that, apart from the gash in my eyebrow, there's nothing wrong. My mind starts to settle.

I've heard apple trees described as angry before. I've also heard Bob Ross, the red-Afro-wearing television artist, use the term *happy trees*, but neither is a good description of a tree's true character. *Happy* and *angry* only describe temporary states of a person's being; they speak nothing of true character as Aristotle or Jung would have it. Of course, I don't extend that level of analysis to a tree, much less to a person, but I do look for expressive and quirky habits when I work on pruning. And they aren't simply visible qualities, either. Sometimes (and I'm sure other apple growers will mock me for this) a tree's character can be interpreted by how you feel and what happens to you around the tree.

Twice now I've been banged in the head at this location along the East Branch of Callicoon Creek. It's never happened elsewhere, so I know the trees are trying to tell me something (by the way, the cider from these trees is equally assertive). I trust it's not an anger; rather, it's more of a school-of-hard-knocks way of communicating with me. I think the trees are actually embracing me in that tough-guy way that hooligans extend to their gang. It's that razzing culture that John Travolta ran with in the movie *Grease*. The culture of these apple trees creates a weird juxtaposition against the homeowner, who looks like she's straight out of a German fairy tale, though a later-stage Sandra Dee might be in her, too.

Trees in other locations have a sense of humor. In my home orchard there are two trees in particular who are constantly yukking it up at my expense: They pull the hat off my head and either dangle it behind me or throw it to ground. I feel like the dumb hunter in a Warner Bros. cartoon: I curse my luck, not realizing that some hammy character has been messing with me. And the rest of the trees must think it's funny, too, or these class clowns wouldn't keep doing it. Clearly they're being rewarded for bad behavior, or perhaps they are still miffed about my attempts to cultivate them.

And then there's the Denniston farm; these apple trees have a totally different aura to them. Tall and elegant, they have total confidence about who they are. Denniston Red, the quintessential example of this, rises like a phoenix from her once-fallen trunk and never looks back or acknowledges her stumble. She hums Edith Piaf and silently commands adoration like a 7-foot-tall drag queen of the Jackie-O temperament. She's neither greedy for light nor hasty in her decisions, but she gets what she wants: humans to serve her. John and I couldn't reach all the grapevines in the high branches, so after we severed their lifeline the leafless ropes still dangle from the canopy. On any other tree this would seem to detract, but on Red the vines are like the buzzing of flies or the flashing of paparazzi. She sees past it, long into the future and long into the past.

Perhaps another tall and severe model could be used to describe Red, too: Snow White's nemesis, her towering stepmother (the new queen). Both offer apples that take their victims to another world, and in Red's case this is a forgotten land.

The apple is medium-sized, squat, oblong or round; it's blood red and doesn't ripen until October, remaining green and unsuggestive until the fall equinox. Then in the last few weeks, the apple quickly colors, it sheds some water weight, and the fruit begins to feel hollow. A waxy sheen builds on the surface and soon attracts sooty blotch, a minor fungal "disease" that layers a black wash over the skin, a mix of colors that conjures up thoughts of Dracula. When it dents like Styrofoam, you know the apple is ready to pick.

As your teeth break past the initial resistance of its skin, plunging deep into the light yellow-green flesh, you effortlessly snap off a bite and introduce it into your mouth. As you chew like a cow, you start to break up the fruit and think to yourself, *Does this have any flavor at all? Why, this is blander than a Red Delicious!* You try to dig past the crispy texture and bright acidity to locate the familiar, but only a faint aroma begins to emerge. And it's *decidedly* not apple-like: You're now in a cold limestone cavern sucking on the collar of your wool sweater . . . you can hear the siren voice of an apple somewhere but it's impossible to locate given the echo of the barren cave. Notably absent are your favorite apple compass points: tart cherry, table grapes, celery soda, flowering wisteria, birch syrup, or bursting tangerines.

Then the texture becomes grainy, releasing more limestone as it mixes with your saliva to form a low-foaming washing machine full of raw linens, scarlet napkins, lacy panties, and a burlap sack that ruptures to spill its contents: lemons, avocados, super-ripe mango, and a quart of sesame oil. Now that Jackie-O drag queen has just morphed into something curvaceous and showy. The apple is the Chiquita Banana lady chasséing to a Caribbean drum, but just when you rise to join her you hear the rumble of distant thunder and the fruity beat fades away, as if in the hands of a teasing deejay. On the other turntable: an approaching army. It's the tannins! You might try to spit it out, but it's too late, the apple has already released a chalky, woody quality that acts like the little people of *Gulliver's Travels* tying down a tingling sensation to the front end of your mouth like a 9-volt battery. *Shit, this actually hurts!* you unexpectedly say to yourself. You're used to juicy apples exploding in your mouth before swiftly falling off the back waterslide, but this apple is setting up shop like a sadistic dentist and you're alarmed at what the Novocain precludes. Maybe the bitterness means the apple is poisonous! Maybe Denniston Red was the model for Snow White's witchy queen after all? Maybe this is why the fruit is forbidden! Doomed, you just tasted a cider apple.

Hey, You Forgot Something

A whole slew of outside interests are now tied to cider's fate. It's increasingly unlikely that farmers devoted entirely to cider agriculture are going to dominate the resurgence of the drink in the coming years. There's too much at stake to insist we go back and bring the cider apple with us this time. Government is now invested, nonprofits, academic institutions, the tourism industry, Big Beer, Big Ag—all of them have skin in the existing game, and not one of them wants to see cider devoted to a new form of old agriculture, not until it exists at a large scale. Many people feel that it's best to suffer their presence and siphon money however possible into the cause.

In the meantime, "cider as beer" commands nearly all cider sales, and it dominates the public's perception of the drink's taste and value. Fed by the excesses of unwanted culinary apples, as well as by imported juice and juice concentrate, the beer model of production has gladly grafted itself over the rootstock of real cider. Used to market the modern industrial product is the feel-good history of old apple trees, old cider mills, and a closed-loop culture of non-specialists who realize the drink from soil to bottle. But what a vicious form of irony this is: What Modern production wants to look like is the very thing it nearly made extinct and currently undermines the value of. While some of those specialized orchards are now grafting cider varieties for perhaps more pennies on the dollar, frankly I don't see specialized cider-as-beer producers wanting to pay more even for excellent fruit. So long as cider is produced like a beer, the ingredient bill will have to compete. And beer, after all, is 95 percent free tap water.

The mission creep of the trade associations has served cider agriculture only in the grafting of cider varieties; it has deflated the hope for an actual cider agriculture. In fact, those few big farms that did graft cider varieties *insist* that the same sprays, same production quotas, same rootstocks, same soil inputs, and same field practices be applied to cider apples. In other words, the cultivation is the same.

Now I hear the opposite of everything I read historically about good cider and personally know about it from my own experience. Pomologists and culinary apple farmers are claiming, "The best apples for cider come from rich soils and well-maintained trees." Could it be that Thoreau and Chapman, and all of America prior to 1900, as well everyone in hill country in the twentieth century, were wrong? Should history surrender its cider apples now that universities, big farmers, and Big Beer is on the case? Will Johnny Come Lately dethrone Johnny Appleseed?

"But I know what cider is," you say. "It's a refreshing alternative to beer or wine, one that's light and crisp, with apple sweetness and a soda-like effervescence!" No. No, it is not. What you're thinking of is the equivalent of a wine spritzer, a drink intent on diverting attention from itself. That version of cider (and I'm not being facetious here) is a compromise of nature. From its conventional orchard start, to its filtered and forced-carbonation ending, that drink (that maybe you even like) is a contrivance unrecognizable to those who have tasted the real thing.

Anyone who's ever made plain ol' home cider knows what I'm talking about. The end product tastes nothing like an apple spritzer: It's dry and vinous, tart and maybe slightly funky; ultimately it resembles a Chardonnay more than it does the juice of Honeycrisp apples. But you love sweet apples and you were hoping your drink would have that Honeycrisp taste just like those beer-can hard ciders from the quicky-mart. So you try your hand at cider making again, this time getting serious and following strict online instructions: You add potassium metabisulfite and follow it with rehydrated lab yeast; you use acids and recommended tannin powders;

you add flavorings and you back-sweeten with sugar; finally bottling and capping it for a later date. This waiting period, you read, is supposed to carbonate the cider, but because you have a SodaStream machine at home you also try some with instant bubbles. This option forgoes the drying sensation of bottle conditioning, and when you drink the cider you discover, *Hey! It worked, this tastes a lot like those hard ciders from the quicky-mart!* But when the bottles that you forgot about start exploding in your basement three weeks later, you finally conclude: Cider was not meant to have residual sweetness. You've been fighting nature all along.

Cider made naturally can be infinitely deeper than what the North American market currently offers, but producers are hell-bent on making it into something that it's not. In doing so they've lowered our expectations and encouraged us to think of cider as an alternative to more popular drinks, particularly wine and beer. Hoping that it could inhabit the middle ground, cider producers have downplayed its agriculture similarities with wine while emphasizing the sweet side so that it can appeal to beer drinkers. But cider basically *is* a wine: fruit fermented. Any alteration to that formula is simply that: an alteration.

As conventional cider has followed conventional agriculture with its limited number of varieties, limited number of growers (commercial), and limited soil types ("agricultural"), the customer became deprived of knowing what could be. But with a new focus on exploring locational attributes, and with an interest in the apple's infinitely diverse genetics, cider can be every bit as complex as wine—if not more so. To repeat myself: What's missing for a fair comparison are (1) the agriculture and (2) proper consumer expectations. The two are culturally intertwined in a chicken-and-egg sort of way, but it's certainly not helpful to further pigeonhole cider based on underwhelming fruit and drink options. Unfortunately, the more cider becomes associated with a kiddy version of itself, the more it will discourage new farmers and artists from taking on the very long-term challenge of growing apples correctly and restoring cider, rightfully, as America's daily drink. (My apologies to those who like unchallenging ciders, though you can rest assured that the wine industry still has its spritzers.)

But don't look to me to tell you how "high-end" or "fine" cider is made. I don't know myself. I simply make traditional cider and try to stick close to its natural form. If you're a potential producer (even if just on the home level), I would suggest you read Claude Jolicoeur's *New Cider Maker's Handbook*. His engineering mind and love of science allow for careful navigation of the details that I follow only as superstition. Plus he's more open-minded than I am and accepts that outside pressures (like taste expectations or the need for farms to scale up) can be positive influences on cider making and cider growing. *My* understanding of cider is exclusionary this way, but Claude and I share a fundamental belief that is now described in two contemporary books and hundreds of older texts with still no absorption from modern apple farmers or cider producers: The best ciders come from apples grown in low-productivity orchards (or in the wild). Whereas I use the word *uncultivated*, Claude uses the term *minimal-intervention*, but we mean basically the same thing. Both of us know from personal experience that the dominant *cultural practices* of North American apple farms are bad for cider. They're bad for the quality of cider and ultimately for the good name of cider, as a whole. I'm sorry, but there's no other way to say it. We either start a new culture (which looks like the old one before Prohibition—small farms and all) or we accept a compromised version of cider. You're the customer, so you're the one to decide.

Location, Location, Location

I'm sure you've heard the breaking news: The Book of Genesis makes no mention of the forbidden fruit specifically being an apple—it may have been a pomegranate! It's likely northerners tweaked the biblical story over time to revolve around the fruit common to colder climates. That seems fair to me. The important thing isn't the fruit type. Whether it was an apple, a pomegranate, or a banana tree makes no difference—is the rest of the Bible supposed to be interpreted literally?—what's truly significant about the Tree of Knowledge is that (1) it was a *tree*, and (2) its location. If the Bible (and the *Apple* Tree of Knowledge) is to hold any significance to people, we need to *localize* it.

Expanding on the above points: Trees are symbolic in that they live between worlds, aboveground (the terrestrial) and belowground (the subterranean). We know and relate to them as terrestrial because that's the world we share. We share their air, we both react to the sun and the seasons, and we both interact with the flora and fauna of the ecosystem. But trees also live underground, which is a curiosity in the same way the dark side of the moon is intriguing to us. We know it's part of the whole but we never get to see the other half! (Well, actually we *will* see the subterranean world one day, and knowing our fate we are haunted by trees for being able to live in that world, too. Whoever picked a tree to represent "Knowledge" was surely referencing this as well.)

And another thing: The Tree is significant as an ambassador for its specific location. Though we can't see what's going on underground, the geology, moisture levels, biological composition, potential toxins, and nutritional levels are all communicated to us by a tree's apparent health. In other words, a tree is able to communicate that which we *can't* see about a location, the other half of the whole. In this manner, too, whoever picked a tree to represent Knowledge was surely suggesting that the Tree was communicating locational secrets about Eden. What we saw aboveground, the apple, was representative of the significance of that location.

I have *no* idea what the modern religious significance of Eden is, so I can't say what the location of Paradise means. I only know that Eden was a place where Adam and Eve ran around free and naked, without concern, and that the Garden provided everything: beauty, shelter, and nourishment. Man and Woman never had to search, work, or prepare for the future. Religion, I don't know, but in terms of agriculture I can say that Voltaire would browbeat this concept as unsustainable and therefore "unrealistic." However, there is a world of non-Western thought that may not be so dismissive of Paradise on earth. On a philosophical level this location might serve as inspiration to Zen practitioners seeking *no-thought*, or being in the moment. But this school of thought is also over my head so I'll stick to a simpler reading: The Tree of Knowledge was chosen for its "treeness," that which is able to communicate invisible worlds to humankind, connecting those worlds, and spanning different generations. That in itself is complex enough.

But all good things must come to an end. It was the snake that first implanted the now-perpetual "grass is greener on the other side" neurosis in our heads. He convinced Man (specifically, a woman) that we could be like God with the power of creation, thought, and consciousness.

With one bite we were expelled from Paradise, cast east of Eden (maybe to Kazakhstan?), and cryptically told we couldn't return "in our earthly bodies." Our next shot at Paradise comes when our bodies are underground. Perhaps in death we become part of the famous Tree itself and can communicate with the living. But what's most interesting about this story to me is that apple trees were soon found on this earth, too, and not just in Paradise. Apple trees are telling us these locations are one and the same! The lesson to take away from this is important: Don't listen to the snake, listen to the tree; the grass is greenest here, so love where you live.

Denniston Red, Part 3

We've been cleaning up the orchard and have it so that it actually looks like one. John has it now so that he has to mow or we'll lose the apples in the tall grass. I doubt this makes it a better environment for cider, but it's a better stage for parties. On the summer solstice we burn all the pruned and diseased wood in a giant bonfire at the north end near Mike's hunting stand. The fire seems appropriately pagan on this celestial day, as do all the naked partygoers after their mud bath. When you're covered in a thick paste of drying clay, there's no need for bug spray, but I've observed something great having bathed in the earth at the feet of Denniston Red. I've never felt more connected with a tree than after wallowing in the mud just beyond reach of the roots. As orchardists we judge a tree mainly by the sense of sight, and this bond is formed in the common airspace we both share. But half the tree lies underground, and it's impossible to relate to it with our eyes. By utilizing the sensation of touch, and by sinking to that level, a mud bath in a mudhole gives us the sense of what it's like to be in the earth, not on it. In fact, I've been inspired to dig a similar pit in my home orchard to get a sense for what's going on there, too. The verdict is interesting: My farm offers a contrast with the Denniston orchard that I would never have considered. At home, thousands of little sharp rocks (the flaking of slate and shale) make for an almost medieval mud bath: Sinking in must be done oh-so-slowly, as if lying down on a bed of nails. But my soils are creamier and "cleaner" in a sense, almost like lotion with the aroma of baking soda. By contrast, here in the river flats along the Neversink, Red's soils are a silky medium with a sandy grain, if you choose to rub it on. And there is a slightly swampy nose to it, suggesting it's more "alive" in the way kimchi is. Maybe it's for this reason that agricultural experts recommend John's soils over mine for growing apple trees.

Don't worry, we aren't pagans or especially hippyish (despite being only 15 miles from the original Woodstock festival). Our solstice party isn't supposed to be meaningful on some higher level, except the mud bath has a way of drawing out primal considerations. I only mention it in this book because there's a benefit to relating to apple trees and to all agriculture via the common ground (literally)—to walk a mile in their shoes, so to speak. But I also need to caution you to research the land first! I don't want to be a downer, but during the twentieth century *most* agricultural soils (especially orchards) were blanketed in chemicals known to cause deformities and irreversible health problems. Those chemicals are still measurably toxic, especially in the prime soil regions that saw the most farming, so I'd be especially careful to do my sleuthing before digging a mudhole.

Humans are a cerebral lot with a tendency to use this power to safely distance ourselves, but to anyone who speaks of terroir, the sommes, the growers, and food enthusiasts, I highly recommend feeling the soil, not simply reading about it. Feeling helps connect feelings, too. Because if we did relate to locations this way, we'd not only find food more personal, but we'd also be more critical of our treatment of the medium. Whether we swim in the soil or eat its food (which most of us do), one way or another we are physically connecting to it and making ourselves part of it. We can't think our way above the earth. Thank God for trees to remind us of that.

SIX

Natural Cider

*T*his year the snow cover didn't fully recede until the first week in April, and now we're in the height of mud season. Up in the trees, silvery buds are swelling back in the homestead orchard, showing the first activity of the crop year. This is one of the most critical months for apple farmers: It's the prime time for proactively dealing with the overwintering pests and diseases that threaten to destroy the upcoming growing season. Whether you are a conventional or organic grower, you need to deal with emerging insects and bacterial cultures at this critical moment before their populations boom with the coming spring warmth.

In addition to the busy spray schedule, a farmer has also to deal with a rush of spring orchard tasks, including planting trees, grafting, and pruning. Add cider bottling to the mix and things really get crazy. But without all this prep work, there will be no harvest and nothing to sell in the summer markets. Orchardists must be in full cultivate-our-garden mode.

I say this about April, that it's a laborious and frantic month for apple farmers, but why then am I in a Whole Foods Market in South Beach, Miami, right now? I should be hard at work staring down aisles of silvery-barked apple trees, their limbs still bare of leaves; instead I'm staring down aisles lined with bronze-skinned Floridians, also mostly bare. I really ought to be in dreary upstate New York right now surrounded by gray skies, muddy soils, and pale brown grass; instead I'm in the produce section surrounded by bright lights and fruit of every color. At this very moment my hands ought to be dirty and chapped, gripping a pole saw or pruning secateurs; and instead my clean fingers are grabbing a massive green orb known as a Crispin apple. How, again, do I call myself an apple farmer?

This particular Crispin wears a sticker reading CERTIFIED ORGANIC. It was grown in the Midwest, it's as green as a lime, as big as a softball, and as shiny as the freshly waxed Lamborghinis out there in the parking lot (for some reason, there's a lot of them). I might be 500 miles from the nearest apple tree, and several months from the nearest harvest, but here I am holding what is surely an abomination of nature—in a natural foods store, no less. But looking around, I'm no longer sure I know what natural is anymore. It's not just the apples that seem abnormally bodacious; it seems humans have also been evolving while I've been away on my farm.

If you can picture South Beach, you know where I'm going with this. There are obvious parallels between this big, round, juicy apple and some of the *other* displays famously detouring our eyes on the beach in Miami. (Do I really need to spell it out for you?) These adjectives are applied to nouns that are instinctually eye-catching despite the fact we know they aren't natural. Okay, *sometimes* these attributes are found in nature, but their availability has become so prevalent that they're now the norm, not a rarity, and I'm *sure* this isn't representative of a natural cross section. Humans have created this abundance, not nature, and it seems the midwestern farmer and the South Beach plastic surgeon have a lot more in common than you'd think.

Don't get me wrong, I'm not above the impulses. Everything here is making my eyes bug out like Roger Rabbit. I mean seriously, look at those Crispin apples, they're massive! I wonder how I'd ever be able to grow such a crop back home with my tired old soils and trees, but there are bins and bins of these perfect apples and probably millions more where they came from. Every last one of them is without flaw, which actually makes choosing a challenge. But my impulses are highly activated here, and I've got to grab something! I select this one, and motorboat my way to the checkout line.

Like I said, there's no excuse for an apple farmer to be in Miami in April. If selling apples is a competitive market, and I know it is, I don't stand a chance growing fruit akin to these Triple-D beauties. But luckily, *my kind* of apple does have a market, and it's found right here in Whole Foods, too. You won't find them in the produce section, though; we need to move on over to the wine section.

Fancy and flashy labels aside, wine bottles seem to engage people's intellectual side a bit more than eye-popping fresh fruit. Whereas one aisle is about impulses, and customers suck in their stomachs and stick out their chests to parade in that environment, here in the wine section consumers appear studious, as if parsing books from library shelves. The guy next to me has slipped on bifocals to read about the vineyard history, what region the grapes are from, what varieties are blended, and what the soils and growing climate are like. In the wine section we intellectualize. The marketing of these products may never mention the shriveled, bacteria-laden grapes that went into some of the finest, most expensive wines here, but even if customers saw this they'd still be able to wrap their heads around it and place a high value on the crop. In fact, I know of no other place in Miami that celebrates visible imperfections and the concept that a challenging environment can add up to something ultimately beautiful, something great . . . something natural.

This all holds true for cider just as it much as it does for wine, and apples might even have a special ability to surpass grapes in some aspects of "natural wine," but we US cider makers have a very serious deadweight keeping our industry from being all it can be. Cider should be a world-class drink, and many Americans can proudly claim to be living in the Bordeaux or Loire Valley of cider, but the drink has long been tethered to low-quality production and the completely wrong form of agriculture. It's a chicken-and-egg scenario involving commodity apple farming, industrial drink production, and (let's face it) lazy customers, who might just prefer cheap and perfunctory over the hassle of bifocals. All of these forces combine to shirk responsibility for a lackluster North American cider market that speaks of craftsmanship and human innovation instead of the apples' true form. But there are still regions in this world that show cider to be deserving of the same respect given to wine, and luckily I've spotted bottles from those places right here in Whole Foods!

The Forchard

I have two orchards on my property. Both are about 4 acres in size. One, I've already written about in chapter 2: It started as reclaimed pasture, and I went about repopulating it with 350 apple trees (mostly with semi-dwarfing rootstocks), which I bought from several nurseries. I planted them in straight rows, tried to keep deer off them . . . yada, yada, yada, you know the outcome already: epic fail. But just when I threw in the towel, I started another orchard farther up the mountain. This orchard is also carved from newly cleared woodland, except I kept many of the tall trees so that grass is not able to move in, there's a heavy leaf mulch still, understory bushes remain, and branch debris litters the ground like in woodlands. This new orchard I call my forchard, or seedling forchard, and it most resembles the havoc of a logging track. I did, in fact, log most of the trees hoping to build a barn, but the real objective was to have a place to throw my pomace after pressing apples each year. Ultimately, I want this place to look and function like Bill's wild apple forest, a mix of many species. I want it to seamlessly blend in with the entire ecosystem of my region (not just my property), so if it looks like something is there on Google Earth I'll know I'm laboring too much over it.

As Bill's farm is my role model, an example predicated on cows dispersing the seed, you could say my grinder and press function as the cow's mouth, while my shovel acts as the cow's back end. I start by emptying the apple press in the bed of my truck and driving up the hill, stopping every 20 feet to toss out about 10 shovelfuls. For six years I've been doing this, trying to evenly cover the 4-acre space, and by now I'm repeating myself in some locations.

Here are the numbers: My cider operation and barn are scaled for 30 barrels. That's 1,500 gallons per year. To make 30 barrels, I need to gather about 40 bins of apples. Forty bins of apples equates to about 800 bushels (20 bushels per bin), and there are about 125 medium-sized commercial apples per bushel. That means there are about 100,000 apples in 40 bins (800 × 125). But since my apples are significantly smaller (and this is without even considering my use of crab apples), I can conservatively say I go through about twice that number—about 200,000 apples per year.

More numbers: In each apple there are 5 seeds (though some have 10). Each seed has its own genetic material (again, the five seeds in a McIntosh apple will not become McIntosh trees). So if I have 200,000 apples, I have the potential for 1 million new apple varieties per year. Granted, some of those seeds might be damaged by the grinder, but at least half of them pass through unharmed, and I estimate about half a million viable seeds in my pomace each year. As I've now been spreading seeds on my hillside for six years, I've introduced nearly 3 million new varieties to a 4-acre area. If these seedling trees were to grow into full-sized spreading trees, they'd have to compete with new birch, maple, oak, and pine seedlings, plus they'd have to fit between the ledge outcroppings and under the remaining tall trees, which make this less of a woods clearing and more of a thinning. In all, I don't expect more than 200 or 300 to survive (which, by coincidence, is the same as with my other 4-acre orchard).

We say that challenges build character: A person emerges from a challenge a better person whether they succeed or fail. Character, however, is a hotly contested topic for those still entrenched in the nature-versus-nurture debate. But it doesn't matter whether character is predetermined, à la Myers-Briggs, or if we are born as tabulae rasae—either way the maxim still holds true: Challenges build character. The only debate is what foundation character-building adds to.

On a subconscious level people and trees both know this about challenges, but there's a fundamental difference between us that makes trees look courageous in comparison. This fundamental difference builds from the fact that trees are stationary and we are not. When the going gets tough, a tree can't run and hide or live to fight another day. A tree must stand its ground, and its first instinct is to dig deep. In times of war, or even in sports, we understand the home advantage, but part of that advantage is spurred by a psychological conviction that actually has great metaphoric parallels to the tree's defense response: When humans fight, we fight "on the grounds" of something. We, too, have the ability to dig deep, even if we rarely employ this conviction.

A tree builds character from its roots. We use roots metaphorically, too. We say roots are where we came from; roots provide us an anchor to our location, to our community; roots define our character; and roots nourish us as we grow up (away from the roots). On a gut level we know that the deeper the roots go, the deeper all those virtues hold true. (Which is why a tree was chosen to represent Eden and not the shallow-rooted Bush of Knowledge.) But if we know all this based on gut instinct, why then are cider makers planting trees on shallow-rooted clonal stocks and not as seedling trees? Isn't character achieved by digging deep, exploring the challenge, and developing far-reaching roots? If roots define the virtues of character, aren't roots what we ought to be growing?

I'm not going to win this argument with commercial growers any more than I'm likely to settle the nature-versus-nurture debate, but there is an impurity in the counterargument that must be addressed. Farmers are in need of money now, and this immediacy begets the recent shift toward clonal rootstocks more than anything. If this pressure were a non-issue, I think the argument would find less resistance within today's agricultural communities (in fact I think orchardists all prefer real trees). But I don't think it's the cider maker's place to concede this battle. In fact, they should be the ones fighting the hardest against agricultural shortcuts! The wine world embraces a healthy battle between growers and vintners; the same should be occurring in cider. Fruit farmers get paid by the ton, which creates an incentive to grow fruit exactly opposite to what a vintner wants. (Good wine comes from quality grapes, not large, watery fruit on high-yield lots.) Growers are the ones pushing for dwarfing rootstocks because of immediate economic pressures, and they are also the ones pushing for the popularity of select grafted cider varieties for reasons of efficiency, while the cider makers are putting up no argument. But we want cider to have character, not "cider properties," so we need the focus to be on the roots. A person focuses on cider varieties for *characteristics*, but they plant seedling trees for *character*.

Ledgey and the Forchard, Part 2

I have one seedling from a 2015 apple that survived its first year emerging from a protruding rock ledge the size, shape, and color of a blue whale. Somehow this whale got beached along the key line of the lower forchard slope (parallel to the topographic lines on a map), and it acts almost like a massive retaining wall for the mountain above. The ledge comprises mostly bluestone, but it's a compacted rock that doesn't appear layered or flakable. Nonetheless, a hairline crack runs top to bottom through the ledge, and if it weren't for Ledgey, the Seedling Tree (that's its official full name), I would never have noticed the crack. This little pippin emerged dead center on the exposed rock face, yards away from the nearest layer of soil (which isn't but paper-thin dirt anyway). So how in the world is this tiny seedling surviving?

To top it all off, 2016 was marked by severe drought in the Northeast. Its first year as a tree, Ledgey had only two months in spring to get moisture before the baking heat set up for the duration of summer. By June I could still see the split-husk clinging at the base of a young sprout that jutted upward the distance of 2 inches. Twin leaflets were spreading out at the top, and in the opposite direction was the hair-like rootlet the color of bone. A few failed barbs could be seen along the way as it snaked in search of an anchor. The path of this root hair went down, then up, curled like a roller coaster, and then finally found its sliver of a home—all in the matter of 2 inches—which tells me it spent a little time during the spring without any anchor at all before finding the hairline crack.

As the sun beat down and the season got drier, I checked in on all my seedling trees to see how they were growing. By August the Northeast United States was one big forest fire waiting to happen. It was so dry that even full-sized pine trees couldn't suffer the drought any longer. More than 100,000 seedlings died on that slope in 2016 (a big number because 2015 was our biggest cider year ever), but of the few thousand to survive, the most unlikely, Ledgey, captured my heart. By September it topped out at 4 inches and the tiny leaflets became dry and crispy. I thought for sure that the drought had claimed another casualty, but for good measure I put short-mesh rabbit guard around the tree just to give it special winter protection.

To my surprise it greened out again the following spring, and by then the rabbit guard had trapped a dusting of leaf mulch. Still, the crack is no wider than a hair, so I didn't want to be emotionally invested in this little tree. Fat chance of that: Over the following summer I checked on it regularly and started taking tour groups to visit Ledgey. Against all odds, it continued to grow another 4 inches that year, and by the harvest it was the same height as the rabbit guard, 8 inches.

The slightest tug would be all it'd take to tear the tree from the hairline crack (or break the tree altogether). In spring 2018 I found deer had discovered the forchard and were browsing it like kids in a candy store. The leader shoot of Ledgey was missing and the stem end was browning, characteristic of an immune response (similar to human scabbing), and yet the tree survived the munching. Soon another bud sent a shoot up to replace the leader, which at the time of this writing is growing at the same rate—by September it will have set a terminal bud about a foot above the rock ledge. And although I vowed not to interfere in the seedling forchard, I most certainly will try to keep the deer away from Ledgey somehow.

Half forest, half orchard, the forchard was meant to be a place where apple trees can live independent from my *un*-green thumb. Having my fondest memories of early adulthood attached to the wonder of wild apple trees, I'd like to know places will continue to exist where people can discover this for themselves. Polly and I don't have kids, so whoever takes over this land is going to have to buy and support this property with real-market money. But how do we create a place that's wondrous enough to compete with financial pressures and development? And the one relief extended to other apple farms, agricultural tax exemption, is entirely based on production. In the end, there's truly no social recognition for the value of wild apple trees. *Everything*, it would seem, must be subject to human economy. In the Land of the Free, even nature is in servitude.

Yet wild apple trees have profound spiritual, emotional, and companionship value to anyone who escapes the pressures of keeping up, and at the physical level they offer food to animals (and to people who have been spit out from that economy). Aside from free fruit, I personally can trace much of my inspiration, many of my ideas, and many of my insights to simply being with wild apple trees. I place their highest value in the pricelessness of companionship. In this sense wild apple trees live in *other* economies, ones that prioritize beauty, uniqueness, nutrition, taste—just to name just a few things that are often in direct conflict with a growing financial economy.

And then along came cider, and suddenly consumers found yet another alternative value to wild apples. Cider started to develop an art-like market where customers began placing value on originality, authenticity, preciousness, love, the limited, and the difficult. What strange concepts these are for Modern agriculture! In a hybrid between seemingly conflicting economies, cider seems to have found legs, and it's in this precarious market that I currently hold my hope for the immediate survival of my forchard, and for wild apple trees everywhere. At least for now, people can derive financial benefit from the uncultivated apple.

Nonetheless I'm very uneasy about pinning my hopes on anything connected to a financial economy dependent on growth. After all, some things cannot be scaled up. Imagine, for example, assigning a dollar value to the love of two newlyweds and then insisting that their marriage keep pace with the growing economy for 60 years! Love, wonder, true art, inspiration—all these things are about the intimacy of direct relationships; they exist in unscalable worlds, and it's in those worlds that wild apples have their highest value. So I'm hoping to keep wild apple trees and artisan cider independent of the pressures of conformity. In fact, neither the wild nor true art would continue to be themselves if they were in any way compromised.

Who knows what the apples in the forchard will taste like when the future landowner stumbles across them? I've given up hope of seeing this hillside fruit given just how challenging this soil is and how exceptionally slow growing the trees are in this location. Only a handful of my oldest seedlings (started in 2007) have produced fruit, but they are growing in my best soils down along the driveway. I'm sure it will take twice as long (or longer) to get the forchard seedlings to that state.

I was careful not to use common fruit varieties as the seed source. In the forchard I only spread the pomace from wild apples and pears because I like the idea of the tree running feral for multiple generations. What's interesting about the forchard is how many red-leafed, red-stemmed seedlings are coming up—about 1 out of 50—and I don't recall having many small red-fleshed crab apples in the cider mix. This might be telling of what other trees (possibly ornamental crabs) the wild fruit is cross-pollinating with, or it might speak of the ancient apple lineage before it arrived in America. Either way, I like that the apples are more deeply removed from agriculture than fresh-off-the-boat seedling trees from Macs or Goldens.

To belabor this point: Independence is the most important thing I could cultivate (or uncultivate) in the forchard. When I discovered how much effort it took to keep my cultivated trees alive down in my first orchard, I knew I had sabotaged my goal of having this farm survive Polly and me. Nobody in their right mind would want to inherit my burden, much less pay the equivalent monetary value of a development site. As a reminder, we live 75 miles from one of the most developed places on earth, so apart from an emotional, intellectual, or aesthetic appeal the forchard needs to survive by virtue of thrift. Wild apples are free in more ways than one.

That future apple collector on my property might disagree with me on this point. They might have to deal with what I deal with in many of my foraging spots: standing in poison ivy, hanging over cliffs, or navigating thick wild roses (sometimes pinned down as if in a magician's sword box)—all in an effort to collect difficult fruit. They won't say these apples are free at all, but they will be engaging in character-building challenges and becoming one with the environment that created those apples. In my mind no apple worth collecting is without challenges, and I'm inclined to think no person worth listening to is without them, either.

But this might just be my own history talking: I hail from a well-positioned "Washington-insider" family, and it was clear my personality was a poor fit for that world. After years of severe conflict I finally managed to retreat from that lineage, go back several generations, back from progressive cultivation, and emerge my proper self: an apple farmer. I did this on instinct, but I recently discovered my grandmother's parents were farmers in upstate New York, too! And isn't this *exactly* what we discover when we plant apples from seed? How interesting it is that by following the apple, we can be connecting with our own roots.

Jeff Bezos → Babysitters → *Absolutely Fabulous* → Ayn Rand

Forget, if you can, that the word has been commandeered by a mega-corporation: The word *whole* still means a great deal to those of us down on the farm. We're not about to forfeit it to Jeff Bezos's natural foods store just because he's figured out a way of profiting from our association. Cider is part of a whole, and I'd like to emphasize the take-back of certain words as a theme in this book. If cider is going to round the corner, we need honest communication, full transparency, and customers to believe us. *Whole, natural, farm-based*—even the word *cider* itself—have been eroded by commercial truthiness, but I am no pessimist. I have complete faith that consumers will eventually demand the full meaning of those words and somehow navigate around the misleading, the smoke and mirrors, and the intentionally omitted content.

How can I make it clear that cider is either whole or it is nothing? Whole means complete, and in the context of food that means complete life (the life of consumers, of the food, and of the planet and soils). Something is either alive or it is not. How did that become a slippery-slope argument? For cider to be whole it must be alive, one with the life of the trees, the people, and the microorganisms. It's not a representation of those things, it *is* those things. No part of this can be missing, in the same way the circulatory system cannot function without the respiratory, skeletal, and the complete systems of the body. Cider is whole or it is nothing; cider is alive, or it is not.

To that end, cider is *not* a product, and cider making is *not* a job. I think the correct way to see it is that cider making is a responsibility. Although that statement might send some entrepreneurs running for the hills (or *away* from the hills, in this case), those who embrace the responsibility will witness complexity, beauty, and joy a thousand times richer than someone who starts with apple juice and hopes to soon be cashing checks. Babysitting, for instance, might be fun for some people—it might even seem more enjoyable than actually being the parent—but the emotional and spiritual fulfillment of being the babysitter is in no way comparable to the joy that comes from accepting the responsibility of parenting. And I get it: Some people might want only a peripheral association with kids; after all, it's no secret parenting sucks (I can say the same of apple farming), yet only a parent can experience the greater joy of the child's whole life. And only an apple grower gets to witness the spirit of specific trees awaken in the bottle and then in their glass.

If this is the goal of cider—and it *absolutely* is!—then *unnatural* alterations to cider are off-topic, self-important, and ultimately self-defeating. And I would include the concept known to winemakers as stretching as among the most unnatural alterations. (Stretching is when farmers take their estate grapes and stretch them with mass-produced fruit for the benefit of scale.) Imagine raising a beef cow—maybe even getting to know it on an emotional level!—and then seeing its meat ground up and stretched with the meat of millions of other cows raised with indifference on a mega-ranch. How, if you *truly* care about your crop, is stretching wine or cider any less than stretching the truth?

But I digress. What I want to say in this chapter is that natural cider is not made that way to comply with any criteria; it's made that way because there is no other way. Life is whole, or it is nothing. There are no formulas, regulations, watchdogs, or rules concerning natural cider, except for this one: to see the life of a particular location (the soil, and then its trees, then its pickers) continued uninterrupted within the drink that you now sip. We let that apple life into our own, which to me is the reason for cider.

The fictional fashion junkie Edina "Eddie" Monsoon (*Absolutely Fabulous*) once claimed, "My whole body just hangs off these cheekbones." This, in her delusional mind, was the reason her looks were holding up after years of excessive drinking (in another episode she flashed back to a young teenager, her mother standing over her asking: "Is that cider I smell on your breath?"), but I like how Eddie's cheekbone comment seems to conjure architecture. In its purest form, architecture is about bridging structures with the life of the inhabitants within. That, I'll run with.

There is only one definition of cider, but there are degrees of quality and examples of great beauty. The key to a good cider hangs on the architecture of the apple and the right coalescence of chemical, emotional, and biological components. Age will eventually bring out the quirky, unique, and stunning characteristics that we look for in the drink, but without the proper framework of alcohol, acidity, and tannin (all of which are preservatives) the cider is vulnerable and will likely turn nasty in short time (much like Eddie's pal Patsy). That tripod structure is nature's way of building a home for the preexisting life of the juice while protecting it from clumsy microbial turns. This isn't to say some acetobacter, malolactic, or other Johnny-come-lately microbial notes are entirely bad for cider, but most of these notes tend to stomp all over the more delicate dance of fruit. Cider should be led by the apple and its place of origin, not the microorganisms or the human hand. Again, the hope is to have a structure that stands the test of time and fosters a favorable community inside, one that's rich in life. And this life is safest within the earthquake-resistant tripod of tannin, acid, and high sugars (converted to alcohol).

Those are the physical properties many producers, academics, and wine lab guys describe as the components of a good cider apple, but there's much more to a building than framework. I would argue that when a truly hideous human culture inhabits a building, it can turn even the most beautiful architecture into a house of horrors (someone tell that to Ayn Rand). Good cider apples have a good culture, with or without great bones. These biological components are less well understood by all those involved, but there's no doubt they play as big a role (perhaps the biggest) for the long-term well-being of cider. For that reason it's no wonder that the nuke-it-and-reset-it approach of conventional production leads to a Barbie of a drink: nothing behind those eyes. Good cider apples will have had a healthy life and they will continue to support that life. To lobotomize it with chemicals or violence just doesn't make sense.

And then there is the emotional life of cider. You can dismiss this as bullshit if you want, but human idealism and biases *do* play a huge part in the drink's taste. They can, and will, shape our experience of it. Try doing a blind taste test between two ciders or two cheeses: one from an actual mom-and-pop producer, the other from a multinational corporate producer. Unless you're some sick Earl Butz type, you'll probably be rooting for the little guy, but even if you blindly choose the mass-produced product, chances are your disappointment will alter your perception going forward and your tastes may change. Or you might rationalize your choice—*Well, the big company does do good things by hiring lots of people*—but either way your mind is desperately trying to reconcile physical and emotional likes. It's going to do that automatically (except of course if you're a sociopath).

I love this about food and drink: The story behind it cannot be separated from the objective. Nor should it be, since both your mind and physical health are encapsulated inside your one body. And if you still feel it's possible to divorce your emotional and intellectual self from your objective experience of food, then go ahead and state your case to the CFO of any major cider or wine company. I'm sure they'd like to know why they spend more money on branding than on agricultural development, facility infrastructure, equipment, and packaging combined. If you can convince the CFO to spend less on manipulating people's hearts and minds then I'm sure they'd be all ears, but so long as small producers are allowed to tell their stories those big companies will be forced into paying huge sums of money to counter with their impersonal one.

I, at least, have no intention of relinquishing my subjective perception of food and drink, and I pray that others don't, either. In fact, I hope consumers spend more time digging deep, fact-checking, and asking annoying questions. Being emotionally attached to the whole product is important, and you don't want your farmer or drink manufacturer withholding information or dishing out half-truths any more than you would your doctor. This is your body we're talking about. You want the *whole* story.

Natural Cider

It's worth noting that the root word of both *artifice* and *artificial* is *art*. Human direction and human expectation are entirely at play. Hugh Williams, of biodynamic orcharding fame, reminds me of this fact at least once a year when I praise wild apples and how they should inspire us as farmers. He tells me, and rightly so, that there is nothing natural in my uncultivated approach; that really what I'm trying to do is cultivate something, an artifice, the same motivation as anyone. Farming, whether it be biodynamic, conventional, or quote-unquote "natural," is an effort to satisfy our will.

And this is absolutely true with my take on natural cider. There are aesthetic, ideological, and health reasons behind the natural wine movement (which in many ways is a reaction against the evolution of artifice in conventional wine production), but it can't be said that a perfectly natural wine or cider is ever possible. Blending, to name just one simple practice, is an art, and as Hugh points out: Art does not happen on its own. Apples don't just fall from the tree straight into bottles, so how can anyone claim it's truly natural?

This paradox tethers natural cider's artists, scientists, and moralists to the masses of industrialized wine and cider producers who care as little about the natural taste of fermented fruit as they do the natural form of the cultivated plant. For them, the priority is something different, happily progressing toward something "new and improved," something innovative. But there is a key difference to the natural wine / natural cider ideology, and this distinction is exactly parallel to the ideological choices presented to growers: We drink makers can face a horizon achieved through finely tuned cultivation, or we can face the unaltered horizon. Which do we idealize? Cultivate or uncultivate . . .

And now, for the sake of clarity, let's return to a table to spotlight the exact choices posed to a cider maker. Table 6.1 is similar to table 3.1, this time for cider. I've included a middle category to show the emerging middle ground known to the market as natural cider (a spur from the natural wine market). This is not a regulated term, nor is *wild*, *raw*, or *uncultivated*—they are used for marketing purposes only. *Organic* and *biodynamic*, however, *are* certified terms, and practitioners are subject to fees, inspections, and/or legal requirements. As the above discussion shows, it's no surprise that the middle column has more in common with the "Conventional" column (left) than it does the "Non-Cultivated" column (right), but it brings up an interesting rift among practitioners of the natural cider movement: Do they want their products more unaltered (more "minimal intervention") or more finely cultivated, more "artistic"? A huge dichotomy exists within the middle column alone, but to me the most important divider is the ideological sympathies: In which direction does a producer face?

Yeast

Would you rather drink from a spring-fed pond with a few frogs and water bugs swimming around, or would you rather drink from a chlorinated swimming pool? Here's another one for you: Who seems cleaner to you, a person wearing deodorant (perfumes, metals, and chemicals) or a person who smells of their natural body odor?

What is and what isn't clean has been turned upside down by a cultural germophobia, and nothing exemplifies germophobia better than our modern cultivation of apples (which, of course, leaches down into modern cider). Take, for example, the apples you see in the store: They are without the discoloring of fungal layers (like sooty blotch), without dirt or bruising, and without insect holes or scab marks—in all, these apples are "clean." But in order to achieve that level of cleanliness they must be doused in copious amounts of chemical sprays and fertilizers, stimulants and hormone blockers, and killing fungicides (not to mention post-harvest waxes and cleanser residues). Is that your idea of clean?

These choices, trusting nature versus limiting our exposure to it, are the same two options given to cider and winemakers at the start of fermentation. In fact, they must decide on it twice: preceding the fermentation and just prior to bottling. In the first stage conventional producers fear that natural yeasts on the fruit (or in processing equipment and the environment)

Table 6.1. Natural Cider Between the Gradations

	Conventional	"Natural Cider"	Non-Cultivated
GROWING/HARVESTING			
Plant origin	From conventional nurseries (includes cloning and all conventional culturing practices listed in table 3.1).	Conventional and/ or organic nursery starts. (This is not yet regulated, but growers tend to support like-minded nurseries.)	From seed or from long-abandoned trees (which may also have had conventional origins).
Growing practice: classification	Farmed: conventional agriculture (but also includes "lighter" versions such as IPM, "Responsibly Grown," etc.).	Farmed: certified organic or biodynamic as well as uncertified bio-intensive or holistic. (Also includes trees converted from conventional practices with regulated time off.)	Non-farmed or from long-abandoned trees (with a much longer amount of off-time required for the tree to go wild).
Examples of growing practices and inputs	Irrigation / chemical fertilizers, chemical and biological pest/ disease controls, herbicides, etc.	Dry farming (mostly). Only certified fertilizers, herbicides, and pest and disease controls.	No inputs, few human influences (see table 3.1).
Harvest practices	Hand harvested from tree and/or machine-harvested from tree or orchard floor.*	Mostly hand-harvested from tree, sometimes from orchard floor.*	Mostly gathered from the ground, or they are shaken out.
Farm source	Large, medium and small-scale farms, usually a mix of many farms from many locations.	Usually from small farms, but not always limited to a single source.	Non-farmed (ideally limited to a single well-defined location, but this is only my preference).
FERMENTATION STARTING AND STEERING			
Juice source	From concentrate and/or "freshly pressed" (apples in CA storage can be pressed any time of year).	No regulation, but usually seasonally fresh-pressed. Rarely from concentrate.	Seasonal apples pressed as they naturally deteriorate (+/- October).
Biological starting point	Dead: SO_2 and/or UV, heat, HPP, or other sterilizations.	Alive (trace amounts of SO_2 sometimes allowed).	Alive.
Biological steering	Mostly with rehydrated "lab yeasts," often with added nutrient, pectin, finings, and/or other enzymes.	Ambient and/or home-cultured yeasts. Certified additions only (e.g., organic yeast nutrient).	Apple and ambient yeasts only.

Chemical steering	Copper, sulfite, potassium, calcium, etc.	None (or regulated trace amounts).	None.
Environmental steering	Heat start, glycol chill-down, and cold-stabilized.	Not regulated (could include artificial chilling or heating).	Ambient temps (or stabilized by ground temperatures).

RACKING/AGING ADJUSTMENTS

Clarifiers	Common: Filtration, chemical and biological finings.	Rare, but filtration is allowed and some regulated clarifiers, like bentonite.	None.
Corrections	Common: Nutrients, color agents, tannin and acid corrections, sugar additions.	Rare, but the same agents are allowed if certified organic (e.g., certified organic yeast nutrient).	None.
Flavor adjustments	Common: Direct flavor additions, which include ingredients, vessel (barrel) influence, and enzymes ("Bret", MLF, etc.).	Rare. Vessel influence and/or organic flavor additions only.	None. (Though influence may unintentionally derive from the vessel or yeast notes.)

BOTTLING

Biological protections	SO_2, sorbate, sterile filtration, pasteurization, and other artificial protections.	Trace SO_2 is allowable but natural CO_2 needs no regulation.	Relies on natural CO_2, higher alcohol levels, natural acids, and tannin.
Gas technology	CO_2 gas infusion (forced carbonation).	Can be natural or forced-carbonated. (Sugar dosage allowable if organic.)	Still or bottled with residual sugars to create natural carbonation (Pét-Nat).
Bottle clarification	Usually fined, racked, and filtered (sometimes disgorged).	Can include sterile filtration ("polishing") and disgorgement.	Racked to bottle, undisgorged.

Note: Conventional means typical, modern cider-making, especially industrially made cider. "Natural cider" is certified as biodynamic or organic. Non-cultivated can't fully exist but is listed for reference opposite conventional cider.

* Most commercial orchards do not, or cannot, use the apples that fall to the ground. Recent toxin and bacteria scares, especially E. coli, have made the use of "drops" prohibited at mills that also press "sweet cider." There is however no biological risk to a drink with 3 or 4 percent alcohol because at that level coliforms are killed. But another unregulated reason for excluding the drops has to do with the apple's exposure to toxins on the soils. The use of herbicide strips at conventional orchards, as well as the runoff from the chemical sprays, means you wouldn't want to use orchard drops anyhow. (One of the more compelling arguments for segregating cider agriculture from modern culinary apple farms.)

will steer the fermentation in an undesirable way, so the option to limit the microorganisms weighs heavy in their decision whether to sterilize or not. Yes, it's true that natural yeasts will colonize, cohabit, and influence the fermentation, but the decision to sterilize (usually with SO_2, but also with sterile filtration, UV machines, and like equipment) involves not only added work but added expense, too. Conventional production then proceeds by reculturing the juice with a select lab yeast (which becomes no less alive than natural yeasts, though commercial yeast culturing involves a plethora of practices no natural food enthusiast would support), but by first killing the microflora on the fruit they have severed the living link to the agriculture. This is unacceptable to a natural cider producer, who sees the transformations through pressing, fermentation, and barrel aging as akin to the cocoon stages of a caterpillar and butterfly's life. The goal is to see the same life of the tree awake in the glass; keeping the product alive at all stages is what distinguishes natural cider from conventional.

Maintaining a consistent ideology (from farm to fermentation to bottling) is important for the natural cider maker, but on the flip side it's also perfectly logical (and consistent) for a conventional cider maker to sterilize the juice, use SO_2 throughout processing, and filter out the remaining yeasts at bottling. Assuming the apples came from conventionally managed orchards, why get all natural at the eleventh hour? It always befuddles me to see conventional orchard cider marketed as "wild fermentation." Meanwhile, all those wine-making technologies, those manipulations and additions, have an identical twin in the practices of conventional agriculture, which uses herbicides, insecticides, and especially fungicides to control the outcome. In the end what's important, in my mind, is that cider and wine production remain consistent with their culturing practices. Or said another way: A cider should taste as the apple was grown.

I've made the point that agriculture is the same as personal culture several times already, but I feel I must repeat it so that this book doesn't become pigeonholed as a cider book or an apple book. I'm addressing *all* people here because cider and apple production are deeply related to the vast world of topics other people struggle with. Human agri*culture* is an extension of our culture; conventional farm practices are simply an extension of conventional wisdom. So if you want to know why apples and cider are less than what they can be (which I hope I've demonstrated), then don't blame the farmer or cider maker. It has all to do with our complacent wisdom, and we will need to challenge this if we want food and drink to rise to new heights. Don't look to chefs, farmers, and food activists to lead the way: The changes will come from the larger culture first.

To that end, a sneak preview to common agricultural practices or common wine- and cider making practices is always first seen in our cultural approach to health care. As all of these practices exist now, an obvious parallel runs between conventional agriculture (and conventional cider making) and the Purell-the-planet approach to medicine. Whereas the tree has survived in the wild for millions of years by learning to adapt to new and changing environments, now Modern orchardists seek to eliminate those variables, amend the environment, and then replace the tree's immune system with a prescription of supplemental nutrients, antibiotics, and physical isolation. Those are doctor's orders as much as they are farmer's orders. It would seem outrageous for a society that cultivates itself in one way to expect anything different from its farmers and drink producers.

Why, then, are natural wine and natural cider becoming popular in the marketplace? It has all to do with modern health problems and our gut feeling (no pun intended) relating to our isolation from nature. We don't feel good about the lives we lead and the foods we eat, so technically we started making natural wine the moment society started challenging Modern medicine. But my point is, don't look to natural winemakers or natural farmers to lead the way: It's all on you, the consumer, to figure out which medicine you believe in. Food is all about consistent ideologies, and if you want your body to function independently, free from dependence on Modern medicine, wouldn't you want *your* agriculture to function similarly? Americans are their apples; we are what we eat. Our cider says everything about who we are.

Wine Flaws

One of the reasons I go to Miami each winter is to surround myself with the internationally good looking. After a year in upstate New York, I can't stand the sight of personal flaws any longer—all those love handles, big noses, and the occasional missing tooth. On South Beach, where the men are sculpted as if by Michelangelo and the women seem painted by Botticelli (except with larger boobs, of course; fifteenth-century Florence wasn't as advanced as we are now), you can instantly tell these are people you're going to like. That's because they've done the work to prevent "flaws" from standing in the way. The same can't be said of upstate New York, where directly relating to other humans requires first putting a bag over their head. In fact, I carry a handful of them in my truck so that I can hold a conversation and judge a person's character without all those imperfections getting in the way.

Sense any sarcasm? When it comes to being a looks-driven culture, Miami is far from the exception; it's just an exceedingly good example of the norm. This American norm (and increasingly it's international—when did the British start having straight teeth?) isn't just evident in our advertising models or in our love for stupidly good-looking musicians and actors, it's a phenomenon that's deeply permeated the cultivation of everyday personal appearances. Case in point: social media. Scroll the feeds from amateur and professional posters: The images have gone through a selection process (of dozens of photographs), and then pass through a post-production of cutting, cropping, Photoshopping, and enhancing. The purpose of all of this, of course, is the same as with any advertisement: Instantly appeal and control the message. But what is it about our culture that makes this necessary? Why can't we appeal and communicate directly with flaws in the way? Is our culture really that shallow?

This approach is *exactly* the thinking behind Modern wine: After the flaws have been airbrushed out, consumers will better see the wine's character. But how ironic is that! It's like saying people will be able to see the real me if I were just to clean up and look like Barbie or Ken. This desire to look polished doesn't just rule the visual aesthetic of wine making; it has become its taste, too. Viewed from the distance of time, the eradication of flaws may very well be the defining character of current-day wines.

I took a class back when the second Bush was still president, "Identifying and Preventing Wine Flaws." For those unfamiliar with the term, a *wine flaw* is one of dozens of spoilages that upset the balance of an other-wise desirable drink profile. More often than not, a flaw is caused by a microorganism colonization that imparts a foul note or ester. In the class I remember tasting through wine samples that were jarring: wines that tasted like the bottle was home to a mouse nest, wines that reminded me of nail polish, and wines that smelled like a wrung-out T-shirt worn by Chewbacca after a hot night of heavy drinking in Tijuana. This class started to feel like a *Clockwork Orange* training session, preparing students to take up arms against something. But what?

When biology is to blame, as it usually is, it puts the winemaker in a catch-22, because the fertility that encourages good yeasts can be the same fertility that causes bad microbes. After sitting in class for a day listening to theories on how to control the life in wine, I got the sense I was listening to theories on stomach probiotic health: I was hearing conflicting reports from doctors who claimed to know the answers, and did so with such vehemence that it bordered on religiosity, but in the end they couldn't all be right. With wine the consequences are less dire to our health (perhaps), but it still leaves the question unresolved: For what are we so concerned? Is it just for "bad" notes? And could this judgment call just be a cultural hang-up? Is it all in our minds?

I still don't know the answer to this, and I'm also still torn on how I'm supposed to proceed. I want to believe the inevitable biology of wine to be a natural and good thing, but I also trust my instincts when I think something tastes bad. Miami, of all places, actually helps to clear this up for me. There I know that the beauty aesthetic is the result of cultural conditioning, and I also know with 100 percent certainty that many forms of beauty are overlooked by this culture. And so this is the attitude I try to bring to wine-flaw theory: I've attempted to appreciate, even find beauty in, what's being grossly overlooked.

Over the years I've subjected myself to my own *Clockwork Orange* training, and I can claim some success in the reconditioning. This is especially true of flaws that are earthy and farmy in character. Anyone who's ever had real (non-industrial) French or English farm cider knows that those barnyard and briny notes are part of their charm. They ride alongside the profile of the finished apple like dolphins to a race boat, adding glee in an interaction that would otherwise feel mechanical. Those notes enhance the drink, rather than detracting from it, so to my mind removing those flaws entirely (although I'm open to lessening them in some instances) would be to assimilate those ciders with lesser drinks. And the same can be said of vinegar-esque Spanish ciders and of the acetone-like Quebec / New England ciders (the natural ones) where the things people consider flaws are actually benchmarks of character. They complement the drink (if the drink is worthy of being complemented).

It doesn't take a genius to realize that our tendencies in one practice are transferable to other parts of our lives. Just as with our apple agriculture, just as with our business culture, the microbial culturing that we practice in wine- and cider making is one and the same, consistent also with the way we make it through daily existence—that, too, is a practice. The question is: Are we challenging ourselves with this culture? Are you so set in your plans that you can't look other subway riders in the eye, lest your whole day be detoured? Are we trying to accept more, or are we trying to box out? And where does that leave us on the topic of discovering character through challenge? When we approach a drink, are we trying to meet it on its own terms, warts and all, or are we trying to church it up with a shave and makeup to present a constructed image?

You'd best believe the latter is more often the case. It's apparent in our daily wine choices as much as at the highest level of wine criticism. We dive into a drink not to engage with it, but more like building inspectors looking for something not up to code. This predates the winemaker. Naturally, wine and cider producers will end up building the same structures again and again, strengthening this approach, and soon we will find that our wines have become the vacant equivalent of mannequins.

Look, no one is saying that spoilage is desirable. Foul-tasting microbial colonization, foul-smelling compounds and chemical taints—they *do* distract from the experience of cider. Again, the goal of cider is to see the life of the apple reborn in a glass, not to celebrate the dominance of a particular microorganism. Still, there is something fundamentally unnatural about our exclusion of flaws. The word itself is alarming. As a now-converted wild apple grower, it reminds me of *weeds* and *bugs*; I've discovered both to be more beneficial than detrimental. What's good for the goose is good for the gander, and I can't help but think flaws might actually contain moments of beauty that we just haven't figured a way to see yet. If we judge our ciders and wines like we judge ourselves, character is tied to the whole. That includes flaws.

PART III

Between Living and Making a Living

SEVEN

Growing Business

I was an artist first, a homestead farmer second, and a cider maker third. Nowhere in that sequence would I insert "businessman" into the equation. To me, business was about money, and many pursuits (particularly artistic pursuits) needed to be protected from this corrupting force. Business taints the pure development of our craft, it contaminates our relationships and makes us distrustful of one another, it forces us to compromise our ideals, and ultimately it consumes our precious time. This opinion of business was especially fueled by my experience in the art world. Other artists would snicker and call your work "professional" when they sensed you were pandering to the audience, playing it safe, or sticking to a formula. Artists often feel obligated to defend talent and creativity (two things money can't buy) against business pressures. We were extra careful not to collaborate with wealthy clients. Nothing is worse than a sellout.

But one night the ghost of an old homestead farmer came to me and my opinion on the subject was changed. Sharing our labors, and getting compensated for it, have always been integrated within this type of living, which is also a form of business. Does anyone associate a homestead farmer with the greed of today's business leaders? Why should we suffer the stigma? Small farm businesses not only predate the insatiable growth of modern businesses, they are one of the better examples where income is incorporated into the whole of the operation. In other words: The pay is part of the farm, *not* the reason for it. By accepting money, putting it back into our cultivations, we are making our living with the land, not "off the land" (a phrase I hate), and completing a looped relationship.

Money, as repellent as it first sounded to me, is our culture's main way of putting back into agriculture.

Rather than retreat from it, I was excited by the idea of having business enrich my experience on the farm. Many of history's best artists came from cultures that supported the arts—fifteenth-century Florence, late-nineteenth-century Paris, and ancient Greece and Rome are clear examples—but was it possible that modernity could support a cider artisan like the culture of eighteenth-century America? If I opened up, engaged in business, could I become a better cider maker and a better apple grower? I was excited to try.

However, my business didn't start so simply. In fact, it started as a complete failure under another name, The Cidery (an obscure word in America at the time). I blame the fact that I began my business education just as I began my agricultural education, and art education before that: by following the advice of professionals, books, and academic programs (classes). This path is not uncommon; in fact it's pretty much what all students follow when learning about something new, and I had no knowledge to challenge it. But I later found that I was being led farther from where my personal goals lay. My professional cultivation—which is what it was—mistakenly focused on success within the "outside" world; I was encouraged to look "centripetally," to figure how my craft related to greater and greater spheres. But my art process was always a *centrifugal* one: My successes were always achieved by relating the outside to myself. This was the blind-sight destined to frustrate my educators and so-called experts.

Oh, I tried to keep up at first. I looked into equipment and facilities that would allow me to increase production, because it's automatically assumed "growing larger and making more" is the future of any successful enterprise. I talked to large-scale farmers about securing an apple source, and I participated in trade associations determined to grow the whole sector's production as well, but the main thing that attracted me to this world, the old ways of growing and making cider, was disappearing as my business grew. I found myself cutting corners and becoming frustrated with "the job." Finally, when I weighed the advantages of business growth against the connection I enjoyed with apple trees, it was clear the jig was up. For me, things had become unrecognizable, and I got the strong sense that the booming industry's growth wasn't the desired evolution, either. How could I support the thing tearing me away from an intimacy with the trees?

There will always be pressure to conform to conventional models for success, but it's also a mistake to retreat from business or concede to pennilessness. The conventional model doesn't "own" business or financial success any more than convention's idealized woman owns beauty. Sticking true to another vision—withdrawing into art—can, in fact, attract alternative forms of cultural support. Led by those principles, money can even help develop the arts, not ruin them.

2008: The Year of the False Start

Early spring, 2008. Just about the time America was waking up to the impending recession, I found out about a state grant/loan program designed to help small farmers and local start-ups. I said to myself: *Hey, I'm both these things, I got a real shot at that money.* This was also the year taxpayers were forced to swallow government bailouts of private businesses. I had always thought ag grants and loans showed favoritism or bias, plus they were disruptive to market pricing, but surely this level of intervention couldn't measure up against the bailouts given to the largest banks, insurance, and auto companies. This was the new reality, so why not try for some of that taxpayer money myself?

I filled out an application with the county economic development office and they soon sent me a letter saying that I had won the grant. Or so I thought. When I showed up to attend the required training course, I found out that I was just one of 100 other "winners," and the earmarked money was limited to $200,000. Next, the officials announced that with 100 people eligible, only about 10 of us were going to see a portion of that, so the average grant recipient would get about $20,000. And then more news: This training course was 10 weeks long and it wasn't free. Each of us had to pay $100 for the *opportunity* to win the grant/loan money. Luckily, 10 people, feeling duped and angry, walked out then and there, bringing the odds of winning down to one in nine. Those of us who stuck around attended classes presented by local business owners, banks, venture capitalists, regulators, and county officials. They were known as The Team, and their mission was to help us craft a business plan worthy of winning the award money and/or finding some other funder of our business. For the next 10 weeks I was going to be a businessman-in-training.

It was never my goal to be an exclusive high-end cider producer. This reputation was assigned to me largely because of the dismal state of cider from 2008 to 2012. All I wanted was to make well-made plain ol' country cider, simply because I didn't know where else to find it in stores. We knew lots of folks up here in the Catskills (and where Polly's family is from, in Maine and New Hampshire) who had barrels and jugs of the same kind of stuff in their basements, but why wasn't plain cider in stores? Sure, there were cans of "hard cider" around, but that drink bears hardly any similarities to the drink I'm talking about, the one very common throughout apple hill country. It's nothing fancy, it's just table wine: dry, bright, earthy, and tannic, only slightly carbonated (if at all), and usually hazy from yeast and apple sediment. But in my research the only cider examples I could find were factory-made, not farm-made. These hard ciders were usually sold in cans, not in jugs or wine bottles, and the apples they used were leftovers from the commodity apple market. Their apple sources were far and wide and very rarely from the same region—much less the same region the producer was in.

Step one of the business plan was to research this industry. The Team wanted me to look up data on cider and call as many cider producers as possible, asking for their sales and production figures (like this was a normal thing shared among businesses). Unfortunately, assertiveness is not my specialty and I got very little help in my responses, except from one farm-based cider producer who made it clear to me that they were going to switch over to beer production just as soon as they got their brewer's license. The research phase was off to a bad start.

The biggest problem was that I couldn't find examples or figures from cider companies that made the type of cider I made. All the data was lumped into one sector, hard cider, and I wasn't yet aware of good role models that could have served as isolated examples in my business plan. The research was leading me toward the realization that cider—as a beverage category—was poorly defined (not that it's much better today). I didn't locate the simpaticos that in retrospect might have given the plan legs, and so long as mass-produced industrial cider data was lumped in with real farm cider data, how was I, or anyone, to know if the business was viable?

This worried The Team, who set out to craft my business plan using *only* concrete examples of cider success. They were especially concerned about the number of apples I intended to grow and forage. The solution, said The Team, was to do both. They wanted me to make the cider I wanted to make, but to offset this naturally small volume with cider from apples grown at large commercial orchards. It's called economy of scale. And I needed cans. Research showed hard cider customers think they are getting a better deal in this format; plus it reconfirms a link to the profitable beer market and not the slow-growing, stodgy wine industry.

I was watching my vision of my cider bend to the expectations and advice of the professionals: My little barn, less than 400 square feet, was going to need to be upgraded with an extension and a loading dock; I needed new electrical hookups and a separate meter; I needed new and expensive stainless steel equipment to do my cider making in; I needed employees to work under me; I needed insurance for them; I needed training on regulation compliance and managerial responsibilities; I needed a marketing specialist, an accountant, distributors, and sales reps. At this point I had no idea if the cider was even going to sell, but if I wanted to find out I needed to shell out the big-boy money. Said and done, The Team determined I needed $113,000 to get started.

This was based on a minimum of 10,000 gallons of production per year. And it was based on a retail price that was in keeping with, or only slightly higher than, the industry standard. My six-pack of cans had to retail at about $12 to customers, while my "other cider," the one I wanted to make from homegrown or foraged apples, could sell for a little more, although it was assumed to be at a loss given the labor that went into it. It was all about scale, and my volumes had to rise to 50,000 gallons in the coming years, and the canned cider was truly what my business would revolve around.

But with a maximum of $20,000 available from the grant money— assuming I won the funds—I was still in need of nearly six figures to get started with this plan, and finding an investor or lender was my only option. I spent much of the first half of 2008 attending class, doing research, and writing—all at the expense of time spent out in my orchard. All the while I was working two part-time jobs, and in the end I had a business plan that, alas, was denied the award money. For the rest of the year my plan sat on the desk of the county economic development office while they and I were hoping it could gain the interest of a bank or venture capitalist willing to fund the full amount. But in the fall of 2008 the stock market officially crashed, and nobody wanted to take a chance on my vision.

And thank God. I can't say I didn't learn something valuable with this experience, but I couldn't be less cut out for running the business like the one I wrote out on paper that year. *That* type of business (which is really just a *formula* for success) would have crushed me. I lose sleep over a simple credit card bill—imagine the wreck I'd be paying investors $1,000 a month in interest alone! Or having employees to manage, and production quotas to fill! I wanted to sell cider because it was part of my life; I wasn't looking for a life sentence. A business formula such as this would have been the equivalent of wearing down a square peg to fit a round hole, and my personality is such that the compromise would have created unrest within me. I couldn't put the plan before myself, and the plan couldn't work with me in front. It was doomed to fail.

Spirits

The start of 2009 felt like the start of the Great Depression. The stock market had just crashed and a dull, uneasy feeling hung in the air like a late Sunday afternoon. There was no escape behind the orchard walls, either. Not our farmwork, nor even a walk in the woods, could keep the mess of the outside world from pressing in on us. That's not what "home" is.

Just a few years earlier, when we bought the farm, we felt as though we'd made it. Polly and I had served a collective 25 years in the subways, coming and going from nine to five, and having our sleep disrupted by car alarms and city noise. With dutiful savings and with our growing IRA investments, we were certain we had achieved the financial security that allowed us to start a new life on the farm in Wurtsboro. We had no idea how exposed we were.

Our perilous situation started with the housing market in 2007. The value of our home fell significantly below what we'd paid for it, erasing our 30 percent down payment and nullifying equity. Then, when the stock market collapsed, too, our available cash and retirement nest egg fell like Humpty Dumpty. Our debt now outweighed our savings, and without urban income to ride out the storm, our dream of country living had turned into a cold-sweat nightmare. In fact, just to live on the farm was costing us twice what we made each month.

We tried to find work in the county, but the rural local economy was depressed even before the stock market crash, so despite a combined 14 years of post-graduate work, and several master's degrees, Polly and I could only find part-time jobs in unrelated industries. Collecting from five scattered sources of income, we saw our debt ratio rise only slightly, but it was still much lower than our living expenses. There was nowhere else to look. Except home.

To turn to farming as a possible savior felt ludicrous, but we had no other choice. Nothing illustrates poverty better than Dust Bowl images of farmers during the Great Depression. But in the 70 years since the Depression, the association between being poor and farming had only grown. Workers were reduced to supporting roles on industrialized farms performing dirty, dangerous, unhealthy, and economically thankless jobs. They worked twice the hours for a fraction of the pay.

On January 17, 2009, a week after my 38th birthday, I woke before the sun and directed the flashlight out through the frost-covered window to read the porch thermometer: -15°F, an exclamation point to a year of lows.

The sun retires beyond the western ridge by 5 PM in February. There is still a working 45 minutes of cobalt-blue sky before it's totally dark, and at that hour an amber glow emanating from the windows of the house contrasts against the cool, electric color of the atmosphere, giving beauty to both the interior and exterior worlds. The bare old maple trees appear as black silhouettes against the first stars in the sky. Their branches cast a network of bony shadows across the snow cover. It is a lonely scene, here. But a good kind of lonely.

I bring in tonight's fire logs. Polly is preparing an extra trout that a neighbor brought by earlier. Paul had a good day ice fishing but he probably shouldn't have been driving. As I work the two cast-iron stoves at opposite ends of the house, I can hear the fish skin sizzle in the pan.

The smell mixes with parsnips, garlic, and other herbs. It's now time to pick out the table wine: cider. We keep it in half-gallon jugs stored in the cellar, which presents a bit of a challenge getting to it. I must go around the side of the house to the cellar's only access: bulkhead doors, which are now snow-covered.

I suit up in the mudroom, which does not benefit from a heat source. My boots are cold. Then I pull open the outside door and am met with prickly air that feels like a splash of cold water across my face, the effect of a wake-up slap. The path around the side of the house is exactly as wide as my snow shovel, and it's now the depth of 14 inches. Hardened like canyon walls from the thawing and refreezing of snow, this path glistens in the moonlight. When I get to the bulkhead, I lean over to brush off the new dusting that accumulated over the previous night. I use my gloves. Throwing open the double bulkhead doors, I peer down the stairwell to where another door encloses the cellar. It's black as onyx underground, but I make my way down the steps, through the bottom door, and close myself in, keeping out the cold. There's not even the slightest bit of light now; nothing can serve as my bearings. Feeling around for familiar bumps in the stone walls, I navigate toward the center of the room where I know a pull-chain is dangling from the cellar's only lightbulb. With a tug, 200 years of history comes into view: a low ceiling of hand-hewn beams and a dirt floor. Spiderwebs drape the corners where the light won't reach.

Along the base of one wall are the carboys from 2008. But 2007 was such a good apple year that we still have plenty to drink. I'll leave that newer vintage to sleep in the 5-gallon glass jugs until I free up enough growlers to bottle it. Air locks are poised to omit gas, but there's no activity during this cold spell. The dark amber ciders appear clear above a 1-inch-thick layer of compacted yeast sediment, the lees.

Along another wall are shelves with Mason jars full of Polly's garden stores: everything from pickled string beans to homemade kimchi to applesauce, all canned safely under sealed lids. I know them to taste great, but in a scary old basement lit only by a single bulb (shadows as harsh as if from an interrogation light) these jars look like weird science specimens. They could be medical oddities from the Mütter Museum in Philadelphia. I look away.

I find what I came for on the third wall, my 2007 cider hiding within stacks of cardboard boxes. I was careless not to put a vapor barrier between them and the damp floor and stone walls, so now a three-dimensional mold grows on the surface of the light brown boxes, making them appear bone gray. I peel back the limp cardboard, grab two growlers, and head back to the center of the room beside the dangling light chain. Taking a moment to get my bearings before summoning the darkness, I yank again and carefully step back toward the door.

It was at this particular stage of my nightly cider-fetching routine that I experienced a life-changing event. Having shut the bottom door behind me, I made my way up the stairwell to the open bulkhead doors where the nighttime sky was comparably brighter and coming into focus. As I took my first step out at ground level I could see everything: every tree in the moonlit orchard, every rock in the stone walls, every shadow across the snow. A timeless beauty filled me with appreciation. Then, suddenly, I became possessed.

I don't know how else to say it: It was like an intense déjà vu came over me—*I have been here before*. But it wasn't "me" who was here; it was someone else's memory as much as it was my own eyes looking at this world. We were *both* here before, and we've always been here.

People say they believe in reincarnation; people say that a person's soul continues to live on as other people after they die. I even once had a man tell me he was a Confederate soldier in another life, but I don't believe any of that. To me, ghost stories are a sure way of filtering the crazies and the overly passionate from society; I avoid ghost conversations like I avoid talking about religion. But there are times on the farm when I tune out all the distant sounds of cars and airplanes and find myself acutely focused on the wind in my ears and the sensation of temperature. Pruning the trees in the winter, for instance, brings me into this trance-like state. And when I sink into that groove, when I become completely *in the moment* with my work, I get an unworldly feeling that I am leaving my body. It's haunting. But it's beautiful.

Perhaps I've been interpreting people too literally when they say they believe in ghosts or reincarnation? Perhaps I've misunderstood their claims when what they really are experiencing is an authentic connection with history or an acute sympathy with other lives? Life is a river, extending beyond our time. That, I can believe.

When I tell you this, I'm not claiming to be physically possessed by the ghost of an old homestead farmer, but I am saying that I'm experiencing something that somebody else experienced—take what you will of that. I've had similar déjà vu experiences since my experience at the top of the cellar stairs that night, and pruning apple trees, for whatever reason, especially brings them out. I *know* that there are ghosts here at this old homestead, but they are good ghosts. They have reached out to me and included me in their realm. I *am* this place now.

That's what home is.

2009: The Year of the Basher Kill

My initial plans for a farm cidery dashed, I gave up on the Monopoly Man or Uncle Sam jump-starting my cider business for me. We returned to the day-to-day farm stuff and plowed along with our part-time jobs. But our faith in cider, the pure and simple drink, never diminished. It became more of who we were with each passing night as we consumed it. The dream of sharing our cider never died.

That winter, the "Hope" president had just been sworn in and the stock market finally stopped tanking. For almost a year our savings and retirement funds had been stomped out like a teen's cigarette butt under the foot of the hall moderator, but finally it now appeared that the markets had reached their low and had stabilized. The irrational and the exuberant could see the glass as half full again.

Strange as it sounds, I found myself similarly optimistic for my cider business in early 2009 when I, too, dropped my lofty expectations and reached a financial low. Without much to lose, the important things stood out more. I saw the base things for starting a business without all the extra niceties; I saw the fundamental work I needed to do without all the complications involved with hiring a staff; most of all I was able to see the resources I already had. It turns out there was help *everywhere*; I just needed to learn how to look.

No greater inspiration could come than simply observing our hometown, tiny Wurtsboro, and how it conducted its business during the

Great Recession. Herb and Traci, for example, had just opened up an independent health-food store when the market crashed. They adjusted by keeping their shelves lean and their infrastructure simple. They couldn't grow their business for lack of capital, and people just weren't spending like they used to, but by developing a personal relationship with each customer, finding out what they wanted, and calling them when the items came in (et cetera, et cetera), they created a loyalty that made the clientele go out of their way to support them, even when similar items were cheaper elsewhere.

And then there was Paul, sole employee and proprietor of the new vineyard across the Bashakill from our house. Polly and I heard about the vineyard but never knew exactly where it was, having driven by dozens of times without noticing the rows of grapes being put in. It turns out we were transfixed in the opposite direction. The Bashakill (or Basher Kill—*kill* means "creek" in Dutch) is a lot more peaceful than its name suggests: It's a wetlands formed by a dammed creek, and it's now a protected nature preserve—home to bald eagles, great blue herons, and osprey. (So, yeah, it's nice to look at.) Finally vowing to visit the winery one winter's day, we found the sign in a residential area and rolled up the driveway toward a two-car garage and a door with a sign: OPEN.

Where the hell are we?—we thought. Even having followed two signs, it felt like we were intruding on someone's home, and when we opened the tasting room door we found ourselves right in the middle of a conversation among four strangers to us.

We made our way past them, disrupting the dialogue, and took an awkward seat at the far corner of the bar. *Maybe nobody will notice?* But there was no room for invisibility at the newly opened, sparsely populated Bashakill Winery, especially not with 6-foot-10 Keith towering above. Extroverted, confident, and perhaps three sheets to the wind, Keith's forceful sentences ended in punctuation like a finger-poke to the chest. We were 75 miles from the nation's great melting pot, a place where you never know who you'll offend, but Keith couldn't give a shit about other people's sensitivities, and naturally I kept quiet for fear of inciting an anti-liberal rant. But Keith, we soon found out, is a goodhearted soul, and many of his opinions stem from him being the protector type. He insisted on drawing us into the conversation, and it was Keith, not Paul, who introduced us to winery regulars: Smiling Joe (because Italians need to know which Joe they are talking about); Christine (Paul's vampy childhood friend—also from Jersey); Elwood (who looks circa 1957, exactly like an Elwood is supposed to look); and then, of course, Paul.

A Larger Symbiosis

In my mind a healthy culture or ecology is one in which community members support one another in a circular pattern, not a linear path as in a hierarchy. If a bird eats the bug that eats the tree, then the tree ought to support the bird so that it's not just it versus the bug. Another example of community support, speaking of birds, is when birds take naps. Being light little creatures, bones as fragile as toothpicks, they can't survive the slightest violence. Be it a predator or the falling of a tree branch, they need to keep watch. When my ducks are napping, they tend to take turns sleeping and won't close their eyes until they see someone else has their eyes open. But it's not just the other ducks they are on the lookout with: Blue jays and rabbits will also send the alarm, and our ducks have become assimilated within the wild culture, too. In fact, I've seen the wild animals adjust in reverse: They come to the duck yard to take naps and even sleep around me, knowing that the ducks don't perceive me as a threat. Of Irish descent, I can't be "made" (if you get the Italian mafia reference); the animals still keep me at a distance, but my ducks have sponsored me and they are all unusually relaxed around me. I've been made privy to a secret society.

All this relates to human culture and apple culture, I promise you. It relates both to our individual ecologies and to our combined role in the broader ecosystem. Think of health. Apple growers can foster both good and bad health in people, and they can do this for the trees, too. They are not unrelated. A healthy community of trees helps keep an eye on insects and disease pressure, and just like the ducks they will signal one another to prompt an immune response when threats arise. (Credit the modern forestry community, not apple growers, for most of these discoveries.) So it's up to an apple grower to observe the broader ecosystem and promote *its* methods of communication. The primary method is simply to *not* break the system of communication, for a disconnected system begets further bad health, which ultimately makes us unhealthy. A severed system forces farmers to hand-pollinate, spray antibiotics, fungicides, insecticides—all that.

But it works in reverse as well: An all-around healthy human society will create a healthy agriculture, too. I'm not just talking about our physical health here, and in fact mental health is one of the better examples. Someone famously said: "Neurosis is a contagious disease." (If you've ever lived in New York City, you know *exactly* what that means. And stock market panics are another example.) But interestingly, an orchard culture is evidence of this hand-me-down mental health. When the trees are living in fear of the outside world, when they are without good communication with it or with one another, and they have grown dependent on human intervention, this condition has arisen out of a parallel human psyche: Farmers feel isolated from the larger culture, they feel in competition with the market and with other farmers, and they are increasingly dependent on government or outside intervention—how could they *not* transfer these pressures onto the trees? It's like when the boss dumps on you, and you dump that on another driver on your way home from work—next thing you know you're propagating a whole culture of road rage—flattening animals, eating poorly, careening along toward the next dump site. Where does the buck stop? It doesn't, it just rototills back into the food chain.

Expenses

Paul's my age. He grew up down in Jersey but used to spend his summers at his grandparents' house just outside Wurtsboro. In his 20s he was trained as a mechanic (a skill that's still a passion), but he later got a better-paying job in the IT department for some company down in the suburbs. He said he didn't know what he was saving his money for exactly, but he always knew this is where he'd end up.

A born outdoorsman and productive in nature, he likes having something to show for his efforts, which include hunting, horticulture, and fishing. Then one day the house across from us on the Bashakill boat launch came on the market and he knew in an instant what he wanted. It was time to take action. He bought the property and immediately mapped out his acreage and plans for a winery. He was off and running like his Italian greyhound who soon patrolled the vines for rabbits.

Though he didn't have much money left over after buying the property, and that he didn't invest in vines and fencing, he sank into converting the two-car garage into a production facility and tasting room. When Polly and I walked in that winter's day, it looked more like a man cave than a tasting room, but Paul saw nothing wrong with this. In fact, it's precisely the world he wanted to live in at the time, a place where he and his friends could hang out, maybe meet some new people and make a little money. What's wrong with that? I, on the other hand, had the predisposed impression that wineries were luxury businesses started by rich landowners or entrepreneurs good at spending other people's money. Maybe they were tax shelters or wedding venues and not actual farms, but I saw them mostly as places of privilege and fantasy. And although this was a gross generalization, it was, until then, in keeping with my experience of wineries.

When pressed about this Paul told me, "It's just wine, remember." Shrugging, he continued, "I had no money after I bought the property but all I needed was a farm-winery license and that's practically free. It's got me this far—what you see now—but maybe it will grow into something else; we'll see."

I was captivated at how relaxed about business he was. We told him of our plans to make cider and he couldn't have been more supportive. I had already planted several hundred trees by this point, so he was impressed with my seriousness. And although we were just a mile apart (as the crow flies), not one ounce of competiveness emerged from him as I eventually zeroed in on my plans at securing the same farm-winery license. To the contrary, Paul helped me over time and recapped the steps he took in starting out.

We first needed to form either an LLC or a DBA business entity, because the winery application requires such. The former, the LLC, would require a lawyer, which would run us about $1,200, but it would give us more legal protections; the latter, the DBA, was a simple form I could turn in at the county office, plus $20, and it's instantly done. Good enough for me. Then we needed to submit a farm-winery application with the

TTB, the federal government's Tax and Trade Bureau, which oversees alcohol regulation. Because organized crime long ago controlled alcohol distribution in America, there are still a million regulatory hoops to jump through, including getting fingerprinted, but otherwise it's not very hard. I needed to draw a map of the "winery premises" for their records, and we needed to purchase a $100 bond (securing whatever that secures). Plus we needed to submit tests for alcohol levels and submit cider labels for approval (they have very tight rules on wording that, dare I say, ill fit true cider). But in the end, if we complied with all the rules there was no reason to think we couldn't get the license in a few months—for a fee of $200.

It's that easy, said Paul, except now we would have to do the same thing again for the state liquor regulators (plus another $400 fee to New York State). And as far as basic expenses were concerned: Plastic fermenting barrels cost about $60 and used oak barrels cost about $100. Paul said we'd need a pump with hoses (about $400), but that was really about it. "Put a lock on the door and wait for the inspector to come and tell you what else they want to see."

Neither Paul, nor I, had fruit from our new plantings by this point. His solution was to buy grapes and juice from the Finger Lakes ($10 to $20 per gallon), and I found local sources for apple juice in the Hudson Valley to be considerably cheaper, between $2 and $3 per gallon (from culinary apples, of course—no one sold cider varieties at the time). The costs in fall amounted to less than the springtime expenses, which included bottles, labels, corks, and corker, plus I needed to buy a filling machine for $600. (This machine sucked, by the way; I ended up selling it and buying the one I have now, which cost $1,800.) In total, it looked like we were going to spend about $9,000 for our first year, making 500 gallons. And as we eventually sold through this cider (still without a license), our plan was to take profits and reinvest them in better equipment. Ultimately, and by my calculations, we could live off a consistent production of 2,000 gallons per year, not the 50,000 that The Team had predicted was a bare minimum for cider production.

In the darkest days of our greatest financial insecurity, $9,000 was still a lot of money to us. And as table 7.1 shows, I underestimated the actual costs, but I was able to spread the expenses over several years while selling cider on the sly. Nonetheless, that amount of money felt like a high stakes

Table 7.1. Expenses, Starting a Micro-Cidery

Category	Type of Expense	Approximate Costs (dollars)
Corks (cages) / caps	Bag of 1,000 Belgian beer corks (3 at $130 each)	390
	Box of 2,700 caps (biduled for méthode champenoise) (2 at $250 each)	500
	Box of 2,700 cages (2 at $150 each)	300
Capper/corker	Italian floor corker designed for champagne corks (2 at $150 each)	300
	Universal capper (also used for installing wire-cage)	90
Bottle filler	Enola vacuum filler (optional for bottling tiny batches)	350
	Stainless five-spout filler	1,800
Filtration	Filter unit with filters (an unnecessary option)	
Bottles/kegs	Champagne glass (250 cases at $12 each, $700 for shipping)	3,700
	Wine bottle / beer bottle (less heavy)	
	Kegs / keg accessories	
Labels	Peel-off stickers (two sided) (6,000 labels at $0.20 each)	1,200
	Roll label machine (purchased later for $1,800)	
Apple juice	50% bought (300 gallons at $3 each), 50% grown (free-ish)	900
Additions	Yeast, SO$_2$, yeast nutrient ($100, optional)	
	Finings, sugar, other lab additions ($100, optional)	
Fermenting vats	55-gallon plastic vats (12 at $60 each, $400 for shipping)	1,120
Aging tanks/ barrels	55-gallon used oak barrels (400 gallons) (7 barrels at $120 each)	840
	Glass carboys for small batches (includes shipping)	1,000
Other	Air locks	20
	Pumps	350
	Hoses	50
APPROXIMATE EQUIPMENT COSTS*		12,910

Federal TTB	$100 for $1,000 bond, $1.07/gallon tax (~$0.90 small) = 100	200
Lab fee	University wine analysis	100
State NY	Farm winery ($175 per year), market fee ($130)	305
State excise / sales tax	NY excise ($180), sales tax ($700)	880
Insurance	Insurance on property	600
LLC	File for LLC by lawyer ($1,500), DBA filing ($30)	1,500
APPROXIMATE WHITE-COLLAR CRIMINAL COSTS		**3,585**
Building rent	In our case: land taxes and portion of overall mortgage	6,000
Sinks/ plumbing	Three-bay sink, faucets, plumbing	500
HVAC	Insulation, AC, CoolBot, electric heater	1,000
Waterproofing / food safety	Plastic panels, light covers, sealant, etc.	300
Utility bill	Electric	840
Security	Locks, etc.	20
APPROXIMATE FACILITY COSTS		**8,660**
Web presence	Facebook, Twitter, web host (basic)	100
Advertising	Business cards, pamphlets (5,000 count)	600
Farmers markets	Booth fees ($500), umbrella, props ($600)	1,100
Wholesale cut	Typical wholesale rate is ~30% bottle price	
Organizations	Cider associations, events	800
UPS/shipping	Boxes, protection, freight ($500, optional)	
BUSINESS COSTS		**2,600**
APPROXIMATE TOTAL FOR FIRST YEAR START-UP		**27,755**

Note: This table shows our actual costs during our first few years selling cider (minus all agriculture costs). Over time we have figured out how to eliminate some of those expenses but any new businesses should factor in some "learning costs."

The figures in this table are (1) for equipment that is entry level, designed for no more than ~2,000 gallons per year, (2) based on 600 gallons producing 250 cases or 3,000 bottles (750 ml), and (3) a mix of annual and one-time costs. Legal fees, service, and rents will vary from state to state.

* Equipment fees can be spread over multiple years.

poker move. We were just going to have to bluff our way through at first: *Dress for the job you want, not the job you have.* Soon people were going to start calling us a business. And by the end of the year, 2009, we had our winery application submitted to the federal government.

Table 7.1 was compiled in collaboration with Steve Gougeon of Bear Swamp Cidery (Ashfield, Massachusetts) in 2014. Annually, we hosted a talk during Franklin County CiderDays called, "So You Want to Be a Commercial Cider Maker?" Both Bear Swamp Orchard and the Aaron Burr Cidery are microscopic by even small-winery standards, with 5 acres of apples and producing approximately 2,000 gallons per year. Some states recognize this as a micro-winery and tax the wines and ciders less (the average small winery by comparison makes about 20,000 gallons per year).

Some attendees were (and are) critical of the fact that two micro-cideries were offering advice to budding commercial cider makers. (We have an "impractical model," they would say.) But the Gougeons and Polly and I share a conviction that cider production should be farm-based (and should especially be viable for small farms), and we make no bones about the fact that this is a separate type of cider—one that should not be considered akin to the average "tap-room" cider or canned ciders, which are conceived for very different reasons, and a different type of cider business. The primary similarity small-farm cider has to those types of businesses is the desire to serve the local population with a drink that is rightly their local table wine. But a major division arises when considering how this goal is best reached. Whereas some producers want to make more cider, the Gougeons and we feel it's best to encourage thousands and thousands of other small producers to provide that volume instead. Our model is based on a scale limitation and we want to see others adopt similar principles.

There is more to this argument:

Company A makes 200,000 gallons per year and might employ 20 full-time workers. This equates to 1 employee per 10,000 gallons of cider.

Company B makes 2,000 gallons per year and has 1 full-time employee (both companies need occasional helpers that I'm not including). This equates to 1 employee per 2,000 gallons (which per gallon is only one-fifth the volume of Company A's example).

So if 100 micro-producers each made 2,000 gallons of cider, bringing their volume up to equal Company A's production (200,000 gallons), then they would employ five times the number of people. *And* the employees would be owners of their business (fully invested in the company), not just employees serving a single owner or outside investors.

Company A claims that they have the ability to lower the price for the customer. We can't dispute this, but we can trump it with a better argument. Given our human advantage (100 employees instead of 20), Company B's are able to have a much greater impact on numerous local economies instead of just one, and offer 100 times the artistic expression to customers. *And* apples from individual farms and microclimates would be free from homogenization. This allows the land and farmer to sing without being blended into white noise. Perhaps a cider industry comprising thousands of micro-producers would never be able to offer the same kind of cost savings as Company A, but the product diversity of Company B's makes for a far better trade-off: Environmentally, culturally, economically, artistically, and ethically, the limited-scale Company B's are the better choice for cider.

2010: The Year of New England

If starting a business at the height of financial insecurity was a gamble, the whole of 2010 unfolded like our all-in hand for us. At stake was the real possibility of losing our savings and home. But the stress of trying to launch a business also meant risking our psychological health, risking even our relationship and losing touch with what's important. While awaiting approval for our federal wine license, our financial security dangled by a thread and it felt like any day could be our last afloat. It was nail-biting. Stuck in the state of limbo, we couldn't improve our situation without the green light. It was in this state that we learned Polly had cancer. We had to fold.

Looking to the future was not an option at this point. During the beginning stages of treatment, our focus was entirely on the job at hand, beating the illness. What had been localized as financial worries now consumed the whole of our lives. It was all-encompassing: worry, as a state of being.

The nature of cancer and cancer treatment, as it unfolds in hospitals, insurance bills, waiting rooms, and on living room couches, is a tedium of uncertainty dotted with flashes of anger or acute despair. It unfolds over many months, and there's never a moment when a doctor can say what's going to happen next. Tests, and more tests, only conclude with their best guesses. It's always a guess. They won't even venture to define the extent of the cancer; instead you just have a bunch of statistics to weigh when deciding the treatment plan. The patient, naturally wanting as little invasion as possible, is given the odds of that route, while the doctor's recommendation is likely to go the other route, with the best statistical scenario. No matter the decision, it's sobering to think Polly's life boiled down to a statistical probability. The weight was indescribable.

In the time between the operation and the chemo we finally got the letter from the government informing us our winery application was denied. *Oh yeah, we were going to start a winery,* was about the extent of my reaction. The Fed was confused about our application; they thought we needed to apply for a "cider producer's license" not a "farm-winery license," but by this point what did it matter? I knew they were wrong about cider (and they continue to regulate it like beer), but I lacked the strength to push forward. We weren't getting help with grant money or loans, the government—as much as I liked Obama—wasn't helping to lower our medical bills, which eclipsed $20,000 by autumn (coincidentally the exact same amount our local government *didn't* give us to start our business), and now federal regulators weren't going to let us proceed with the business, either. If ever there was the feeling of being an outsider, it was then.

Every logical, legal, financial, and physical obstruction to our farm cidery had asserted itself. Still in my 30s, living in a part of the world we had no friendly or family connections to, my wife with cancer, and now with impossibly high medical bills, the farm business seemed fated not to be. And yet the dream of living in a cider landscape still lingered. This is the power of idealism. It provoked me to keep weeding around the base of my newly planted apple trees and discover other people who made their living this way. Even when I tried to put cider out of mind, coincidental observations provided me with lessons. Sometime between my failed 2008 cidery attempt and 2010 I learned to survive setbacks. If something was meant to happen, it would happen. But by then a bond between me and the apple trees ruled my determination, laying out the track for my stuck business. I only needed time and a little serendipity to power the wheel's first spinning.

Polly's parents live in the Monadnock region of New Hampshire, where we annually spend our winter holidays. While she was undergoing cancer treatment, I drove Polly up there during the warm months. The state change helped disassociate us from our troubles, which were, fairly or not, attached to our New York location. But when I was up in New Hampshire, I often felt in the way of family time; plus, being away from the farm made me antsy. So Polly's parents arranged for me to help a local gardener, Roger, to install bird netting around his cherry trees. Roger, it turned out, was not only a famous horticulturalist but also a cider apple grower and had a number of trees in his backyard. I had read about these varieties in the Cummins Nursery catalog, where I had the same varieties on order that year, but here they were, growing in real life. I had a sneak peek into what I was going to plant.

Back in Roger's kitchen after a surprisingly hot New Hampshire day, the horticulturalist opened his refrigerator and pulled out samples of his cider and a jar of vodka-soaked cherries (from the very trees we'd just netted). He popped the caps on the cider and poured it into Mason jars, where the color was intensely richer than anything I'd seen in stores. I told him about my failed business plan and my research into the industry, and Roger was incredulous: "You don't need a license and why do you want to sell cider anyhow? It's always best when you make it for yourself!" Drinking from the Mason jars, I understood what he meant. "Look, you need to come back in autumn and go to the CiderDays festival," Roger continued. "And read Ben Watson's book, *Cider, Hard and Sweet*. He lives right around here. In fact, those are his trees I'm growing for him right there in my backyard!"

Leaving Roger's, driving back through town, I passed a thrift store called Serendipity, where, true to its name, I found Ben Watson's book. But the serendipity didn't end there. The following week we were in New York City for a follow-up surgery, and just outside the hospital doors was a city park with a farmers market in progress. In it, I discovered Eve's Cidery.

And befriending their salesman/orchard helper, Andrew, I was able to take my mind off the worries, passing the waiting room time sipping fine cider and sharing farm experiences. In the heart of the concrete jungle, I found a simpatico obsessed with bittersweet apple trees—so many layers of irony.

But *Cider, Hard and Sweet* brought my attention back to New England. I couldn't wait for CiderDays, which wasn't until November, so I planned a return trip that summer to visit some of the producers mentioned in the book: Farnum Hill, West County Cider, and Flag Hill (Vermont Sparkling Cider). On a three-state tour I found everything I was hoping the cider business to be: mom-and-pop business owners, the cider fermenting at home (in either the basement or the barn), and always the apple trees located just outside the door. I returned to New York inspired to make their life mine, but I also wanted to storm back into my county economic development office and let them know what I thought of their business plan, their delusions of grandeur, and their fetish for industrialization. I now had proof that actual farm cider lived on its own, entirely untethered from the industrial version they'd insisted on.

Then came the weekend I'd been waiting for all year. The Franklin County CiderDays is a two-day event that takes place over numerous locations with overlapping talks and demonstrations. Predating cider's recent popularity by a couple of decades, this event has emerged as the Super Bowl weekend for cider nerds in America. Though I've yet to see face paint, you can often find tailgaters leaning against parked cars with plastic cups in one hand and a tap line in the other leading to a keg in the trunk. In fact, when I arrived in Shelburne Falls, Massachusetts, I parked directly behind this sight, and I knew instantly I was in the motherland.

A 9:30 AM pint of cider delayed me a few minutes from the first talk presented by Canadian cider maker Claude Jolicoeur. Claude is not a commercial producer but instead a true enthusiast. He grows his own apples and makes his own cider, but without a brand he's free to explore the craft with his engineer's training. What stood out about this first talk (and it's still the most inspirational I've heard on cider) was that he wholeheartedly defended what he called "run-down" apples, from wild and long-abandoned trees. This came as a shock to most everyone in the room, people who likely knew of dozens of such trees but never considered them valuable.

And his support for the bacterial condition known as apple scab, as well as for low levels of soil nutrients, sounded almost like a provocation to commercial growers and cider producers. But having a scientist's mind, he came equipped with samples and statistical evidence to prove his assertions.

I also made stops at the annual bring-your-own cider tasting guided by local legends Paul Correnty and Charlie Olchowski, who paid homage to (and made fun of) some of the best and worst ciders unleashed on the planet. They brilliantly picked apart the amateur drink, which reveals New England's regional preference for dry, high-alcohol ciders aged a minimum of one year. I also stopped by Bear Swamp Orchard in nearby Ashfield to view the tasting room and their Oesco milling equipment. I hadn't yet heard of the proprietors of said orchard, but they stole the show for me that weekend. In Steve Gougeon and Jen Williams, Polly and I were witness to a homestead operation exactly our size but operating in calm, patient financial order. They became our heroes as mom-and-pop producers in the Yankee tradition of thrift, do-it-yourself-ness, and taking the long view of farming. And before leaving CiderDays I also met author Michael Phillips, who happened to write my orchard bible, *The Apple Grower*. His holistic (and organic) approach to apple growing is what convinced me it was possible to give up conventional orchard sprays. Meeting Michael, I was eventually introduced to a network of Northeast apple growers that I continue to count as my favorite people on earth, even if we meet up only once or twice a year. I had found my community, and I also found my apple and cider culture.

When I returned to New York, I had the wind at my back: A community was there to support us. I wanted to make better cider, I wanted to help expand a similar culture in lower New York, and we immediately applied for the farm-winery license again, this time under a new name, the Aaron Burr Cidery (don't ask). In 2011 we got that approval. Now we were in business.

If You Want to Make God Laugh, Tell Him Your Plans

You've heard my assessment of "predetermined agriculture": Instead of working with the natural variations and limitations in the soils and climate, growers jack the environment to achieve otherwise unachievable results. I call this the Miracle-Gro compulsion. It's an understandable approach given who and where we are in history, but it does warrant introspection. You want your tomatoes to be one way, but your garden soils will grow them another. Solution? *Pour on the Miracle-Gro.* Could it be there are other solutions? Could you change your expectations, or grow something more suitable? Is buying a bag of synthetic quick-grow fertilizer from the Home Depot what "cultivating our garden" has come to?

For the chase of a predetermined outcome, a similar pour-on-the-Miracle-Gro response dominates *all* the practices of our culture today. From medicine to education, and especially to business, the knee-jerk response is always to manipulate the environment. As an example: It's considered old-fashioned for a business these days to build from just the local resources or to finance its growth from just the earnings. It's *way* more common to plan it all out, acquire a huge capital to turbo-boost the launch, and secure prior commitments, government incentives, and customer hype before the business is even officially in business. It's who we've become: Before taking any steps, the environment must meet with our approval for a predetermined outcome. The environment must adapt, not us.

The conventional approach to agriculture has a perfect brother in the conventional approach to business, and for that matter conventional cider and wine, but on the flip side, parallels could be made between organic agriculture and organic business growth. There is such a thing as a "natural business," although I might not be the one to best describe it.

I, myself, have tried to follow a more natural path (which, needless to say, is a highly subjective quest) into the practice of commercial cider making, but I must confess that when comparing this approach with natural apple growing or natural cider making, running a business organically is harder than the two other practices. Human realities— money, law, insurance, government (all artifices)—make it impossible to break free of artificial inputs. Although they don't exist in nature, they are tangible realities to us now. You can't tell a lion it's illegal to kill, but you can tell a cider maker it's illegal to sell cider. So natural cider makers must work between these two worlds if they decide to be commercial, making our entry into business a duplicitous venture trying to navigate the artificial with a mind set on coursing a natural path. In the end, we *must* collaborate with the artificial inputs.

Nonetheless, I am certain there's a way to quarantine that influence and still proceed with a consistent natural-facing path. In fact, looking back at the evolution of my business, I don't see how I could have overcome all the human-made barriers or have contrived a predetermined version of success anyway. It just happened organically. Polly and I owe at least half of our success simply to going with the flow, and I would have sabotaged the whole mission had I ignored all the chance occurrences that brought us to where we are today. And it's scary just how fragile those encounters were! The slightest thing, like stopping to pick up a penny, could have made all the difference in meeting someone or not meeting someone who played a huge role in pushing our business forward. Retracing the bread crumbs, I can track every sale we've ever made to the flush of wild apples in 2007. We could just as easily have ignored them.

It was one of those mast years in the Mamakating Hollow. The wild apples were so plentiful in 2007 that we became like squirrels, desperate to make use of them before they rotted. But how could we possibly keep up with the applesauce and/or juice them with our countertop juicer? (Have you ever used those things? They're useless beyond the 4-ounce scale!) We needed help, and this is when we located Soons Orchard, just 20 miles east of us. "Old Man" Art Soons quoted us an impossibly low price and told us to drop the apples in one of their field bins, along with a dozen carboys in another. When we got the call a week later to pick them up, the sweet juice was cold and unpasteurized, dark as marmalade. This was to be our first attempt fermenting wild juice, and we were equipped with at least five different lab yeasts, which are available from wine supply stores (several carboys were earmarked to ferment using wild yeasts alone).

Apart from the cider, which I'm not going to obsess over in this section, what developed most of all was a good relationship with the Soonses, particularly Jeff Soons, the primary orchard director. Three years later Jeff (who also happens to be a lawyer) helped us form the Aaron Burr Cidery (Hamilton's killer was also a lawyer), and he informed us of a cider talk down by his alma mater near Charlottesville, Virginia.

We met Jeff in the spring of 2011 at the Albemarle CiderWorks, where cider legends Steve Wood (Farnum Hill) and Diane Flynt (Foggy Ridge) were leading an all-day discussion on cider making. With breaks given between presentations, we roamed the orchards and production facilities and introduced ourselves to other attendees in the audience. The cider talks were great, but of equal value was our meeting Sara and Thomas, who were also down from New York that day. Sara told us about her project working for a nonprofit, Glynwood, which by sheer coincidence was working to promote cider production in our Hudson Valley area!

First, a little background: Glynwood is a farm-based organization 40 miles east of us in lower New York. Their mission is to strengthen agriculture in the Hudson Valley. One of their trustees had just returned from Normandy, France, where she witnessed one of the world's most bucolic apple cultures and she asked herself why the Hudson Valley didn't have something similar. With an already thriving apple industry and 20 million people within in an hour's drive, not to mention stunning scenery, the region just needed a little push to become the Napa Valley of cider. It made perfect sense. Thus the mission of Glynwood's Cider Project was born.

My orchard was too small to be considered for most of the cider program opportunities, but since I'd met Sara in Virginia that day she kept us in the loop and did her best to include us in the general Cider Project mission. When a new farmers market in downtown NYC approached Glynwood for sponsorship, Sara put us in touch with their market manager, and when we interviewed with Robert we were a perfect match for the New Amsterdam Market. After a five-year absence, Polly and I were going back to work in New York City.

By this point in our personal history, we'd been humbled financially. Compacted dirt blacked the crescents of our fingernails, and the cracks in our hands made us look 80. We weren't New Yorkers anymore, not *that* kind of New Yorkers, so when we drove down on opening day of the New Amsterdam Market we felt like the Beverly Hillbillies bopping up and down the FDR Expressway with our dented Kia station wagon overloaded with cider. As we rounded the 14th Street bend, the downtown skyscrapers appeared larger and more menacing than I remembered. And when we approached our final destination under the Brooklyn Bridge, butterflies were fluttering in my stomach.

Parked, we then unloaded the cases. I felt just as I did preparing my work for a gallery opening. Would anyone like my cider? Is $20 or $25 too much to ask? The butterflies felt more like a flock of birds now, and I needed to find the bathroom across the street at the bar. Taking a shot of bourbon on my way out the door, I returned to our booth just as the market was about to begin, as it always did, with the ringing of a bell. Another Wall Street tradition.

We were off: our first cider sales.

But the New Amsterdam Market, it turns out, was not an environment to be intimidated by; it was, in fact, very welcoming. I had dreaded something like the trading floor pits at the stock exchange, but this particular market ran and looked like a cozy ship. Visually well organized, and adjacent to the historic port of New York, it complemented this history and garnered great community support. It cooled my nerves. The other vendors were like old friends, and if you needed to step away from your booth they watched over your stuff and would even make sales for you while you were gone. I had just discovered another layer in which farmers markets are *truly* supportive.

Time flew as we got busy with sales. Our cider was clearly a hit; many customers, too, wondered why dry cider wasn't "a thing." Wine store owners and restaurant managers stopped by, gave us their cards, and requested we drop off cases on our way out of town. By our third market a sharp young man by the name of John presented himself to us and handed over his business card: Rowan Imports. John had just come back from that part of Spain where they make *sidra* (cider), and he was in the process of getting a license to bring it over to this country. He loved the dryness of our cider. He felt that with its tannic makeup and tartness, it was similar in character to Spanish sidra and would pair with his "book" (a term distributors use to sum up the their portfolio of producers). In other words, could he represent us?

We considered his offer. But we were small, and giving up 30 percent of our income to a distributor was a hard choice. Add to that fact that we were local to NYC and could distribute it ourselves. However, a year later we concluded that if we wanted to remain focused on apple farming and cider making, we needed to limit our direct-to-customer sales to local farmers markets (we still don't sell from our home property). We signed with Rowan Imports, and we couldn't have been more pleased with our brief partnership with them.

A rush of memories came back to me as the closing bell rang out at the last New Amsterdam Market of 2012 (a special holiday market), closing out also our first year in sales. I remembered writing my first business plan in 2008, nearly four years earlier, when we had only the vaguest concept of business. I remembered The Team asking me to research my distribution options. I remembered them saying I needed to put cider in cans and offer a cheaper option. And I thought about the six-figure debt that I would have carried through my years of unexpected hardships, 2008–11.

Nowhere in that old business plan did there appear the words *by chance*, *serendipity*, or *because it feels right*. And yet those were the things that guided me to our first successful year in sales. It was truly by chance: We have the New Amsterdam Market to thank for meeting our distributor, Rowan Imports; we have Glynwood to thank for connecting us to the farmers market; we have Sara to thank for insisting the Cider Project help us, too; we have Jeff Soons to thank for our run-in with Sara; and we had the flush of wild apples in 2007 to thank for discovering Soons Orchard. Try writing that into a business plan!

Even so, I wouldn't recommend forgoing business planning for the new farm enterprise. But I would recommend writing a *fluid* plan that keeps options open. Like in the way the US Constitution or wedding vows can't or couldn't predict the future, business plans shouldn't be followed like the maps from previous explorers; they need to be constantly rewritten to fit with changing times and sentiments. Maps are good, but if you're a sea captain following one and you don't have your eyes open for storms or icebergs, you're going to end up like the *Titanic*. Creativity, and doing what feels right to you, should find equal representation in a business plan. After all, those are the traits that inspire most entrepreneurs into business in the first place.

EIGHT

UnGrowing Business

*I*t's said that there's an intersection between humankind and nature. If so, which way are we facing?

Washington Irving, of "Sleepy Hollow" fame, wrote another ghost story sometime in the early 1830s, "A Marvelous Tale of Mamakating Hollow." In it he introduces the town later to be known as Wurtsboro:

> *The traveler who sets out in the morning from the beautiful village of Bloomingburgh, to pursue his journey westward, soon finds himself, by an easy ascent, on the summit of the Shawangunk. Before him will generally be spread an ocean of mist, enveloping and concealing from his view the deep valley and lovely village which lie almost at his feet. If he reposes here for a short time, until the vapors are attenuated and broken by the rays of the morning sun, he is astonished to see the abyss before him deepening and opening on his vision. At length, far down in the newly revealed region, the sharp white spire of a village church is seen, piercing the incumbent cloud; and, as the day advances, a village, with its ranges of bright colored houses, and animated streets, is revealed to the admiring eye. So strange is the process of its development, and so much are the houses diminished by the depth of the ravine, that the traveler can scarcely believe he is not beholding the phantoms of fairy-land, or still ranging in those wonderful regions which are unlocked to the mind's eye by the wand of the god of dreams. But, as he descends the western declivity of the mountain, the din of real life rises to greet his ear.*

Irving's introduction of the Mamakating Hollow is more bucolic than what my prowess as a writer allows. I will say, as a ghost story his "Tale of Mamakating" lacks the suspense, fantasy, and drama of the other hollow's legend, but as a setting for an early-nineteenth-century fable the hidden valley deep in the wilderness is unrivaled. That's why his impression of the town doesn't sound right to me. And it doesn't jive with modern-day Wurtsboro, either. We are not awash in "the din of real life" (trade, gossip, human buzzing, et cetera); rather our culture is, on the whole, dominated by insulated nature lovers, making this a more accurate fit for the name sleepy hollow. Irving wasn't the man to tell our story; it would have been better left to someone like John Muir to describe a people focused on nature, not the supernatural.

My first glimpse of Wurtsboro was from the same spot just beyond "the cut," a massive engineered wedge taken from the ridgetop along Route 17, which has been posted as FUTURE INTERSTATE 86 along the highway for the past 10 years (presumably it will be just I-86 one day). Traversing the summit, just as Irving did, I could see from high vantage the postcard-like image of a town below: the small Main Street with a single traffic light, two white steeple towers, and a baseball field. Apart from the Mayberry-like impression, which attracted me immediately, the surrounding landscape was relatively untouched: two forested slopes cradling the town like a marble in a dark baseball glove. It's more fitting for a painting than for prose, and Washington Irving should have brought along some of his contemporaries from the Hudson River School.

As I made my first descent from the Shawangunk on Future Interstate 86 and reached the valley floor I found myself perpendicular with Route 209 traveling north-south in harmony with the parallel topography of the hollow. Route 209 is the evolution of the Old Mine Road, which was developed in the mid-1600s by Dutch settlers. Some claim it to be the oldest extended "wheeled road" or commercial highway in America, but the Old Mine Road was the evolution of a much older Indian trail before it—a path rising from the mouth of the Esopus Creek in the north that connects to the mouth of another river, the Neversink, 100 miles west. As an unusually gentle span between two great rivers (the Hudson and the Delaware), it's no wonder it's been well traveled for hundreds, if not thousands, of years.

But I knew none of this history at the time. This was my first entrance into the Mamakating Hollow, and I hadn't heard of the real names for Route 209 or Route 17. I had no idea I had come to the intersection of *the Old Mine Road* and *Future Interstate 86*. I couldn't have guessed the metaphoric significance of this crossing over to the place I now call home.

The Boom Years

I was pulled from an East Village bar amid the uproar. Momentarily yanking myself free from the fist grabbing my jacket, I wanted to look back one more time before getting tugged across the sidewalk. The clamor from behind the red door was euphoric. This evoked in me a strange feeling, like I was a bank robber just handed an extra sack of cash and a pat on the back by the security guards. Dazed, I struggled to make sense of what had just happened.

Between 2011 and 2015 cider's popularity skyrocketed. Nationally it went from being a long-forgotten segment of the food and beverage industry into something akin to digging in the backyard and finding oil. Even multinational beer companies were rushing in, hoping to make a dime. In terms of growth percentage, statistics showed an industry that topped all others—even the wildly popular microbrew movement. But what the data didn't show was the street-level hype or sudden media presence given to cider and cider makers. For the moment, it was the "It" thing.

During that stretch, particularly in 2013 and 2014, no cider business saw the attention and uncanny demand more than our own Aaron Burr Cider. Earlier interviews with Geoff Gray, Alice Feiring, and Steven Koplan (to name a few journalists who discovered us early on) helped to transform us into darlings of New York's foodie world. We made the menu list at Eleven Madison Park, Union Square Cafe, Gramercy Tavern, and Blue Hill, and next thing I knew I was on the cover of newspapers, featured in popular magazines, and even seen on network and international television news programs. With a measly 30-barrel output, I joined the ranks of both veteran and gargantuan cider producers as a leading figure in the industry.

Naturally, this fed my ego. The winds inflated my sales and energized me, bringing me to consider ambitions I'd never thought I had. Time would tell which the right moves for our business would be, but it helped me address personal barriers, too. Whereas introversion and self-doubt had long obscured my art-making process, now with the popular support of cider I found my work justifiable, confidence-boosting.

Among the notable hurdles I faced was my fear of public speaking. I had my good moments and my bad in front of crowds. Gearing up for that night's event, I wondered: How was I to address a bar full of people? Would my newfound confidence put me on par with the natural showmen or the born entitled who naturally gathered an audience and told them about themselves, their ideas or work? I had to remind myself what a friend at Stone Barns once told me: *If you really, truly believe in the cause, speaking about your work is easy.*

That night I had just completed a guided "flight," a sampling of numerous ciders. Cory, the bar owner and manager, arranged this event with the help of Anthony, John's brother and co-owner of Rowan Imports, my NYC distributor. Their promotion had combined with my recent media attention, and the result was a bar packed to taste through our 2013 vintage.

This was in fall 2014. Cider was at the peak of its hotness (probably mine, too). Those in the audience might have been drawn by the buzz, but these were no casual drinkers—not even close. This was a gathering of sommeliers, bar and restaurant professionals, food writers, and hard-core cider enthusiasts. They had come to sample cider from quote-unquote "cider apples" that were foraged local to the New York City area and sold legally in the form of a traditional dry cider, for perhaps the first time in a century.

I started with a Golden Russet cider. Cory helped pour shot-glass-sized samples and distribute them across the bar as I stood behind the rail and described how it was made. The Golden Russet is an apple of historic significance to upstate New York. It survived commoditization as an obscure heirloom apple, but given the abysmal lack of commercially available cider varieties at this point in history, the Golden Russet had reemerged for having adequate cider properties, especially its high sugar content and alcohol potential. It has a fair degree of tartness, crunchiness, and aroma, too (it happens to be my favorite eating apple), but being smaller, russeted, and a late-season apple, it's always been sought after by amateur cider makers, who then receive the wink from the farmer selling it. In the Finger Lakes region of New York it had been made into a single-variety cider, which is a daring feat to accomplish, countering historical advice supporting diversity as the key to a good cider; having notes that wander in different directions, the apple is rather complex on its own. I tried it for a few years, too, and tonight it served the purpose of introducing people to the single-variety concept well paved by New World wine.

Next I poured the Appinette cider, which is a blend of three varieties —two of which are apples, the other being a grape. Again, the premise of this cider was to draw attention to New York–origin cultivars, as well as to strive for the complexity any good cider should hope for. Golden Russet is also featured prominently in the Appinette, in equal measure with Northern Spy (apple) and Traminette (a New York hybrid grape that closely resembles its parent, Gewürztraminer). The result is something floral and bright, a bit hazelnutty in the middle, but all in all reminiscent of a dry Pét-Nat-style Alsatian wine or some Proseccos. Whether or not a cider mixed with grapes is still a cider remains a debate annoying to cider purists (among whom I include myself) and government regulators alike, but the fact it's mostly apple makes it mostly cider, and I don't know what else to call it. (Incidentally, my cider purism forced me to quit making other concoctions like our ginger-cider, which was our most popular product from 2011 to 2014. We also capped our second-most-popular Appinette at no more than 25 percent of our overall production because it utilizes commercially grown fruit. With each passing year I seem to be getting more and more insane with my stubbornness.)

And finally I poured four examples of our Homestead Apple line, made from wild apples. This, undoubtedly, is what the audience had come to try, since wild apples were (and are) the thing I'm most associated with. But few know that I use wild apples in these ciders not because they are superior (they are) but because they serve another function: To my mind wild or assimilated apples are best capable of relaying the larger concept of terroir. This is because the soil and environment around the plant have not been altered by agriculture, the growing conditions are closest to nature, and the plant must grow to survive these conditions. The ecology, terrain, and climate are what shapes apples to become unique to a particular location, and the goal of the Homestead Locational ciders is to articulate this as greatly as possible with multiple places of forage. The drinker can then taste the ciders side by side and experience the trees' acclimation (or struggle) in each location. This is my vision of terroir, at least.

Our Locational ciders (because *terroir* sounded a little snooty to me) follow the seven geological bands throughout Sullivan County, which are obviously unique in character. This is evident in the vegetation, soils, terrain, and climate, as well as peculiarities in the ecosystem, which human activity is a part of. Anyone could surmise the locational differences on their own—you don't need to be all that perceptive—but I later found out that these seven bands coincide with a USGS soil study and atlas of Sullivan County. The Geological Survey goes into great depths mapping the bedrock and describing each soil type, but inexplicably they name these bands after towns hundreds of miles upstate. I took the liberty of renaming the appellations, thus the ciders are dubbed: Neversink Highlands, Shawangunk Ridge, Callicoon Creeks, Mamakating Hollow, and the like.

To maintain the integrity of each location, the ciders and apples obviously must be fermented and bottled separately. But there are a number of variables that I wish to eliminate to keep the spotlight always on the location. Above all else: I need to eliminate my stylistic hand. It's for this reason I stick to rudimentary traditional cider techniques and blind apple selections—I don't want to play the hand of the curator and make selections per my tastes. We strive for equal proportions from as many trees as possible. To me, if an apple is late-season and it's growing in that location then it's not up to me to say what should or shouldn't be in the cider. This also relieves me of the art of varietal selection or later barrel blending. Remember: Art is an artifice; it sits at the opposite gradient from natural. So, too, does industrial processing, which is the ultimate sabotaging hand to terroir. To me, locationalism can *only* be sampled by simple, natural winemaking techniques so that the life and locational character are not damaged or removed.

We've already discussed the oxymoron of natural cider (an art), but nonetheless I do feel that the only way to taste the nature of a place is to use minimal intervention within the cider as well as within the agriculture. So it would seem absurd for me to advocate for controlling the variables, and yet that's precisely what I try to do as a cider maker, so that only the locational attributes shine. Just as I don't want human styles to interfere with the locational voice, I don't want yeast or fermentation variables to out-scream the cider's theoretical expression of terroir. One such variable I try to rein in is fermentation temperatures. It's important for me to have them all ferment at the same time of year (October through December), because if the yeasts were exposed to different ambient temperatures they would be prodded differently, and surely the fermentation variables would be among the defining qualities among the ciders. But a fermentation that does not coincide with that season's natural fruit deterioration (late autumn) is unfit to be called a natural vintage, too, so as I see it there is only one time of year to make a natural cider.

And then I try to control the yeast populations so that they don't imprint a dominant characteristic and steal the show. Rather, I want the yeast note winning Best Supporting Actor. But controlling the yeast characteristics is extremely hard to do naturally, as I'm not even sure where the yeasts comes from—are they in the apples, the air, my hands, or the press? All of these combined? So I try to find a middle ground between the chaos of yeast populations and the lab-yeast approach (which I feel is an unfit match for the culture of wild apples and thus self-defeating). Again, you might think this is arbitrary (that's your right), but what I end up doing is using a mix of wild yeasts (which is to say I don't kill them with sulfites or sterilization); I also pitch my house starter, which is a long-term culturing of native yeasts. Maybe this levels the playing field enough among the locational ciders so that at least the home yeast can be identified and appreciated, while still allowing those locational differences from the apples to play the starring role. (I could just as easily end that last sentence with a question mark.)

Lastly, a consistent approach requires that all the ciders be bottled at the same time, either dry or with the exact same level of carbonation (à la Pét-Nat cider). Because I utilize natural CO_2 as a bottle conditioner, I find April to be an ideal time to bottle; at this time the cider's final gravity is either dropping to near 1.004, or it can easily be lifted back to that level with SüssReserves. This ensures that varying carbonation levels don't interfere with the taste comparisons.

In the end our Homestead Apple or Locational ciders hope to show what it is to drink from one location versus the next. The idea has parallels in the concept of single-variety wines: To drink the same estate's Merlot and Cab-Franc is to purely drink one cultivar versus the next because the locational variables have been eliminated (assuming the wines are actually grown at that location). I want a range of single-location ciders like many American wineries want a range of single-variety wines, but for me it's not appropriate to take a leveling hand when it comes to the apple genetics or yeast culturing either. My belief is that true terroir depends on truly acclimated fruit, which is a concept that even most sommeliers do not understand. To them, terroir has always been linked to organic or biodynamic cultivation, or other cultivation methods that look to nature as the guide but are not actually naturalized. These forms of agriculture are good compromises, but I have tried to show that they are not nearly as close to the natural side of the spectrum as actually wild fruit. (This is another reason why I call it our Locational series. All things considered, terroir as it is commonly used in the marketplace fails to recognize just how different farms—even "natural farms"—are from the environment that would otherwise be located there.)

Again, I don't want to be an artist with my Locational ciders, and I'm happy to limit that type of artistry to our other series of fruit blend ciders, the Appinette and our Elderberry-Apple cider (the former isn't from wild fruit anyway). I want my Locational experiment to be representative of the bigger nature of a place, including everything from the unaltered soil to the birds in the forest. It all hinges on the way the apples are *not* grown. The apples must be truly wild or as uncultivated as possible.

As an obsessed, introverted farmer / cider maker, one who rarely leaves his property, one with a fear of speaking in public, how am I to face a packed New York City bar with *all* the above information about our ciders? (Even before I begin I'm getting blank stares when I say I'm from Sullivan County—to them, it's all "upstate." In actuality, 90 percent of New York is north of where I live, and the rest of New York calls me "downstate"!) I have to compose myself and remind myself this is all new to them. And to talk about truly wild apples, I need to begin with the seed and the reproductive goals of the tree—that's a big enough starting hurdle in and of itself. You, the reader, have already read dozens of pages relating to this topic; imagine the difficulties of introducing an infinitely dynamic organism, the dynamics of the various locations, and how the two relate to each other. And now imagine doing all this in short time and in a crowded bar with drinks to serve! Suffice it to say it's a chore that I must be prepared for. As my friend at Stone Barns would say, *I must truly be a believer in the cause.*

For whatever reason, it worked. I was *on* that night. I was bobbing and weaving like Floyd Mayweather, and I just sort of blacked out in the zone. It became like an out-of-body experience, like watching myself on TV. When my senses returned I was standing in front of an applauding group of strangers. I've been in front of applause before, during various graduations, but this was genuine and enthusiastic! Like the end of a Who concert. What did I miss?

"Hurry up, man!" I heard just then. Over by the door was killjoy Anthony. It turned out I was already late for my next appointment somewhere on the Upper West Side, a dinner pairing at a restaurant featuring the same ciders alongside curated dishes prepared by the chef. "We gotta go! You were supposed to be there half an hour ago," he pleaded.

But I was still unresponsive. He had already grabbed a taxi and was leaning halfway through the entrance bridging both me, who stood shocked behind the bar, and the cabdriver, who sat impatient behind the wheel. "Yo!" he tried again. "Let's go!" And then Cory started pushing me along. I grabbed my coat and stepped under the bartop en route to the door. The patrons were still applauding, perhaps tipsy, and I began squeezing through like a tricycle at the carwash.

By this point Anthony was truly annoyed and grabbed me by the jacket and literally threw me outside to speed things along. "Dude, the restaurant tried to stall the customers but they forgot to tell the chefs and now their second course is ready!"

He pushed me in the cab like a cop and slammed the door in my face. "Fourteen Seventeen Lexington, corner of 93rd," he yelled up to the driver through rolled-up windows.

"What? You're not coming with me?" I yelled back to Anthony.

But no answer. He flickered a bemused facial gesture featuring an upside-down smile, and I got the sense he derived some sort of sick pleasure from my confusion. With a swat of the cab trunk he had done his job, and the taxi pulled out.

What the hell had just happened?

The Mamakating Hollow

Our eyes are not just cameras and our brains are not just computers. Information that we absorb—be it through books or through our senses—quickly becomes more than raw data because it's in our nature to contextualize the world to ourselves, to our psyche. It's a profoundly more impressive feat compared to the "personalizing" of information accomplished by artificial intelligence. And it all just happens at the speed of light, without even asking ourselves to do it. It's just "in our nature." And I wonder how that relates to "being in nature?"

The Terrain

Belowground, the rock strata is not U-shaped like the valley is. The modern-day appearance is deceiving: If you could take a giant cross section of the rock layers, they wouldn't parallel the soil surface bending up toward the ridge peaks, nor the bend back down to the Hudson Valley; instead the layers would appear broken by the surface, as if someone took a section of layered cake and laid it on its side. That's because this area was once part of a massive mountain range, 10 times higher than what we see today. As it eroded down, the rocks with the hardest mineral composition wore away more slowly (as you see among the granite White Mountains). Today's Catskill "mountains" don't actually follow the ancient strata or hint at where the old peaks were. At play were the massive forces of glacial retreats, while the wind and the rain continue to carve away at the landscape. In some places sediment piled up and in other places it got washed out to sea.

Being a hollow, the Wurtsboro area is one of those places where eroded rock tended to pile up. We have some areas of pure sand, pockets of lime, and heavy clay soils that are loaded with stones. A backhoe shovel scoop is like a cup of rocky road ice cream. But solid ledge outcroppings are numerous, and when not protruding from the ground they hide below the surface and surprise the digger, ending all hope of progress. In all, these soils (or lack thereof) combine to characterize the area, and it's most pronounced in the deep valley. But the attributes repeat themselves in smaller pockets as the slopes turn upward, and even at the very top of the mountains it's possible to find sandy soils that eroded down from once-higher land.

At my farm the rock ledges dominate and protrude more than in other valley locations. The stone is slate, blue, layered, and flat; it's often easy enough to hammer off sheets of varying thickness. New York City sidewalks were once paved with Mamakating bluestone. As the rocks have been loosened over the eons, many of them slumber in the subsoil along with other glacial debris, and they pop up each spring during the yearly freeze-thaw cycle. It never ends, it makes life hell on lawn mowers, and cultivating the soil is even harder. For that reason alone (although there are many others) the Mamakating Hollow and its hills have never been considered prime cropland except in small pockets. But there is a benefit to all the loose rocks (especially the flat ones) in that they can be collected and made into stone walls for animal pasture containment. Area farmers have been moving slabs of bluestone for over 200 years, resulting in some of the most beautiful rock walls on the planet. Often moss or lichen colonizes the surface, which intensifies in color with the morning mist. And having been without soil contact for ages, the stones develop a satin-finish patina like a varnish darkened by oxidation.

As we continue to add rocks each year, these walls will likely be our only legacy 200 years hence. I like that. It's a collaborative work uniting a community of the dead, the living, and the not-yet-born. (Although if you were to chart this progress, you'd see that the bulk of the stonework was done by the earlier people; contributions have progressively trailed off. And at this rate I wonder if future people will not be too busy to participate.)

Ecosystem

In the heart of the Mamakating Hollow is the Basher Kill or Bashakill. In some areas the Bashakill just looks like your typical woodland stream, but in others it opens up to a vast wetland covering hundreds of acres. Bald eagles and ospreys coast on the mountain updrafts patrolling the mudflats and shallow waters in search of muskrats and fish. Human trespassers are deterred by a quicksand-like mud. Snapping turtles and mosquitoes aren't welcoming, either. Along the edges of the wetlands it's common to find elderberry, grapevines, and staghorn sumac, each with an edible berry attractive to a great variety of birds.

Everywhere else in the valley, the soil is well drained and the terrain is almost entirely wooded, with a good mix of coniferous and deciduous trees. Oak and pine are the two most numerous trees, followed by maple, hemlock, and birch. A dozen or more other tree species are found in areas advantageous to their growth habits. There's also a wide range of bushes, vines, grasses, and flowers, making them far too numerous for me to list here. I only wish to say that the flora is diverse.

And so is the fauna. The animals typical to the American wilderness are all common in the valley and on the hillsides: bears, deer, rabbits, coyotes, groundhogs, and turkeys. Migrating birds like catbirds, robins, and goldfinches actively move in and move out, leaving the hawks, eagles, woodpeckers, and cardinals to wonder. In general, the animal diversity is healthy, and that includes the insect populations. Again, I don't wish to name them all, but I do want to mention that some of the key species are easy to overlook: the red eft salamander, pine voles, flies, termites, and boring beetles. And perhaps the most important of all are the mycorrhizae and other soil-swelling organisms that have yet to be studied or named by science. Without them, the entire ecosystem would spiral out of control.

Climate

Climate zone maps are constantly changing: We were at one time in USDA hardiness zone 4B, then in 5A, and now we're in 5B. Which is right? Who can tell? But gardeners should know that the average yearly temperatures range from -10° to 95°F, and the last frost-free date is usually around May 5. On the global scale of things, that's a medium-to-large range of temperatures. Subzero temperatures *Fahrenheit* begin in late December and extend through March; subzero temperatures *Celsius* are common from late October through the end of April (with exceptions, of course). Rain is heaviest in the spring and it's a crapshoot for summer—it can be either super wet or scary dry. Hurricanes and nor'easters bring days of heavy rain from August through December, and they continue in the form of heavy snows. It seems once a year we get a two-footer, but the winter is otherwise very dry with only light snows to pile up.

Low atmospheric moisture is more common in the valley than on the slopes. Early in the morning and late in the afternoon the two ridges cast shadows across the valley, causing us to lose an hour of direct sunlight on either end of the day. This tends to prolong fogs that set up overnight and sit heavy from ridge to ridge (Irving hinted at this in his Mamakating piece, earlier). This fog plays a curious role in our culture, and if there's one thing I'd like to tell you about us it's this: Below this fog layer our weather is obscured until the temperature rises and the sun burns through the mists. Then, and only then, will we know what kind of day the rest of the world is experiencing, and until that happens, which may not be until lunchtime, we live under the blanket and feel insulated from the concerns facing the rest of the world. We are people defined by our geology, wildlife, and daily weather.

Crabby Activism

After allowing the tannins and acids of the 2012 *Malus baccata* cider to round out for three years, having blended it cuvée-style with a small portion of the aged 2013 and fresh juice of 2014 (all from the same crab apple trees), we bottled the crab apple cider and waited. Finally, by winter 2014–15, we started selling the world's most expensive cider.

Cider was then on a tear, and suffice it to say I was trying to keep up during the first few years of sales. During that time I found myself traveling to major cities doing presentations or history lessons, trying to be an advocate for dry, natural cider. Although I hadn't yet formed my dogmatic opinions on "the right way" to grow cider apples, I knew it called for a separate agriculture that resembled the old ways of farming. I spoke at museums, festivals, restaurants—both famous and obscure— and of course to the media. Wherever I was, I wanted people to support their nearest growers and not necessarily the local cider producer. This isn't beer—was my main point. Unless the *apples* are local, the cider isn't.

My reputation as a cider maker was particularly high at the time and we were selling out year after year, but I knew full well the attention given to me was attention aimed at *all* like-minded cider producers. Customers wanted small, they wanted local, they wanted real grower/producers, and they wanted high quality. I certainly did not have a monopoly on those things; in fact, compared with licensed New England producers I was just the new kid, but because my farm is within the New York City area we happened to be the most accessible and most local of this type.

I understood my role as a stand-in, and I was happy to advocate for other producers whom I admire and who are the living embodiment of traditional cider. But I drew the line at advocating for all cider, because I believed the sector had been tarnished enough by poor quality. No matter what the level of quality is, the reputation of cider spells the difference between customers choosing it over wine or beer, so the overall sector reputation needs to be drastically improved. As I would have it, not another drop of low-quality cider should be added until the overall percentage of good cider reached at least 50 percent. But starting at close to 1 percent (literally), there was a long way to go.

I think most people involved in making cider recognized the period from 2012 to 2015 as a pivotal time for the sector, and most everyone got involved one way or another trying to steer the industry. Most notable was the formation of trade associations. But my earlier experiences with "all-inclusive" cider groups had frustrated the hell out of me because I couldn't comprehend how a good future for cider could suddenly appear without a change in the agriculture for cider apples. This would take decades. And my compatibility with all-inclusive trade groups only waned as their membership began to fawn over large producers, of both apples and cider. Also, their favoritism was not benign to my efforts because of the nature of my scale. Trade advocates saw exclusivity as snootiness, not as I saw it—a focus on ideals. This seemed a direct conflict with their larger goal of "getting more cider out there." To them, the goal was to immediately increase the visibility of the drink, make it an option on the large scale again, but to me I was like, *What is it you want out there?*

It's little wonder industry advocates courted industrial producers capable of mass-producing the drink (beer-style production) as well as partnering with the large preexisting apple farms—no waiting necessary. Some, perhaps not aware of the infinitely higher levels cider is capable of, even saw the new beer-style drink as good cider, and soon enough the marketing of industrial cider reflected similar vocabulary. *Dry, artisan,* and other nods to intimate production became attached to drinks that were everything but. To me, this was a reprehensible sign of our times, a general acceptance of truthiness, and I didn't want this corrupting element to enter the relationship we have with the drink. It encourages distrust, it destroys culture, and it drives a wedge between consumers and their agriculture. Cider's best surviving quality was its reputation as having escaped modernization. I was determined to protect the truth behind those claims.

By 2015 cider-as-a-beer was trending upward, and the markets reflected this. One beer company alone commanded over 50 percent of all cider sales in America (and at the time of this writing it's up from there), while ciders from cider growers remained a stagnant fraction of the overall sector. How could that type of cider emerge in the future with the industry returning to ease of production and standardization? The same ol', same ol' apples, the same ol', same ol' farmers, and the same big beverage companies were peddling a vision of cider while the cider grower was out in the orchard, working on a different future. The beer model seized the momentum presented in the earlier years of cider's revolution, and it reshaped the model for the next generation. Instead of working through agriculture, new cider producers went straight to the factory and followed the microbrewery model. The agriculture behind the product was whatever you wanted to market it as.

I wasn't given a choice. There was no way I, or any other cider maker driven by ideals, could suffer such an extreme setback. To team with advocates of this industry would be to nullify our reputation as the real deal. If I had any currency left from my run in the media, it was most certainly not going to serve the mass exploitation of apple trees. I want apple trees to be cared for like a herdsman looks after a small flock of beef cattle; *no* cider growers I know of want to see their beloved apples blended one to one million in a placeless product. Again, I had no choice; I had to try to disassociate myself and the idealistic vision of cider from the path the industry had chosen.

But in short time the fight looked to be over. Anthony, my distributor, sent me warnings that city people weren't buying farm ciders like they briefly had been. *Cheap and a good story* was what they really wanted now. "They are *all* farm ciders in their eyes, no matter where the apples come from," I even heard one restaurant owner say. "The same thing could be produced for a lot less." (This was while I was trying to tell him about David Buchanan, a truly great grower/producer in Maine. The restaurateur scoffed: "This one costs me one-fifth the price!" he said as he picked up a can of cider with only a Maine-*sounding* name.) The culture that attracted me to cider was now lost to the marketplace. What had happened to cider now that cider growers didn't own it anymore?

Prices were falling. Even cider makers who were long associated with high quality started making industrialized versions with leftover culinary apples, but their high-end ciders appeared to be dropping in price, too. This was not good. I feared that the world of local and intimate production would soon be economically unsustainable, thwarting the potential entry of thousands of new producers. This would only further advantage industrial production. Land costs were going up, taxes only go up, the price of health care was skyrocketing, and workers' wages were going up, too. For the cider grower/producer everything from bottle costs to equipment was up, and yet customers expected our prices to go down? Who but the biggest could possibly benefit from this dubious scheme? Consumers mustn't be misled by the temptingly low prices.

Anthony was the first to pose the question, "What if you sold the crab apple cider on its own?"

I laughed. I told him it would have to cost $100 given how much effort it takes to collect wild crab apples.

"And?"

"And what? Charge a hundred bucks? That would be stupid, no one would pay that."

"But if you truly believe it's worth that much, then why not at least give people the option? Don't try to guess what the market will pay—leave that to me, I'm in the city every day and I know people will support what you do. Those with higher budgets can afford it—not everyone's a farmer, you know. You've sold paintings for hundreds of dollars, right? [More, actually.] And did you spend ten times the effort on them?" He had me there. I once sold a painting for $4,000 and it only took me about three months to complete. This cider had taken three years.

But did it *really* deserve the comparison to art? Didn't that offend me as a painter 25 years in the training? I had to consider it a while, but in the end I thought I had an obligation to my vision of cider.

Why? I wanted to expand the parameters of the drink, to push it upward or at least *not* allow it to be filed down by the trend of streamlining. If $10 a bottle is all you can get for a labor of love, then what's the incentive for an artist or a small farmer to get involved? What's the incentive for someone to do their very best when doing as little as possible is actually more profitable in the marketplace? Winemaking will forever attract the best and the brightest, both the growers and producers, when the parameter range is as much as $5,000 a bottle. And what a fucking shame it would be to have the best and the brightest in Maine, the Catskills, or West Virginia—areas so supremely suitable for apples that they actually go wild!—giving their attention to growing and fermenting European grapes. That's why I did it.

True, we took our punches. A three-figure cider had the appearance of me exploiting my reputation, which was garnered on consumers' love of the homespun. Now at $100 per bottle, this had the glitter and cachet of a Warhol, not a Grandma Moses. I knew the apples to be nothing more than half-dried marble-sized crabs from the edge of fields, but without an elaborate story on the label or website we were simply leaving the taste to explain the eye-popping price. And then anxiety over this bold move set up shop in my head. Just as soon as I handed over the nine cases of *Malus baccata* cider to Anthony, I became a backtracker. I was so self-conscious that I wanted to call him and find out who bought it so I could buy it back. I even did from some stores! (This, by the way, is exactly how I behaved after selling paintings, too.) Rumors circulating in the cider industry didn't take too kindly to this action, either. Still, in the end it was out there. I, like the rest of the world, was just going to have to accept cider could be worth this much.

Late March. It was one of those film-noir foggy nights a block north of Washington Square Park. Water crystals were suspended in the air after 36 straight hours of drizzle, and the glossy surface of the sidewalks reflected the streetlights like one of Whistler's nocturnes. Cars driving by stirred up the wet roads, and an unpleasant mist eddied in the tailwinds while the sizzling sounds from the tires fluctuated up and down in volume with each passing car. This added a tinny melody to the sporadic car horns chiming in from the hollow distance, muffled by fog. Above the four- and five-story buildings a dense gray cloud layer formed like cigarette smoke, and when backlit by the invisible skyscrapers it felt like Martians were landing.

This meeting is to take place at a coffee bar on 8th Street. It looks and functions like your quintessential corner café in Paris with pastries and soups; even a poet is scheduled to read in an hour. I see Anthony already seated. I go to greet him with our customary bro-hug. (I don't know if that's what people still do, but when I lived in the city bro-hugs were becoming the standard.) Polly is next door at my alma mater, the New York Studio School, where she's been taking weekend classes this winter. The more I get into cider, the deeper she digs into art. She needs to keep her independence.

"Andy," he said, "we've had a good run these past four years."

He continued: "Your business is clicking, you sell out each year, we've both had our share of praise, but I'm telling you it's over. It's about to get China-crowded in here, and it's getting so that people just associate cider with Heineken or Sam Adams. They think *they're* the default cider and that traditional cider is new! Some people even think that farm cider is just a fancy product for the food snobs! The two have only one market now, and that, my friend, is a problem on the wholesale level. Whatever you think makes you special can be leveled by marketing, which is done at the retail level. They'll just *say* they're the same thing."

"I don't understand, did you sell the cider? What about the crab apple?"

"Of course. I told you people would buy it!"

"But then why—"

"Economy of scale, kid. It's the same in distribution as it is in cider— maybe even worse. It's too easy for big producers to get their product out there. There's a reason why the same ciders, same wines, and same beers always get grouped together in stores. They are bundled together to sweeten the wholesale deal. In the end most wholesale buyers reward their bulk packaging prices."

He tended to call me kid even though I was 15 years older. Anthony was on a roll, and if a sentence ended in "kid," it was for cadence. He was a charmer by nature—the big-daddy aura attached to him at a young age—but I saw him more as a friend than as a rep or distributor. This was less a business meeting than a confessional. I just couldn't believe that a guy so young, so brash, and so full of confidence could suddenly about-face at the height of his career. Were things really that desperate?

"I'll say it again: It's marketing. The only way you can compete with that is to be down here everyday so that store owners and the newest sommeliers can put a face to your product. Otherwise, customers are just going to buy what was already selected for them. Big distributors and some cider brands have their own reps, and they are in the buyer's faces day in and day out. And who's going to fact-check their stories in the back room where the deals are made? The field is narrowed before the customer even has the option, and I'm afraid I can't fight that fight for you anymore. You're not the newest thing anymore and unless you become the cheapest I don't see brand loyalty emerging in this sector.

"I'm worried about you, kid. My suggestion to you is start selling from home because that's the only way people will be able to see what's real. But fuck, look what's already happening—even the agro-tourism market is awash in deception! I don't know, it's just going to be a hard run for you guys."

And with that he reached across the small white-marble table and slid the check back toward him, peeling the bottom end up like a poker player. Befitting his character, he leaned to reach for a fat wallet in his back pocket and stood up, slapping down two twenties. "When the waitress comes, tell her to keep six and you keep the rest. I'm worried about you. Let's talk next month."

But we never did. That was the last I saw of him.

The D&H Canal

I'm going to leave it to Washington Irving again to introduce the terrain of the larger valley to which the Mamakating Hollow is but a short section:

West of the Shawangunk mountain lies a sweet valley . . . the natural entrance to which is from Esopus. Their farms, some twenty years ago, before turnpike roads and a canal intersected those regions, were stretched across the [Mamakating] Hollow from the Shawangunk to the corresponding mountain on the west. They were thus furnished, at either extremity, with woodland and pastures; while the spacious bed between the ridges, varying from two to five miles in width, was a carpeted meadow.

Some context about this passage:

Esopus is a creek, but it's also the old name for Kingston (capital of the New Netherlands and first capital of New York), and the name of Thomas Jefferson's favorite apple—all of which derive from the local Esopus Indian tribe. But Irving is referring to the creek. Its waters empty into the Hudson River at a spot navigable by ships, thus lending commercial importance to that location.

Irving wrote this in the 1830s so his mention of "turnpike roads" probably refers to both the ancient Old Mine Road and the new Cochecton Turnpike, which was created 20 years prior to his writing. The latter road circumvented the old Denniston Ford with the completion of the covered bridge at Bridgeville, charting the path for today's Future Interstate 86.

When Irving writes, "the spacious bed between the ridges," he's referring to the valley floor, which does generally range between 2 and 5 miles wide, but the Mamakating Hollow is at its narrowest stretch and is not more than 2 miles wide. (In fact, where I live, the valley is only 1 mile across, more V-shaped than U-shaped.)

The "canal" in the above passage I will expand upon, below.

In the very late 1700s anthracite coal, which burns extremely efficiently, was discovered in northeastern Pennsylvania at the same time Alexander Hamilton served as Treasury secretary of the United States, a powerful position at a time ripe for setting the course of American industry. He chose to favor manufacturing economies (some have argued at the expense of agricultural economies), and within a few decades there were advancements in transportation (canals, and later trains) that allowed for this high-energy coal to fuel New York City's rapid expansion in the 1800s (see "Lady Lazarus" in chapter 1). But until then, anthracite was still locked in Pennsylvania mountains and needed to find its way to the coast, a distance of 200 miles cutting against the hilly terrain and two major rivers.

In the early 1800s a Philadelphia businessman, William Wurts, and his brothers first began exploring ways of getting huge quantities of the heavy, cumbersome rock from said Point A to Point B. The wheeled roadways were impractical for that scale of transportation, so the brothers schemed of a canal system to utilize the buoyancy of boats on water. Logically they needed to dig the canal through the easiest possible terrain, and the long valley along the Old Mine Road provided just that. The valley rose from the Delaware River by only a few hundred feet (to its height at modern-day Summitville) before descending again toward the Hudson River. The Wurts brothers began collecting Wall Street investors and in short order chartered the Delaware and Hudson Canal, one of the first businesses in America to exceed the value of a million dollars. Fortuitously, with plenty of Irish immigrants pouring into the country in the early 1800s, the brothers had the money, abundant low-wage manpower, and a natural valley to proceed with their plans. By the mid-nineteenth century the D&H Canal, and the more famous Erie Canal, lay the foundation for New York City's exploding population, which quickly outpaced all others.

Eventually trains would replace the Wurtses' canal system. Soon railways (which the Wurts helped pioneer, too) cut a parallel course through the valley, passing towns first founded as canal stops. Mamakating Hollow was renamed Wurtsboro, but other current-day town names—Port Jervis, Summitville, and Phillipsport—also reference the canal history. Activity returned to the ancient roads in the twentieth century when they became paved and widened, leaving the waterways and railways to become abandoned; now they are both overgrown. Even the "carpeted meadow" in the prime valley floor is "Nothing but Flowers," as David Byrne would say. Actually, it's a wilderness of trees, including apple.

The Investors

On a beautiful June afternoon a few years ago, Polly and I were in the New York's Financial District at the edge of the Hudson River. A block away glistened the new World Trade Center with its towering building designed to remind us *the sky's the limit*. It's a perfect day, warm and clear, and hundreds of tourists and businesspeople crowd the bar and patio seating of an indoor/outdoor restaurant. Polly and I snag a table just before the five o'clock rush. The purpose for our visit: to meet with a venture capitalist and his partner who've been interested in "our brand."

Having arrived first, we now have a moment to decompress with a drink after a stressful two-hour drive. I'm frazzled but also nervous. I'm not thinking straight, I order a beer. Stupid! What kind of message does that send, that even a cider maker chooses beer when out for drinks? Luckily, Polly bails me out by finding a French cider on the cocktails menu. I take a sip of hers: notes of caramelized apple, oak, and barnyard can't be disguised under the unnecessary sweetness that French ciders are known for. But I love the density of these flavors, and I'm shocked they offer such a drink in a Huey Lewis of a place like this. Fuck if I'm not going to support that decision, so I order one, too, and let my beer gather flies.

Here they come.

I like these guys. I met them at our cidery last year during our CSA day: They poured out of a fire-red BMW with two stunning ladies and seemed to be casing the joint, taking in as much as possible before engaging with us. I knew something was up; they reminded me of the way health inspectors arrive, but this was no G-man's car and those gorgeous ladies were too fashionable to be farm-savvy. They proceeded to taste our ciders and walk the orchard with us but made no mention of their business schemes; they were just taking inventory. (Our CSA, by the way, is the one day each year that we direct-sell to customers from our home. Being that it's our home, we've tried to create boundaries for the business, and direct sales would feel like an encroachment on our personal space.)

Six months later Antonio, the Wall Street half of the duo, invited me to a bar uptown to discuss a business proposition. It was winter now. I was recovering from food poisoning, probably not looking too well, but nonetheless he made me a proposal: He and his partner wanted to take our cider brand and grow it into a profitable business. *Um, it already is profitable*—I thought to myself—but I knew what he meant: He was talking about red BMW profitable. He proceeded to tell me about his work in finance, his private investments, and his partner, the Chilean, who was an "everything man" in international wine: landowner, brand manager, vintner, importer, and sales rep. "Think it over," Antonio said, "and we'll have another meeting with him and Polly if you guys are interested."

I did what he suggested and months passed. I thought to myself, *Well, yeah, I could definitely benefit from better financial management*, but did I want to grow the company? Did I want more people involved?

Back downtown, the restaurant starts to fill with traders and bankers. Polly and I are feeling very out of place even though it's also a tourist location. I don't want to be seen as one myself, not in a business meeting, but I'm certainly not up to the standards of the regulars—gold watches and white pressed shirts glowing from under dark tailored suits. I don't look like a hillbilly, but I certainly don't rock the bling like these money-men do. I'm feeling inferior.

When the partners arrive they sit and exude the confidence that I now identify as the ambience of this place. Antonio and his partner look more casual than the rest but they have managed to fit right in. There is a fashion to the wine sophisticate that savvy vintners know. It's a look that says Landed Gentry, Rock Star, Business Shark, and Tractor Driver all at once. These guys have it; I do not. We are not 30 seconds beyond our hellos and I'm already feeling behind in the count. Am I here for a handout? Are these guys my saviors?

Antonio is a sweetheart, though. He can tell I'm feeling self-conscious and positions himself almost like a mediator. I know he's trying to bridge the gap with his Chilean friend who's not at all impressed with me, or for that matter the cider sector. He's asking me to explain how this could work, and I'm at a loss. "We'd have to make more cider obviously. But there are not enough high-quality apples to make the same cider I make; the flavor would be diminished." I go on, "If that happens I don't want my name on the bottle, but I'd be happy to part with Aaron Burr. I'll just do my own thing and let Burr kill without me."

"But you'd be managing the production end, right? Oversee the buying, give tours and tastings, talk to the media, all those kinds of things, right? I mean, we'd still need you to be the face of the cider."

"For how long?" I ask. "I suppose I could do that for a year, but I don't want to be that guy telling people that a second-tier product is the best it could be. I'd rather just be the farmer or forager."

The enthusiasm is starting to fade. Antonio explains that after a few years of steady growth another company will want to buy us out (the four of us), and then the new company would only need me another year or so. "You two [Polly and I] will be the figureheads and make sure the workers are making the best possible cider at higher volumes, and we'll guarantee the growth, the marketing, the distribution, plus provide the capital for all ends of the business. That's where this is heading," Antonio explains.

Maybe I don't appear to be getting it. "It's simple: The money will allow you to do the things you want to do. If not immediately, long into the future. You can still be a grower; you can still forage and make cider. The money is a tool for all those things, not a hindrance. What *is* a hindrance is *not* having money."

As the details unfold and we finish our drinks, Antonio prepares to make a closing argument: "Look, what you're doing up in Wurtsboro is excellent. And it's sustainable for you and Polly, at least for now. But cider is an expansion market now, much bigger than when you got started. What you're doing is essentially a hobby at this point. Other people will take your place in line if you don't grow with the market. You can still be an advocate for small cider, in fact it can help you maintain your reputation, but what *we* want to do is leap-frog the people already scaling up and get you back in place ahead of the game."

The meeting ends amicably. We vow to get together soon and hammer out the details, but I think we all know the idea has cooled. Polly and Antonio are still optimistic but his partner sees through me. I don't have what it takes, and now I have a grudge. The word *hobby* stung.

If you want to piss off an artist, tell them they aren't living in the real world. To say art is made merely for pleasure, that unless it has financial value it has no value, is to deny ideals, beauty, catharsis, and inspiration— all forms of emotions and beliefs. To exclude art from the real world is to make the real world unlivable, therefore not real at all.

But I can totally understand why art would frustrate someone in finance. Certainly the importance of art has no financial equivalent, and artists have long eluded commoditization. The nature of art acts as a market disrupter—even within its own industry. Sure, there are examples of sellouts, but just as soon as a studio becomes a place of business another artist will come along with more passion, more content, and more freedom, and produce without the expectation of making money from it. The moment art becomes a commodity, it loses its importance.

What other industry's economics, besides art, are sabotaged by unpaid workers who just do it because they need to? Apart from wine, there aren't a lot. This passion-led business is so problematic for our money-structured society that art has been the target of stigmas and the cultural equivalent of hazing. But art will not get in line, because it can't. Conformity and the capitalist system have their own positive values (money, for example, can be spent on good causes, too), but clearly there are other values that lead people.

The TV show *The Shark Tank* was not helpful in explaining this. A whole generation grew up watching inventive entrepreneurs and fool-hardy idealists get berated by venture capitalists for not having scalability built into their plan. Television-worthy quips—"If you want to shred with the big dogs, you're going to have to get your chops up"—instilled a cold culture based on the formal tenets of business and not the moral. Guests were encouraged to ditch their small thinking, ditch the idealism, and ditch the aloof uncertainties making capital investment all but impossible. In short: conform. Conform to market pressures, conform to consumer demand, conform to customer tastes—if you can provide all that, and do so for less money than what you get in return, then you have yourself a business, right? But wait, there's more: Now you need to expand because someone else is going to move in and take your success from you; you need to stay ahead of the curve and squash the competition.

Maybe that's what commoditization and expansionism is all about, but it's an awful mistake to think that's what business is about. My "competition" is a bunch of farmers; who would want to squash them anyway? I want to live in a world that allows for us all, rather than pitting us against one another in some sick survival-of-the-biggest competition. If one economy can't do that, then another one can. And it can.

I've been thinking about an earlier question: Does it offend me as a painter to compare cider to art? And I think I understand a little more about what binds the two. It's culture. When people read a lot of books, or go to museums, they are said to possess culture. Our society calls people who expand their intellectual horizons cultured, which is a word that derives its origins in tandem with *agriculture*. The parallels are unmistakable: Crops grow, we encourage our minds to grow, and both agriculture and intellectual cultures provide us nourishment. It's also worth noting that these nourishments—these cultures—have *no* direct financial value (and even indirectly it's hard to place a monetary value on health and intelligence). But here's another peculiar thing about the compartmentalizing of agriculture within the financial economy: Agriculture is more than just the culturing of crops; it's a whole system—an economy in its own right. This system includes the improvement of soils, the creation of farm tools, distribution systems and labor management, and more. These things need to happen for human nourishment; the only question is *how* they will get done. It's a mistake to say money makes them happen, because the need for human nourishment is truly the motivation. It's going to happen anyway. And in that sense, it's a *bigger* economy.

Frustrating financial markets, culture is not "under" anything and art, with its weariness for selling out, is continually reminding us of that. It's true that people can buy and sell commodities of food and art, but their purpose is higher, and they are *not* fueled by them. Money helps, but it's not required. In fact it's a fatal mistake to make money required. Conventional agriculture, for instance, fell victim to that and as a result we now have an increasing number of health issues by way of unhealthy food. With nutritional values tied to commodity values, we neared disaster until a resurgence of unconventional farms sprang from a cultural fight-back. These cultures, however murky they would seem to an economist, have their own economy.

So, no—I'm not offended to compare cider to art. I know of at least 50 people who are going to make cider with or without a favorable financial take. They find it nourishes themselves, their community, and the environment—it has its own bigger economy. What I *am* offended by is the idea of subverting culture to financial systems. Culture is not a hobby, and if you think so, try not eating.

Polly and I left the meeting within the view of the Statue of Liberty and crossed West Street to stand beneath the new Freedom Tower—both are monuments to concepts that I'm 100 percent certain are unrelated to expansionism. We looked up and followed the building contour lines, which meet a quarter of a mile up, taller than the mountains on either side of our farm back home. It's very impressive, and given that the building is a response to 9/11, I understand the Freedom Tower name. But its other name, One World Trade Center, might be more fitting, as it expresses its honest function. Maybe trade and freedom are "One" and the same (what do I know? I'm just a farmer), but I can tell you I don't feel very free in a financial system that forces me to grow beyond my land and squash my neighbor farmer, lest he squash me. As I look up at the architecture I am inspired, but when I look down at the soil back home I am also inspired. Is it necessary to always keep moving, always be climbing higher, always be making more and more money? How much higher is "free"? Am I wrong for wanting to stay the same size?

The Old Mine Road

By the early 1900s nostalgia for old-timey culture brought with it the first leisure tourists to the Wurtsboro area. C. G. Hine, an amateur travel writer and historian from East Orange, New Jersey, applied his pen to the same hollow as Washington Irving, but in the 80-year span between them America had already suffered a Civil War and our fate was decided: We were now careening forward as an industrial nation. Whereas descriptive, and sometimes epic, natural landscapes character-ize the Romantic era (with whom Irving is associated), and this focus on nature was passed to the Transcendentalists (Emerson and then Tho-reau), nature featured prominently in the "insider art" of the early 1800s, both in painting and in writing. But as the century drew on, Modernism began its ascent and realistic naturalism became increasingly fringe. By the time of John Muir, it was downright unfashionable. After the turn of the twentieth century the title of high art was given to the likes of Pablo Picasso and Henry James, not to realism.

But nostalgia for nature lingered and realistic portraiture served a useful social purpose, which continues to survive in the documentary form. C. G. Hine was no John Muir, but his tourist journey along *The Old Mine Road* was a skilled amateur's way of documenting a dying culture, one that faced nature, not progress. Not coincidentally, S. A.

Beach's *Apples of New York*, was written at the same time (1905–08) and with the same intentions: to document a pre-Modern culture before it vanished in the face of industrialization. For Hine that meant the Old Mine Road; for Beach it was apple diversity.

There's a vintage photograph in *The Old Mine Road*: A young man is sitting on a wooden log that serves as a guardrail over a stream crossing. It's a view taken from along the dirt path, which was only about 8 feet wide in 1908. Looking down the road, across the tiny bridge, the path quickly curves off into the bushes and deeper woods. You can't see where the road leads, but the forest enchants with Brothers Grimm–like potential. The man seated on the log is slouched, wearing suspenders and a straw hat. In all, we get the impression time is of no concern to him. He's *stopped to smell the roses* so to speak; he draws the modern reader into his mind-space. It's quieting.

The *Old Mine Road* book gives the best impression of what this area was like before cars and trucks forced the road's eventual expansion, but Hine reached further back in history, too. He gives accounts of the lost years between the Dutch use of the road in the 1600s and the D&H Canal days of the 1800s. French Huguenots began settling that span and lived in obscure isolation, particularly along the Upper Delaware and Lower Neversink Rivers just south of me. These homesteads were mostly fort-like structures designed to protect against Indian attack, but some estates achieved a level of colonial grandeur, too. One plantation was stately enough by the mid-1700s to have developed a sizable orchard, the trees of which were drawn on a map by a teenage boy who was the heir to the land. These apple trees are still there, mostly dead and buried under heaps of wild vines, but at least eight are still alive and one, "Old Pierre," still occasionally fruits. And the unmarked stones of a slave cemetery suggest that this plantation was once productive enough to also have exported goods from the farm.

C. G. Hines's and other accounts of the Old Mine Road indicate that it was commonly used for farm and raw material export throughout the 1700s. Of particular interest to me is the book's mention of cider barrels being transported during this time, headed to the Kingston markets and presumably making their way farther, to New York City, as well. It's very satisfying to know local cider was being made over 250 years ago and traveled by my house (literally just feet from my front door) en route to the city. Has nothing changed?

Well, yes. Now the road is a two-lane highway known as Route 209. It's been expanded to encourage economic development, bringing with it higher speeds. How speed and prosperity have become inseparably linked is sport for certain business owners and lackeys in government, but never mind that it's not true and that thousands and thousands of residents and small businesses along Route 209 are put in personal danger by fast traffic. Everyone knows that speed kills: If safety were the top priority, every effort, every penny, would go toward *slowing* the road, not enabling faster conditions! But progress moves on and the DOT continue to widen the lanes and beat back vegetation (all at the expense, by the way, of homeowner front yards, wild forests, and the rural feel of the area). Now it's "safe enough" for 18-wheelers to travel 60 miles an hour past children 5 feet away waiting for the school bus.

When we first moved to the area, there was only one traffic light at the intersection in town; now there are two more on either end of town. One is designed to allow trucks to pull out from a new distribution plant, and the other is the light at Future Interstate 86. Although this light isn't needed (there has never been a traffic buildup at this intersection), it would seem a foretelling gesture. Build it and they will come.

Like all the steady concessions inching us further and further along, the Old Mine Road is now a blur from a windshield. Drivers race against the clock for not having given themselves enough time to get where they need to be. Or maybe it's not their fault, maybe it's a social indenture that has us on our heels, traveling at greater and greater speeds to keep pace. Maybe it's some macro-cultural tyranny forcing us among work, school, shopping . . . a second job. I'll refrain from speculating on the causes but toss the spotlight on the results instead: roadkill. Deer, turtles, bears, even dogs and cats now pay the price for all our rushing around, dead along the Route 209. That's right, it's gotten to the point where drivers don't stop for pets anymore—we are *that* evolved. It's only when a pedestrian is hit (the driver, having outpaced their reaction time) that society stops and reckons with the consequences. This is where we are now. Now.

Still, you can see faint traces of Hines's world, like at the canal museum in Cuddebackville, or in the small town of Westbrookville, where an old stone house stands by the edge of the road. This "fort" is nothing but a small house built in the late 1700s, but because the threat of Indian attack loomed large, the homes at that time had small windows strategically located for shooting from. And just before the fort is an old cemetery with worn, thin stones made from the local slate. They are covered with lichens now, but you can still read the names. The Browns are buried here, the people who started my homestead.

And just before the cemetery is the stump of an old apple tree. I remember this tree to be about 50 years old and curiously leaning toward the road, seemingly attacking it. Tall trucks routinely pruned back the branches, but still it leaned, Pisa-like, over Route 209 for decades. I heard that road crews were under orders to take it down but didn't have the heart to kill an old apple tree. They, unlike their bosses, are not lackeys to development, so while all the other vegetation was thrust back from the road the old apple tree remained, becoming a humorous topic in town. The peculiarity of her survival got to the point where we were all rooting for her, like a symbol of the old ways. Like the lean in Delacroix's painting, she was Liberty Leading the People.

But alas, one day I slowed to notice she was gone. Did she fall on her own? Not likely. Chain saw dust formed a ring around the freshly cut stump. Looking down I saw not an inch of rot. She was just in the way, that's all. Another roadkill.

Downsizing

The year 2015 was epic for cider in the Northeast. The fruit cycle, having been upset by the 2012 blossom freeze, was on a heavy on-off pattern. The third and fifth years after a freeze can be especially abundant, but this wasn't the only factor—it was also a forest mast year. As cooperative as apples are, they were gearing up to participate with the wild cycle, and they did. Then to top it all off, it was a good growing season, too. Needless to say, I was going nuts trying to collect all the apples I could.

By the first of October, our cold storage room was already full and we had to put a 10-day freeze on all incoming fruit. "*No mas,*" I told the townspeople as they stopped by in the midst of our frantic pressing. We were trying to free up apple storage space, but in doing so we were starting to run out of fermenting space in the barn. And we didn't have enough fermenting vats, either. So I found a winery in the Hudson Valley with five 1,000-liter (270 gallon) "cubes" and set out with my trailer to collect them. But when I returned I found my driveway lined with bags and trash cans full of apples that people had left for me. I'd been gone for only two hours and already I had two more days of pressing as a result. I didn't get back to foraging until after Columbus Day.

For the first time in my life, I was sick of apples. All the racking and barrel washing that winter got me down. I was working 50-hour weeks at a time of year that we're supposed to be hibernating. Cider started to feel like a job, an obligation, an indenture. I had the opportunity to make more money with the increased volume—almost 2,400 gallons— but I felt I lost the intimacy with the product. I was always hurrying and accidentally breaking things—my refractometer, carboys, bottles. I felt like I'd lost my pulse on the fermentations, too, and let some go too hot while others needlessly sat. Tight for space, I had to take off my heavy jacket and hold in my breath to squeeze between cubes. Then, scaling the racks three layers high, I'd reach the top of barrels and slink across their surface like a roof rat pinned to the ceiling. Careful not to bang into the air locks, I'd take hours just to reach all the barrels for sampling the sugar progress. Later, as I racked the barrels, removing the empty vessels became like a giant game of Tetris. I wished I had a bigger space.

Anticipating the spring bottling work ahead of me, I elicited the help of Pastor Mike (one and the same as hunter Mike) and Asher to construct a new storage shed behind the cider barn. They were nearing completion as the most dreaded day of the year loomed: the day the bottles arrive from Quebec. If 30 barrels and five cubes ate up all my usable barn space in bulk containers, imagine all that liquid divided into 500 ml and 750 ml units. The space that one barrel takes up is only one-fifth the space the cases of bottles would eat up. Luckily, Mike and Asher were done with the large storage shed before the shipment arrived, but that's not the part I was anxious about. It's getting the bottles off the truck that's worrisome.

———

Jean Paul (I would later learn his name) lives in northeast Quebec. He knows less English than I know French. When he made it past the border with his Mack truck hauling a 53-foot box trailer, he thought he'd be arriving at a loading dock; he could eat his lunch while the warehouse workers unloaded, and he'd be back on the road in 25 minutes, back in Canada before nightfall, if things went as planned.

That's why Jean Paul was annoyed to see the addresses on Route 209 going down farther away from the address on the bill of lading. He had blown by me at 60 miles per hour and didn't notice for 15 minutes until he turned around and came back up. But again he missed our driveway, and now the street numbers were going up. He pulled over in Wurtsboro and called dispatch to yell at them in a language I wouldn't have understood. So they called me, and with their broken English told me to meet him down at the end of my driveway on Route 209. I stood there as cars, motorcycles, and dump trucks sped past. When I saw Jean Paul round the corner in his massive truck, my stomach trembled with dread. Slowing to a halt, the large French Canadian stepped out, shaking his head. "No—no, no, no, no. Thees is no possible."

"Well, I've done it before, I've unloaded trucks on 209 just where you are now. I've just got to have room to back my tractor out of the driveway."

"Are you mad? Thees a highway! I cannot stop traffic like thees!"

Jean Paul assessed the situation, walked up my driveway, measured the distance between my fence posts, and called dispatch. "*Pas possible,*" is all I understood. He handed the phone to me. "The driver says he can't pull in," said dispatch. "How long would it take you to unload on the road there?"

"Probably about an hour."

"If you can guarantee 60 minutes then I'll instruct him to wait." And with that I handed the phone back to him and he listened in. A few more French expletives later, Jean Paul hung up and sighed.

So we walked back down the driveway but when we reached the truck we found that traffic was stopped up. When a break in traffic from the other direction arose the line of cars behind the truck could go around but many drivers were too nervous to do so on their own and we had to wave them through. Jean Paul then hopped up and moved the vehicle over a few extra feet, and this is what it took to prevent traffic stoppages again, though the situation was still precarious enough that drivers felt compelled to honk as they sped past. Jean Paul met each honking horn with a sigh. As he fumbled for the right key to unlock the cargo door he said to me resignedly: "OK, Let's do this." With one more deep sigh he pushed the door upward so that I could begin unloading with my forks.

Just then 20 or 30 cases of wine bottles came cascading down onto the pavement. The rear pallet had become unstable in transit and was leaning against the door when he opened it. *Holy merde!* we were both thinking as glass shattered all over the roadway and unbroken bottles bounced and rolled out into traffic. What a nightmare! We scrambled to pick up what we could amid the tires of rushing traffic and I grabbed a flat broom to push the glass to the side. After cleaning up the mess and repackaging the loose bottles, we stacked the last pallet upright so that it was ready for me to lift with my tractor. But it wasn't. It was too heavy. Canadians stack their cases nine layers high per pallet (8 feet) and my tractor, I now know, doesn't lift that much weight. So I grabbed an empty pallet from my barn and went back to the truck to remove a layer. Still too heavy. So I removed another layer, and it was still too heavy. I did it again, and even at six layers high the tractor struggled to get them off the cargo deck. Only at five layers high could the forks on my tractor safely lift that much weight, and dread turned to hopelessness when we calculated what this meant in terms of unloading all 24 pallets: We'd have to divide them all in half and make 48 trips to the storage shed. So much for the day.

Luckily I had a stack of unused pallets sitting around, but backing into speeding traffic with my tractor and getting berated by car horns made the task unnerving. Polly and Peter came to the rescue and helped Jean Paul as the three of them labored to remove the top layers of the pallets and create half pallets for me to cart off. We worked at a frazzled and hurried pace as cars and other 18-wheelers blew by, sometimes rocking the whole box trailer. After an hour we found our rhythm, a pace of one trip per 15 minutes, but with 38 more trips to go it was looking bleak. And no way could we keep up this pace, either!

After my 12th trip to the storage shed, I returned to find the flashing lights of a state police car and an officer trying to reason with Jean Paul.

The cop looked at me. "Look, tell him to get this thing up the driveway or get it out of here. You can't be doing this on a state highway."

"State highway? This is my road! I pay taxes like everyone else and this house was here before cars were even invented!"

"You can tell it to the judge after I give you a ticket. And if you still continue to defy my orders you'll be arrested."

Cooler heads prevailed and Jean Paul started measuring again. He closed the cargo door and decided to give it a shot. Luckily the cop also decided to help—he called for another unit to stop traffic. With two flashing state police cars on either end, Jean Paul angled the massive vehicle in a manner I didn't think possible. It was essentially jackknifed, but somehow still moving. Squeezing between the fence posts, he managed to get the beast up to where the tail end of the truck was a good 20 feet beyond the road—enough distance for me and my tractor to work. Hurray!

"Don't try to back out on your own, just call us and we'll stop traffic when you leave," said the cop, and with that we were back at work. I was so relieved to be unloading from the driveway and not the road, but I saw a look in the Jean Paul's face that said my anxiety was now his. If it was hard getting in, imagine how hard that maneuver would be in reverse! And with limited visibility!

And then it started to rain. Through the whole of the afternoon Peter, Jean Paul, and Polly broke down the towers, restacked half pallets, and I drove wet cases to the storage shed. It sucked, but we were making progress.

Sometime between the 30th and the 36th trips the sun had set. What kind of truck doesn't have interior lights, anyways? Flashlights and cell phone lights were called to duty; then someone had the bright idea of parking the Subaru by the road. In the headlights we worked into the night, wet and starving. Finally, trip number 48 came, and when I saw the truck finally emptied I rejoiced. But it wasn't over. We still had to get the truck out of there.

I thanked Peter and stuffed some extra cash in his hand for working in an emergency. Jean Paul, Polly, and I went up to the house to dry off, and I called the police for Jean Paul's escort. From the other end of the phone came: "It can't be done tonight. Call us in the morning when there's daylight." Click.

Luckily, Polly knows French. She told Jean Paul the situation, and the poor man's expression sank. He'd been holding on to hope that he could put this miserable day behind him, and now he was stuck here. People gravitate toward a career in truck driving because they like the independence and time alone—so do farmers—but now we were all stuck together for the night. Thank God Quebec is cider country.

Polly was great: She had unexpectedly spent the day repacking heavy boxes, she made the dinner, she served as translator, and she showed Jean Paul the guest room. But her work didn't end there: The next morning presented perhaps the greatest challenge for us all because we were unsure if getting the truck out was even possible! And when I placed the call to the police, I heard, "No officers are available at this time, try again in 30 minutes." And after half an hour I tried again but got the same response. Breakfast and coffee were becoming a distant memory when I tried a third time and was given cold instructions: "Go figure it out for yourself. Do you have any road flares?"

The three of us returned to the scene, and Jean Paul mapped out what he'd have to do. At least it was a dry day. "You stop cars thees way," he told Polly. "You, sir, go around z'bend and stop cars that way," to me. "I won't see traffic until I'm on z'road. Eet's up to you to keep them from hitting me."

I walked up the road halfway around the bend so that I was no longer in sight of the truck or Polly. I stood by the side of the road waving my arms, but I wasn't having much luck slowing the enraged commuters. I noticed traffic stopped coming from the other direction—Polly must have been convincing—but my efforts were more like those of toreador. It was out of my hands when Jean Paul apparently already backed halfway out and was across both lanes. I could hear cars screech but no crash. Finally, traffic had stopped, and I went around the bend to watch. With a few back-and-forths Jean Paul slowly maneuvered the monster out of the driveway, contorting it like a pretzel. I couldn't believe my eyes when it was finally on the road in an L-shaped position. It took him only 500 feet to straighten out into one lane, and just like that he was truckin' again.

As I watched Jean Paul drive off north I felt the weight of the world lift, but this experience taught me something: I couldn't live like this. Things had to change around here. As I saw it, I was trying to do too much. I could either make it so that my farm could accommodate big trucks or I would have to accept that I was over my limit. In other words: Was I going to keep growing my business or shrink it?

We decided small is who we are. Venture capitalists continued to seek us out and tempt us with offers in the following years, 2016 and 2017, but we had finally become certain of our vision of cider and it had no place in expanding markets. To me that is a totally different market, and I'm fine with that other cider expanding without me. Vermeer painted small, Corot painted small, and Morandi painted small, and they just happen to be three of my favorite painters. Now I suddenly realized why I like them so much! They are from very different time periods and painted in very different styles, yet intimacy is an unmistakable common thread among them. Those paintings wouldn't work at a larger scale. Small scale is the key to this type of success.

Intimacy has a value that must be managed by an economy (*economy* simply means "the budgeting of resources"—think, for instance, of fuel economy). That economy, unlike the modern financial economy, fails when it grows, because it disrupts the values of greater importance. When Vermeer tried to paint beyond the borders of his usual small canvas (as he sometimes did on a medium-sized canvas), the loss of intimacy became as obvious as the red dot in the Japanese flag. They are still masterful paintings, but they are clearly lacking by comparison. I wouldn't say our 2015 ciders were lacking in the same way, but if nothing else, my personal relationship to the process was stretched to where I felt the intimacy was unsustainable. Or maybe it was just that I was so frantic all the time trying to keep up that I couldn't enjoy the intimacy. Either way, the jig was up. We were going to make less cider from now on.

Incidentally, I hope no one confuses large artworks with large-scale cider or wine production. (And yes, I *would* be offended comparing cider to art if that were the case.) Maybe you can compare industrial production with *commercial* art, but please, for the love of God, don't compare it to real art! Just as Vermeer doesn't work at a large scale, Gerhard Richter paintings and Tintoretto murals don't work at a smaller scale. But they still have a carefully managed economy to them based on qualities more important to them. Although they *do* also possess intimacy, their value has more to do with physicality and a rhythm that large spaces create.

Your eye must travel great distances, and that sets up a different tempo. Artists choose the formal qualities most suited for them, but the difference between successes and failures has to do with how well those formal qualities are budgeted. So let's be *absolutely* clear that large-scale art is not the same as large-scale food, drink, or crop production. Industrial is industrial and handmade still means something.

Like a Duck to Water

Cider culture: When we hear these words we might picture large gatherings of cider drinkers and assume that's what a cider culture is. Or we might picture the farmers and cider makers employed within the industry, washing barrels and picking apples, and we might say to ourselves: *That's what cider culture looks like.* These are both correct assumptions, they *are* part of a cider culture, but they are only components of a bigger, complete cider culture that requires more than a few working parts. Let me explain.

A true cider culture is an agricultural tradition that has emerged over long periods of time and transforms entire locations into the living embodiments of the drink. The best example of something similar that I can think of is Maine's lobster culture. By his or her job description, a "lobsterman" is someone who goes out on the boat, sets the traps, harvests the lobsters, and sells them on the dock. But when outsiders refer to "the lobstermen," they aren't just referring to the actual fishermen; they're talking about the whole town, including the dockworkers, the boatbuilders, and even townspeople who have nothing to do with the industry. The place and the people have become defined by the job at hand.

That's what cider culture used to be to many regions in America, and in some locations it even still exists! Cider may not be the one thing that culture is known for, but come September and October it defines the people fairly enough. Similarly, wine culture still exists in small villages in Europe, where whole towns go to the hills to work the harvest. Everyone is involved—the kids, the priest, the whole village; the people's work becomes the embodiment of that location. Perhaps it's the memory of this communal identity that most strongly drives the recent interest in cider, especially in areas like New England where the link is still traceable.

My initial trips to New England in 2010, visiting cider producers and Cider-Days, made me realize what was missing in my life. They also reminded me of my ducks after I dug a pond for them—also that same year. Lucy and Moosey (our geese) as well as our ducks, Senior Splotches, Pagoda, Snowball, Large Marge, Miss Wobbles, Pudge, Patches O'Houlihan, and The Ocho (the eighth) were without a swimming hole since they were hatched in 2008 (coincidentally, the same year The Cidery was hatched). In those two years they frequently developed leg sprains and bumble foot, which is a foot infection making it too painful to walk. Their top-heavy bodies were disproportionately large for their skinny legs, and walking around all day isn't what they are designed to do (even though their breed name, Indian Runner, hints at how natural they seem on land). When at last I was done creating the pond, the ducks—curious little guys that they are—wandered over the banks, and their beady eyes bugged out of their heads the moment they saw open water. They made a quick dash for it and spent the entire afternoon playing, quacking with joy, and diving under the surface to explore the depths. It was as if they had been swimming their whole lives. And they did this every day from then on. But what later struck me about the pond is that it eventually cured their leg issues. Buoyed by the appropriate environment, the strain on their legs was lifted and the problems vanished. A duck was meant to be supported by water, and a cider maker was meant to be supported by a cider culture. I saw this now.

But New York State's culture is quite different from rural New England's. In no place might this be more evident than in our big orchards and wine menus. It's called the Empire State for a reason: A New Yorker's gaze is always outward, engaging with the rest of the world. New Yorkers push the boundaries, and our culture becomes extended onto others. Many growers here, I've heard them say, intend on feeding the world, and this mentality becomes evident in the size of some of our orchard operations. The same is not true in rural New England, where food is assumed not to travel beyond Boston. But the biggest difference is in the attitude. Whereas New Yorkers want to engage with the world, true Yankees just want the world to leave them alone. Community versus expansive markets. Maybe it's due to New York's greater population, or maybe it's the lingering effects of Dutch versus Puritan culture; whatever the reason, these two contrasting cultures now stand as polar influences in the shaping of cider in America. Cider can either be local, or it can be global. Both cultures will reward their farmers for their respective gaze, but it was in rural New England that I first discovered a culture supportive of my approach to cider.

When I returned I was hungry to help grow cultural cider in New York, but ironically I was seated right on the edge of an old cider tradition here in the Catskills. Being from the city originally, I assumed like most people that the place to find advanced culture was in that direction (east and southeast of me), but cider culture was alive and well in my home county. Up in the mountains there were hundreds of thousands of unfarmed (or lightly cultivated) apple trees that had *always* been used for home or small cidery production. But when the small mills closed (the last of them shut down about 20 years ago), there was suddenly no infrastructure for the fruit processing and the age-old autumn tradition was left hanging, with a perilous present or future.

Aging property owners particularly had reasons to fear the dieback of this culture. Trees they had cared for their whole lives wouldn't be of value to the next generation unless the passion for this way of life persisted. These are not clonal trees we're talking about, they're trees that have the life expectancy of a tortoise times two, and they are like a gold mine of character. In the same way antique cars have quirks that only the owner knows about, so the old trees take time to develop a relationship with. But if people in the modern world don't understand the components of good cider (including the culture), who would be able to comprehend the value of these trees? Certainly not the new city transplants who assumed, as I did at first, that times had changed and everything needs to be updated: new trees, new varieties, new growing methods, new rootstocks . . .

In my town alone, 95-year-old Bob had a 4-acre cider orchard that he planted in the 1970s during one of the stronger back-to-the-land pushes. This was a time when cider cultivation was first being re-explored, and just like today people were sharing insights, trading graft wood, and doing community pressings. But when the cider mills closed and the culture dipped in the early twenty-first century, the future of these beloved trees was called into question. Out of sheer luck, we linked up with Bob, and I've become sort of the interim orchardist on his property, but we're talking about just one cider orchard in one town in a vast cider region alone!

I was excited to think (as many people were in these parts) that when small-production cider sprang back around 2010 to 2015, it would birth an army of future apple cultivators (or cultivators of uncultivated trees), but now I wonder if the accessibility of mass-produced cider might actually be making matters worse. At that point, wouldn't cultivating a small orchard or harvesting out-of-the-way trees seem like *Why even bother?* It's not cider's national popularity that makes location-based cider (such as co-op or community ciders) sustainable; it's the care of the culture—what Candide would say to Pangloss.

As luck would have it, I stepped into a void for this culture when I moved to Sullivan County a few years after the last mills closed, but by macro-business standards I was stepping into an opportunity that I was not able to maximally capitalize on. The conditions were ripe for an extremely ambitious plan. Someone could have seized the moment and built an empire by consolidating the wealth of superior cider trees and the community support and turned it into an efficient single-company operation. But I couldn't, and still can't, imagine how that would be good for the actual trees or the personal relationship we develop with them. Scale and homogenization would dilute the pride we have for each community, each property, each tree. No amount of outside pressure—neither financial pressures, nor even artistic standards—must be allowed to get between the community and their trees. And I believe, without the slightest doubt in my mind, that the great cider cultures of this world (and wine, too) originated because the culture was inward-facing and locally focused. Maybe the country as a whole (ahem, England) was aggrandizing, but the agricultural communities themselves were not. Regional styles are the result of regionalism—plain and simple.

Certain areas of New England and Appalachia were able to sustain an unbroken tradition for cider throughout Prohibition and the twentieth century, albeit at a very low simmer, because they had amassed a strong pillar of cider culture. It survived in hiding, but it did survive. What I'm talking about differs from isolated basement wine or cider making in that in these places whole communities openly talked about it, shared it, drank it, traded, boasted, and pursued higher and higher knowledge regarding it. That's *exactly* what we mean when we say a person has culture, too. You might call them hillbillies or Yankees, but they don't mind. In fact, if it buys them some privacy they'd be happy pretending to be "dumb rednecks." They hold on to something that is more likely to be corrupted than helped by economic development and greater awareness. They are an inward-facing people who don't see anything wrong with being called provincial. In my mind these are the ideal conditions for building a lasting cider culture.

As America now looks to grow a cider industry, the hope is that more cider cultures will emerge. That's a fantastic goal! This would guarantee sustainability and create longevity between the generations—two things drastically missing in Modern agriculture—but suffice it to say it's a little ambitious to set our sights on re-creating something like Spanish or English cider culture. Personally, I think it would be disastrous to overlook our own Yankee cider roots still slumbering in backwoods and in the back of our consciousness. But no matter which cider culture we emulate, what worries me about the larger American culture is that we will need to turn exactly 180 degrees in order to face it. I can't help but think our business culture is going to sabotage this mission by insisting its own needs get met first. The way we conduct our business is outward-facing, expansive, and aggrandizing by nature—everything cider culture is not.

Is our dominant culture compatible with cider? We know it's compatible with beer, but will cider culture just be a clone of that? Is our nation still compatible with regionalism, and regional styles? I think the answer to all that is: Yes, but only if we start at a location, build from the core (then the tree, then the fruit), think small, be patient, support local, and above all else disassociate ourselves from industrial production. New cider cultures may not appear in our lifetime, and they sure as hell can't be bought, but we can be happy working toward the goal knowing we started with real trees and not short-lived clones. "Plant a pear for your heir."

Future Interstate 86

From satellite photographs the valley, which includes the Mamakating Hollow, looks like a very long gully along the eastern edge of the Catskill

Mountains, clearly dividing the highland regions of the west from the Hudson River Valley and the coastal sections of southeast New York. (Seriously, check it out on Google Earth. Turn all the labels off and you'll see how noticeable the gully is—even more so with just the topographic settings on.) This long, deep scrape starts north of Kingston and extends more than 100 miles south, past the Delaware Water Gap. But what's also interesting about this valley is that it divides the dense human population (east) from the dense tree population (west), and this, too, is clearly visible from space. Perhaps Google is enhancing the colors, but to my eyes the developed east looks gray while the forests appear green. If those two cultures were at war with each other (and let's hope that they're not), then this valley would be the trench line.

The eastern wall of this valley is formed by the Shawangunk Ridge. The "Gunks," as they say, act as the last line of defense against the buzzing of the human activity on the other side. But because we sit so much lower than the ridge we liken it, not so jokingly, to a levee keeping out New York's urban sprawl. To me a breach in this wall would be catastrophic, but the DOT has already carved a massive "cut" in the mountaintop to make it easier for traffic along Future Interstate 86. This highway connects regions east-to-west and passes through the trench line and continues the length of Sullivan County, seemingly immune to the barriers posed by geological strata. The Shawangunk is not the only mountain Future I-86 has displaced.

As a connector we should rejoice, right? No more obstacles! But it begs the question: Will one culture dominate over the other? Developers are actively building casinos and shopping centers along the corridor, but are wild spaces expanding in the other direction? I believe they are: For every bit of energy thrust in our direction, some backyard or alley gets neglected and wildlife returns. Maybe an appreciation for wildlife returns home with them, too? Modern systems of order become compromised by wild values in the same way wild spaces are destroyed by our human compulsion to develop order. A slow leveling is taking place between the two regions, and the superhighway, Future Interstate 86, is just what we need for this to proceed faster, right?

Actually, the verdict is still out on the success of Future I-86 bringing economic expansion to Sullivan County. There's still one more barrier urban and rural people need to conquer: their fear of each other. No amount of highway widening will facilitate the haves mingling with the have-nots if they see them as culturally backward. And the ill will goes the other way, too: Locals antagonize urban fears with Confederate flags, YOU CAN HAVE MY GUN WHEN YOU PRY IT FROM MY COLD, DEAD FINGERS bumper stickers, and never-removed TRUMP 2016 election signs.

The trench divides two financial economies just as much as it does the wilderness from urban development; a $100 bill means something very different to people from the city than it does to a local Catskiller. But what's really, *really* interesting is that the wealth divide is/was not founded by income or class. Nope, the divide predates all that. Our "poorness" originated from the land. We are who are because of our soils. It was the *soils* that defined our cultural development.

The soils of Sullivan County, if you even want to call them that, are so shallow, so rocky, and so "poor" that historically few settlers chose to live here. When opportunity brought settlers west during the eighteenth and nineteenth centuries (after Sullivan pushed the native people into Canada), most of the settlers bypassed the Catskills and preferred to keep going until they arrived in western New York and the Finger Lakes area. There they found the rich lands they were looking for (the same soils predicating much of Cornell's experiments and advice, by the way). Over time the Catskills became about as valued as Baltic Avenue on a Monopoly board.

Large parts of New England and Appalachia share a similar history. In fact, what people call hillbilly culture today started in New England as Yankee culture. It moved from the rough climate and terrain in the Northeast and spread to similar terrain in the southwest direction. When the first wave of colonists claimed the prime fertile soils located along river valleys, coastlines, or navigable rivers, the next generation (or those fresh off the boats) had no rich undeveloped lands to begin on their own. Unable to afford prime lands, they needed to either go west or climb higher. This pattern continued long into the twentieth century and was described in the 1930s by Ulysses Hedrick, in his book *History of Agriculture in the State of New York*. In a most fascinating passage (spanning pages 92 and 93 of said book, available for free online) he tells how a ragtag group from other cultures came to define the style of agriculture north and west of the Hudson Valley ("upstate," but particularly central and western New York). And he cites migrants from New England, with their "poorness of soil and badness of climate," as having the greatest influence. This "produced certain traits—a shrewd, calculating, inquisitive, thrifty people—lumped as 'Yankees.'"

Be it Maine or Kentucky, Yankees were always without prime flatlands for certain crops. Those rare pockets of good soils they did possess were direly needed for staple crops, what we grow in our gardens today. If you can picture hill country, you don't think of "amber waves of grain" or excesses of money. It was geographically impossible for beer to play a major role in this existence. Apples are the only "crop" that grew well on the steep scarps of rock and snow. And in the end, cider triumphed over wine and beer for agricultural reasons, thus becoming "American." We owe it to our terrain that we became an apple (and cider) culture. This is an extremely important point concerning American identity and heritage if you believe that struggle can be a catalyst for character development, so I'll repeat it another way: Apples, and cider culture, became who we are as Americans because of unfavorable climate and terrain.

Then we found level terrain via expansionism. We overtook the Great Plains and found endlessly abundant good soils. With innovations in transportation, science, machinery, and financial economies, we made every effort to make farming even easier. We nullified the barriers on a macro scale (like terrain and distance) as if we were prepping a monumental "blank canvas"; but this time we proceeded by repopulating with a monoculture—one turbocharged by Miracle-Gro.

In the second section of the book, I explained how almost all wine and cider begins with a similar neutralization: That which the farmer didn't already kill gets neutralized by SO_2 and/or sterile filtration. But this rant is located in the business section because the leveling of terrain happens here, too. The culture in corporate offices is no different from the agriculture on most farms today. Across the board, it's the leveling of terrain, *not* acclimation to unfavorable terrain, that now describes how we proceed and who we are.

Nothing can better sum up our patterns, particularly of business, than the word *expansionism*. By leveling trade barriers and subsidizing fuel and transportation systems, we have achieved a barrier-free market that makes it as easy to buy a banana in New York as it is in Costa Rica. Whereas before the local option was the only option, it's no longer difficult to compare apples and oranges, to hold in each hand fruit from two corners of the world.* Now, that's some leveling!

I can't hide a pessimistic attitude regarding leveling in farming or business, but I don't really have the right to complain, either, since I'm 99 percent the product of the culture myself. I'm too much in the shit to even see my options clearly. And anyway, those of us who make the effort to buy local are just doing so using money from a global economy. Yet I'd like to think that buying local is more than merely a protest against leveling the terrain and homogenization, even if I often despair it's too late. The modern business model, for better or worse, is an homage to expansionism, conformity, and globalism—and yes, it's a celebration of homogenization: One size fits all. And that's who we are now; we are *not* as Ulysses Hedrick said: a culture defined by unfavorable climate and terrain. But if we are still free enough to protest the fact that our landscape has been leveled, I hope we can also appreciate the values of difficulties. Until we are completely leveled (which seems to be happening faster than ever), there will be challenges to every locale. For now, it's what saves regional character and has saved cider culture in some parts.

When I lived in New York, I left for the country as often as possible. As exciting as the city is, it's also boring in another way: Manicured parks don't satisfy the need for wild nature (in fact, I took more inspiration from the way weeds grew back in brownfield sites). The melting pot may support one type of growth, but I learned from abandoned trees the value of another. And I, personally, needed this in my life.

Today, when I see all those cars coming to the Catskills on Future I-86 in the summer, I don't see people "getting away" (although they

---

* Please join me in an appreciation for the word *difficult*, a word I heard described to me growing up. It's a word that doesn't hide its etymology very well: In plain view are both *culture* and *differ* (as in *different*). We've already belabored the word *culture*, but note that *differ* stems from a word meaning "distress," often applied to poverty. Here again we've found a word that connects soil wealth and human wealth, but I, personally, like to think the word *difficult* means "a culture that begs to differ."

might think they are); I see people "going" someplace. Relaxation is *not* the difference between work and escaping work, it's simply a different type of challenge. Urban people come to the mountains for a culture that begs to differ.

And, my!—you should see the traffic leaving the city on summer Fridays. That's how I got here, too, on Future Interstate 86. I followed it through the massive cut in the Shawangunk Ridge designed to level the barriers between town and country. The DOT even used the rock from the top of the mountain to build the ramp up leading to it—what better example of leveling do you need? Maybe it could be said that the cut is the perfect symbol for spanning the distances between humanity and nature, old culture and future culture, or inward-facing versus expansionism? This may seem conceptual to you, but a very tangible transition occurs when you leave the open farmlands of the Hudson Valley with its large-scale orchards and enter the undeveloped Catskills: The cut becomes the gateway to the land of wild apples. I just pray that man does not carry with him the Midas touch.

Sad to say, I'm highly doubtful it's going to end well for the wild apple trees, but Thoreau was wrong about their survival so I could be, too. What if instead of conventional agriculture pushing this way, what if wild farming, forcharding, were to push back and find a home in our larger culture instead? Again, I doubt this based on the fact that the ever-growing financial economy has yet to find the appropriate value and a reason to adjust its expectations. All signs point to "full steam ahead." Pretentiously, people seem to think that the wealth of urban New York is justification for expanding their ways—teach us hillbillies what's best for us. In actuality, we have an economy about us that is quite admirable and appropriate for our terrain, so in the end I've just got to hold out hope that our slow regional qualities survive here along the Old Mine Road. Seeing what wild trees are capable of, we should never lose hope. Maybe the cut along Future I-86 will connect the two cultures without leveling them into one; or maybe the dominant culture will just swallow the other whole and we will all careen faster forward. For now, though, there's hope: From the crossroads we can choose two different directions.

Epilogue

The funny thing is, I don't even really like apples. They're okay, I guess, but I prefer vegetables to fruit. I do like to sample the apples as I go from site to site, try to dig through the array of flavors, but I've never gone out of my way to collect them to eat. It wasn't until I started making cider that I've done this (and now I *really* go out of my way), but what I love is the tree. It's the tree that I want to drink in. I can't get enough of how expressive wild or naturalized trees are, and it amazes me how unique each one is. They radiate "being" back at me, and I imagine I could feel their presence even if I were blindfolded. They also have a way of communicating wisdom (especially the old ones) and the virtues of home; they do so better than any other living creature that I know of. Not to take away from the individuality of the other trees in the forest, the oaks and pines, but somehow apples have a way of articulating their uniqueness to us even in numerous stands where they develop to the same general shape and size. When trees are allowed to be themselves, be.it genetically or behaviorally, no congregation is too large to dilute each tree's individual dignity.

This is the great crime of modern orchards. Somehow we have taken those implicit qualities and subverted them, just as we have chicken or cattle on farms of a certain scale. We try *not* to treat them as individuals in a food system removed from the lives of consumers, and a system based on extreme economic pressures, outside forces. Now when I walk the rows of a mega-orchard, or even smaller orchards planted high-density, I can't feel the presence of individual trees. At the very best, the fruit variety might stand out as unusual, but that's small consolation. It kills me to think we can look in the eyes of a fast-food ranch cow and not see the creature looking back at us, like it's already dead. Maybe that's what we need food to be, inanimate—food that does not look back at us—but what a strange disconnect to nature we've allowed for ourselves. Addressing struggle and death is never easy, but turning it off, excluding ourselves, seems too great a sacrifice. It's downright weird that we can even do it! On a macro-cultural scale we've become the sociopath of nature. (And yet when a true sociopath breaks our human-made laws we suddenly get moral, as if a natural law was broken!)

I wonder if we are the only creature to toggle between this on-off switch, mostly in the off position now. But my greater concern (and the concern of many people these days) is that we are becoming increasingly more sociopathic in our relationship to the rest of the planet. I can say that in the case of the apple this is true. Some 150 years of progress and we've officially snapped. The overall cultivation—our relationship with the tree—has become Ted Bundy–esque, and the focus on varietal selections, clonal rootstocks, and other aids to mass-production further proves to me society is not focused on the lives of the trees but only on our own bottom line. Our relationship is dictated by the outside pressure. We've allowed it. Now all we want out of the trees is workers (maybe because we define ourselves by our work), but thank God for the office romance!

In the prologue to this book I wrote:

> *I'm opposed to anything turbocharged to override the pace of natural acclimation. What unites and distinguishes natural practices is a look away from predetermination. I want to look toward nature, where things happen, they don't happen, or they happen in unexpected ways. Natural practices seek acceptance with these facts.*

Pretty pretentious words for a man who wants to turn away from pre-determination, right? Because let's face it, the connection to a more natural existence conflicts with many hard realities we've created for ourselves. Man's realities are as real as natural ones now, so it's a tad idealistic throwing around the word *natural* as though the new realities aren't part of our nature, too. We can't deny this, and it's for this recognition that most farmers, producers, and business leaders rationalize a growing divide between their highly manipulated practices (their cultural practices) and purely natural outcomes. Maybe the question isn't, *How do we grow the connection between these worlds*; instead it should be, *Is it even necessary?* Who cares?

We now look at nature from the vantage point of what has become a contrived existence: a hybrid of the artificial and natural laws. After thousands of years of Western culture, we exist in the matrix, within elaborate systems that *absolutely* affect the way we relate to the natural world. Money, law, civilities, language—they weren't there until we *put* them there, but they frame our relationship to nature now, in both good and bad ways. The only question is if our relationship is affected for the better. Within financial realities, for example, we can recognize the power of money in affecting environmental causes (solar energy, for example), but we must also acknowledge that being financially indentured (required to work) might not give us the time to relate to nature; the value of that connection can become a low priority. Maybe that's for the best—I don't know. But I do know it's important to recognize we exist between the two worlds and we must constantly reevaluate the safer direction to travel. That's just self-survival 101.

For those who think the natural direction I'm advocating in *Uncultivated* is regressive, that development and progress have happened and continue to happen because they are our best solution, consider that our resolve is not, and never was, a definite 100 percent decision. Choosing to go in one direction might have looked more like going with the five jurors in a split five-to-four case. But looking back at those decisions in light of new evidence, one single vote could tip the scales and make our development look like the unwise choice. And I mean to suggest that in my industries—apple growing, cider making, and farm businesses—this evidence has already surfaced. We thought we were cultivating wisely in the twentieth century, following a good manner of moving forward, but it turned out to be deadening to an important part of our own being. We forgot to include the Whole. We went with the lesser choice, we became sociopathic, and now we must amend this error (especially when it comes to apple trees). This is not regressive, and in fact *not* to reopen the case would be irresponsible. Assuming our whole health is a priority, and we also need to feel culturally connected to our location and to food, putting our efforts into uncultivation is actually a progressive solution. It's not nostalgia if that's where we're heading.

———

Readers of this book might wonder what the hell sweeping glass from the highway has to do with wild apple trees. But I like to tell that story to anyone who wonders what foraging is like, because I don't want to lose sight of the fact that nature, an unaltered one, relates to the quote unquote "real world." Uncultivation is not about reaching for an impossible standard. What I do professionally is both hampered by and immersed in the mechanics of business, same as anyone else. I couldn't forage if I was economically obligated to be elsewhere, so it's up to me to figure out a way to make it work. Everyone has to. Foraging is indeed bucolic, as is cultivating apples on a farm, as is drinking cider, but none of these things exist without the nitty-gritty, the unglamorous, and the slog. It's an obligation we all have: Bridge the things we love about this world with the things we hate, make it whole.

If we allow our daily existence, the din of life, and especially our business decisions to be segregated from the inspiration of art, wild landscapes, food cultures, and our personal thoughts and beliefs, then I'm not sure there's any hope for cider going forward. But if that's *not* the case, and all those things are *one* culture, one practice, then we need to decide in what manner we want to cultivate going forth. There is an economy to be figured out, that's for sure, but it's not going to be a pretty future if the immediate financial realities rule the direction in which we go. We need to rise to ideals. The prisoners behind the orchard fence can't lead us, only the escapees. Uncultivation is about opposing the momentum that took the tree at the center of Paradise and brought it far from where people live to mass-planted monocrop orchards, cloned, sprayed, and homogenized. I'm in favor of a better economy that values nutrition, taste, cultural diversity, and relationships. What better to lead the way than wild apples? They are exploratory, adaptive, creative, and contribute to the culture of every place they inhabit. But what makes them wild is that we allow them to be so.

It's true wild apples set the bar awfully high. I realize this, but I am convinced they are not an impossible target for a working cider industry. It's too easy to allow critics to deride art, ideals, and for that matter love, by using that real-world bullshit. We live in a world with immediate needs and we must have practical solutions, I realize this. But ideals can become real if we strive for them. The apple tree knew this, and it escaped the prison yard; it transcended one reality, and so can we.

Lastly, I want to say a word about the cultural connection to the fruit, not just the tree. Clearly this is the layperson's point of entry into the pomological world, but I pray to God we expound on that and see the apple as a reflection of the tree and the tree a reflection of the place. We need to care for it all. I mentioned I don't really favor eating apples, but as a person of Irish descent I can speak to another point of entry. But that's all cider is, I promise you, simply a point of entry. The greater fulfillment is waiting in our development of a cider culture, which is about participation and finding ourselves in the drink. A cider culture, of course, will lead us back to the apple, back to the branch, back to the trunk, back to the roots—*our* roots in a location, "home." It's All One, to quote Dr. Bronner, whether we start with the general and move to the specific, or vice versa. The death of this culture, when we simply don't care about where the apples are from and how they were raised—*That's what specialists are for!*—spells the death of many things.

The most influential book in all of history begins by telling readers that all the plants and animals were put on this planet to serve us. Some have taken that as justification for the sociopathic mechanics of our food systems, the very thing that keeps us alive, but the Bible makes no mention of, nor advocates for, the psychological removedness that we began cultivating in earnest 150 years ago, both on the farm and in regard to wild nature. To the contrary, the rest of the text seems to suggest we need to settle down and build relationships to this earth, ground ourselves. How did "cultivate our garden" become divorced from emotionally and spiritually bonding to our garden? Or appreciating the dignity of the life that we consume? I don't know, but I know that the apple tree, more than most anything else, has the ability to reflect our options back to us. The question is *not* whether we'll cultivate the tree, it's whether we'll cultivate a personal connection to it. Thoreau addressed this in the nineteenth century when he wrote *Wild Apples*. And then again in the twentieth century, Shel Silverstein best expressed this relationship in *The Giving Tree*. Hopefully soldiers for this cause continue well into the twenty-first century.

———

The year 2018 is shaping up to be one without many wild apples in Sullivan County. It's not that we had a frost or anything; it's just an off-year for apples. But even if I don't make cider this fall, I still know I will be making cider 5 years from now, 50 years from now, and 200 years from now. That's what being part of a cultural tradition does for you. And that's also why I'm not keen on supplanting the still-living culture of cider in America with an amnesiac ruse: Cider is Modern, cider is innovative, cider must be subjugated to the real world. A better world, and a better economy, already exists for the apple, and the goal, in my mind, is just to be the living incarnation of cider past and future. I like that I'll be haunting some other poor farmers in 100 years' time as they do exactly what I do now, and exactly what other farmers did in the past. To find us, those future cider farmers just need to follow the tree down underground. Our spirits will be resting, hibernating like cider does, waiting to rise again in the spring and mix it up with the living. Wherever cider is locally grown, made naturally and in tandem with the seasons, you will find us, living forever.

ACKNOWLEDGMENTS

*I*t took five years and a mercifully light 2018 crop to complete this book. But it took more than time and a clear schedule to hone the concepts, so I'd like to credit the people, places, and things that realized *Uncultivated.*

I'll start with the places: The actual writing took place in Wurtsboro, New York; Isle au Haut, Maine; Miami, Florida; Jaffrey, New Hampshire; Mazunte, Mexico; my childhood home in Potomac, Maryland; and in a cabin along the Neversink River (Sullivan County, New York). This would look like baseless drifting had it not been for the strength offered by those places. In fact, the premise of this book is not to look for greener grass elsewhere but to love where you live, root-down, and acclimate. So it only makes sense that I was able to intimately write about home from a diversity of places, because I was made to *feel* home in all of them. Being one with the environment requires the environment be one, and for that achievement I'd like to acknowledge the aforementioned places—everything and everyone there, including the ghosts.

The people to acknowledge are too numerous to count. I'd sincerely like to thank everyone in my life, including people who probably think their role was insignificant to this book. So for fear of omitting an important name, let me *not* list individual people here (you know who are—the Steves, the Cates, the Bens, Patricks, and Johns, as well as all the family and friends dating back over 30 years who've encouraged me artistically, professionally, and agriculturally). Except Polly deserves special recognition and the honor of being the only person specifically named. It's obvious to me, and to everyone who knows her, how adept she is at bringing out the best in someone. Maybe she plays silent at first, maybe even the enabler, but her sights are on the long game. Her sly navigation around my many "issues" truly makes this her book just as much as it is mine. Seriously: Believe me when I say that.

And finally, "things" deserve acknowledgment. I hope what I'm about to say does not take anything away from my heartfelt human-to-human appreciation, but the muse of this book, and for large part of my life, is the apple tree. Obviously, *Uncultivated* needs a subject matter, but the apple tree is so much more than a thing. In fact, she is equal parts person, place, and thing. I acknowledge her wisdom, companionship, beauty, and sacrifice—without which this book doesn't exist. Truly, she is the giving tree. Please God, I hope what I've written does right by her.

INDEX

Note: Page numbers in *italics* refer to figures. Page numbers followed by *t* refer to tables.

INDEX

ABOUT THE AUTHOR

Noah Kalina

*A*ndy Brennan owns Aaron Burr Cider in New York's Catskills region. His career started as a freelance artist, working in the fields of photography and architecture. Since its founding in 2011, Aaron Burr Cider has become well known among cider enthusiasts for its natural approach to cider making using wild apples and yeasts. As a prominent figure in the growing cider movement in the United States, Andy has been featured in print media and on television, radio, and podcasts. He regularly speaks about natural apple growing and cider production at museums, trade events, festivals, restaurants, and anywhere local food enthusiasts are found.

ABOUT THE FOREWORD AUTHOR

Rowan Jacobsen is the James Beard Award–winning author of *Apples of Uncommon Character, A Geography of Oysters, American Terroir,* and other books.

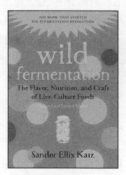